A MILD FORM OF INSANITY

A MILD FORM OF INSANITY

RECOLLECTIONS OF A HELICOPTER PILOT

Mike Tuson

Writers Club Press
San Jose New York Lincoln Shanghai

A Mild Form of Insanity
Recollections of a Helicopter Pilot

Writers Club Press
an imprint of iUniverse.com, Inc.

For information address:
iUniverse.com, Inc.
5220 S 16th, Ste. 200
Lincoln, NE 68512
www.iuniverse.com

ISBN: 0-595-18257-7

Printed in the United States of America

For Ann

Introduction

A form of helicopter technology has been used for hundreds, if not thousands of years. As early as 400 AD there are references to a Chinese kite employing a form of rotary wing to achieve lift, and there are many examples of water pumps powered by wind driven sails. In the fifteenth century Leonardo da Vinci sketched a machine that was to rise vertically from the ground and, if a suitable power source had been available, it might even have worked! In the 18th Century two Frenchmen presented a toy helicopter to the French Academy of Science, using a rotor made from bird feathers. In 1870 a more successful model was produced, again in France.

Many other sketches and models appeared, but lack of a suitable power source and a method of controlling the rotor blades always proved a stumbling block. The arrival of the internal combustion engine alleviated part of the problem and, in 1907, Paul Cornu made what is generally regarded as the first, untethered, hovering flight in a helicopter. It flew for twenty seconds and achieved an impressive altitude of one foot from the ground!

Over the next ten or fifteen years designers continued the quest for vertical take off and landing. In 1919 Juan de la Cierva began to tie together the best parts of all extant research and produced his autogyro, which he flew in 1923. Though it could not take off vertically or hover, it had short, stubby wings to provide some of the lift and a propeller to drag it through the air. The resemblance to a helicopter came from the horizontal rotor system spinning freely in the airflow above the fuselage, which augmented the lift and provided much of the directional control. This rotor lift not only helped to keep the aircraft airborne at slow speeds, but also allowed it to descend and land almost vertically. By 1933 Cierva had come up with, even if only in rudimentary form, the answer to almost all the rotor control and stability problems that were besetting the designers of the true helicopter.

Many regard the Focke Achgelis FA 61, produced in Germany in 1936, as the first practical helicopter. Two years later Hannah Reitsch, possibly the first female test pilot, publicly demonstrated the FA 61 in the Deutchland-Halle in Berlin, and it soon held both world height and speed records for helicopters with an altitude of over eleven thousand feet and a forward speed in excess of seventy knots. It must be said, however, that even with many design improvements in the twin rotor system, this machine was still more akin to the fixed wing of the early twentieth century. The helicopter still had a long way to go.

Igor Sikorsky had tried to build a helicopter in his native Russia, but gave up in 1910 after two failures and turned to building successful flying boats instead. He emigrated to the United States of America and, returning to his first love, designed, built and flew the VS 300 between 1939 and 1941. It was little more than a test vehicle but it was the first machine to use what has become almost the universal layout for modern helicopters—a large, horizontally mounted main rotor, and a smaller, vertical tail rotor. By 1942 Sikorsky had developed the VS 300 into the R4, and this became the first of a long line of helicopters built by the Sikorsky company. The R4 was used during the later stages of the Second World War, mainly for local rescue missions from allied air bases in the Pacific but also for some combat rescues by the Americans in Burma. The Royal Navy became the first of the British military forces to use the helicopter when, in 1944, they took delivery of several R4's for use in the search and rescue role. It was not, however, the first helicopter to see war service; the credit for this goes again to the Germans with the Flettner 282 Kolibri which they used for ship-borne gunnery spotting.

In 1943 the American Bell Helicopter Company began production and, immediately after the war, the Bell 47 became the first helicopter to be certified for commercial use and was also used by the American forces during the Korean War. No one who has seen the TV programme

"MASH" can fail to recognise the bubble cockpit and lattice work tail boom, and so successful was this design that there are Bell 47's still being used more than fifty years after they first flew.

The arrival of more powerful and purpose designed piston engines, and in the 1950's the turbine engine, as a power source for helicopters, produced massive advances. No longer were helicopters limited to carrying little more than the pilot and a verbal message over short distances! They could now lift commercially viable loads. Most major military powers used helicopters from shortly after the end of the Second World War, but the machine really came of age with the American forces in Vietnam. Among other models, the Bell UH1 Iroquois, commonly known as the "Huey," were used in their thousands. They transported troops into the front line, they re-supplied them with food and ammunition, they provided gunship support against the Viet Cong, and they recovered the dead and wounded when the battle finished. The "Huey" was a tireless workhorse, comparatively simple to maintain and able to absorb much ill treatment, both from the enemy and from the many, many thousands of pilots who were catapulted from training straight into the front line.

In Britain, the Royal Navy was the main user of helicopters. They provided the Search and Rescue for the fixed wing aircraft carriers, and naval helicopter squadrons flew in support of the military during the Malayan anti-communist campaign. By the end of the 1950's they were being used in numbers for antisubmarine protection of the fleet, and early in the 1960's specialised squadrons were formed to support the carrier-borne Royal Marine Commandos in their world wide role. The Royal Air Force used their helicopters for shore-based Search and Rescue, and later provided the majority of the helicopter support for the Army, alongside the Army Air Corps who were initially used for communications and spotting.

The commercial use of helicopters remained focused on areas where more conventional forms of transport were unusable, and tended to be limited to those organisations for which the high cost could be under-pinned by the potential savings or profit. A prime example of this is the oil industry. Whether on or offshore, a drilling rig is expensive to run, even when it is not drilling. The ability to fly in spare parts to keep the "down time" to a minimum far outweighs the cost of maintaining a hel-icopter on permanent contract, and the aircraft is now the preferred means of transport for almost any item that is within its lift capacity. In more recent years, following successive defence cuts, civil helicopters outnumber military ones in the U.K.

The more general use of civil helicopters was led by the USA. Few if any of their police forces are without their own helicopter element, which they use for everything from traffic surveillance to riot control. Many hospitals have their own, dedicated Helicopter Emergency Medical Service. This has been shown not only to save life by transport-ing the emergency medical team to the scene of an accident more quickly than other means, but also, by reducing the delay between the accident and treatment in a fully equipped trauma centre, thereby shortening the period accident victims may have to spend in hospital. In many cases the helicopter is the preferred means of transferring patients between hospitals for specialist treatment. These uses were mirrored, if somewhat tardily, in Europe and even later in Britain.

The future of vertical takeoff and landing aircraft is assured. Whether it will continue to be developed solely in the form of current helicopter design, or by a vehicle which will combine the versatility of a helicopter with the speed of a fixed wing aircraft will be decided, primarily, by the requirements of the military forces of the world. The United States has already put into production the Osprey, a tilt wing vehicle which can lift a viable military payload vertically into the air, and then transfer to speeds of forward flight that rival almost all other propeller driven aircraft. Civilian use of such machines could follow, but only as long as production and running costs can be controlled, and the general public assured of their safe operation over city centres and other heavily populated areas.

Chapter One

Flying has been described as ninety-nine percent boredom and one percent stark terror. I prefer the word monotony to boredom, and have had my share of it. I have also been terrified—most pilots have, even if they seldom admit it other than to themselves. I learned to live with the fear and used it to improve my flying and to stay alive. I have always been a firm believer that complacency lies in ambush for the pilot without fear, and that complacency leads, inevitably, to a very sticky end.

I had no particular aviation heritage. My father had served as a regular officer in the Royal Tank Corps, but my parents had split up when I was three and I had been brought up by my mother. One maternal uncle, Alick Montgomery, had flown as a pilot in the Royal Air Force, but I had seldom met him and knew little about him. Almost every other male relative had served in the Royal Navy.

At the start of the "phoney war" in 1939 my family was evacuated from Birchington, in Kent, initially to Wedmore in Somerset. From the comparative safety of the depths of the Somerset countryside I watched the contrails of high flying aircraft in the summer skies; but although we could hear the Germans flying overhead on their way to bomb Bristol and South Wales, we rarely saw them. The closest I came to an aircraft was at the age of eight during the summer of 1941. We had gone to the beach at Burnham-on-Sea in our little Morris Eight, a rare visit with petrol rationing in full force. My mother was asleep while my sister, three years older than myself, and I built sand castles. We heard the sound of aircraft engines and, almost immediately, an aircraft appeared under the low overcast. Confidently identifying it to the world as a Hurricane, I continued my construction work. My confidence received a nasty knock when the twin-engined Heinkel jettisoned a bomb on the nearby mud flats! My sixty-seven year old grandmother remained sitting in the car throughout the whole episode—very Victorian, very upright.

I was staying with relatives near Lee-on-the-Solent, in Hampshire, when the war in Europe ended. On the coast, just outside the town, lay H.M.S. *Daedalus*, a Naval Air Station and the headquarters of the Fleet Air Arm. I was invited to look over the airfield but can recall little of the visit, apart from being rather unimpressed by a battered old Supermarine Walrus which was the only aircraft available for me to see. A year later I had a fleeting desire to be an engine driver, but ultimately it seemed quite natural for me to join the Royal Navy. This I did in 1947 as an officer cadet.

With thirty other thirteen-year-old children I went to H.M.S. Britannia, the Royal Naval College perched high on a hill overlooking Dartmouth and the River Dart. I was there for a four-year course designed to churn out Naval Officers, but within a couple of years I began to feel that I had made a mistake. My mother was, by then, in partnership on a small farm near Exeter. I spent all my holidays there, loved the life, and by the time I was sixteen had decided that I wanted to be a farmer.

I had joined the College on a scholarship and my education was free. This financial arrangement had been an essential, since my mother's income was described on my application form to join the Navy as "a fluctuating overdraft." I suppose it was only natural that Their Lordships of the Admiralty insisted that if I was going to leave their employ I would have to purchase my release. The two thousand pounds they demanded was way beyond our means so, reluctantly, I stayed and completed the training.

It was a good education if, on occasions, a trifle parochial. Some subjects that could be given a naval twist were twisted; history was a series of naval battles, all of them as far as I can remember, won by the Royal Navy. The exception to this was, perhaps, being the tale of Admiral Byng who was shot on his own quarterdeck for cowardice, and whose fate could be used as a salutary lesson for us all. Mathematics was less concerned with how long it would take a certain number of men to mow a given acreage of meadow, as to how long it would take them to scrub a similar area of quarterdeck. It had compensations, the sports facilities were unrivalled and I was fortunate in not only enjoying all forms of sport, but also in achieving a small measure of success. On completion of the final exams, and the requisite nine months as a seagoing cadet on board the heavy cruiser, *H.M.S. Devonshire*, I was promoted to Midshipman and appointed to *H.M.S. Eagle*.

Eagle was an aircraft carrier. Laid down in the Harland and Wolff shipyard in Belfast during the early years of the war, her completion had been delayed by the final victory in 1945, and it was not until 1951 that she was handed over to the Navy. Displacing nearly fifty thousand tons, she was one of the newest warships in the world. With her airgroup embarked she would be, arguably, one of the most powerful. I joined her, with six others from my Dartmouth term, in Devonport Dockyard in January 1952. She was still carrying out acceptance sea trials and we were visited frequently by trials aircraft, but it was to be another three months before she was ready to join the Heavy Squadron of the Home Fleet, and embark her full Air Group.

The RAF had operated jet-powered aircraft during the final stages of the war, but the Navy had only just taken delivery of the Supermarine Attacker, its first single-seat jet fighter. Apart from the Attacker, the remainder of the airgroup were equipped with the best of the British wartime-vintage, piston-engined machines, among them the Hawker Sea Fury, Fairey Firefly, Blackburn Firebrand and the De Havilland Sea Hornet, this last a navalised version of the Mosquito. The Lease-Lend American aircraft that the Fleet Air Arm had been flying during the war had either been returned to the States, or dumped into the sea after VJ-Day.

The angled deck and stabilised landing aid had yet to be invented. *Eagle* had a "straight" deck and two wire nets—euphemistically called safety nets but more often referred to as crash barriers—separating the landing area from the forward deck-park. The aircraft were launched either from the hydraulic catapult or by free takeoff. They were guided back to the deck by a "batsman". He stood on a small platform near the rear end of the flight deck, from where he signalled with a pair of "bats" to direct the pilot on to, and then to keep him on, the correct landing glide path.

The aircrew were all Naval Officers, many of whom had served during the war when survival itself could be regarded as a victory. Losses among Fleet Air Arm aircrew had been very high. Not only did they have to cope with enemy action, both from the air and the surface, but during the early years of the war they also operated antiquated equipment like the Swordfish, affectionately known as the "Stringbag." It was said that one reason for the losses of the Swordfish not being even higher was that the enemy could not believe that an aircraft could fly so slowly, and always laid-off their guns too far ahead. The original specification for this biplane had been laid down by the Air Ministry in 1930, but the design became amalgamated with one for an aircraft for the Greek Navy and it first flew in 1934. It was still on active service in 1945. It was to be a while before the more purpose-built carrier aircraft arrived, some of them American like the Corsair.

The pilots also had to cope with the problems of finding a postage-stamp sized runway in the middle of an unfriendly ocean. There were few, if any, navigation aids and, when they found their floating airbase, frequently in atrocious weather, the runway could be lurching up and down forty feet or more, making a successful landing a combination of art form and luck.

The other pilots in *Eagle* had been recruited since the war. All had volunteered, an act that required a deep and very personal faith in their own ability to survive in the face of continued losses, and a mild form of insanity. The war might have ended, but the weather at sea had not changed; nor had the decks stopped pitching.

As a result of their working environment, naval aircrew tended not only to work hard but also to play hard, taking each day as a bonus. Even to me, a lowly Midshipman, the gulf between aircrew and the ship's officers was very apparent. Although we lived in our own quarters, known as the Gunroom, and were not members of the Officers Mess, the Wardroom, occasionally we would be invited there for Mess Dinners. After the meal the aircrew would let down their hair and indulge their high spirits in such traditional games as Mess Rugby and High Cockalorum. The combination of alcohol and the ship's movement inevitably led to injury, and in later years the more violent of these pastimes was forbidden. It was very noticeable, however, that the main participants were always the airgroup and less often the ship's officers. Many of the more senior of these had been brought up in the pre-war era, when naval aircraft were all flown and maintained by the RAF. It was obvious that some of them regarded the specialisation of "Aircrew" as beneath the dignity of a true naval officer, and the Fleet Air Arm as a wart on the face of an otherwise elite body. Others seemed to find it difficult to reconcile themselves to the demise of their beloved guns as the main armament of their equally beloved Navy. This was an attitude that remained with some of them until the scrapping of the conventional fixed wing element of the Fleet Air Arm in the late 1960's. It did not advance the cause of the Fleet Air Arm in their eyes that many of the more junior aircrew were also Short Service Officers. They were in the navy for four or eight years and were on board for flying duties only. Many were using the navy as a stepping-stone to a more lucrative career in civil aviation and this made the insult even harder to bear.

Much of our time as Midshipmen was spent working with the air department. I watched with admiration as the aircraft were thrown off the front end of the flight deck by the catapult. I marvelled at the cool, competent way they returned to the deck, their approach guided by the elegant ballet of the batsman. I held my breath as they reached the point of no return, throttled back their engines, put their wheels on the deck and were pulled up short by one of the arrester wires stretched across the landing area.

Of course, if they failed to pick up a wire there was little chance of going around again for a second try; a crash into the barrier, then, was almost inevitable, but fortunately not necessarily fatal. Most pilots climbed unaided from their cockpit, while the wreck, if too badly damaged, would be dumped unceremoniously into the sea to make room for the next aircraft in the landing pattern.

It was early on in the first months of the Air Group's time on board that an Attacker took to the barrier. For jet aircraft, in which the pilot sits far closer to the nose and does not have a massive piston engine and propeller in front of him as protection, the two barriers were made of vertical strips of nylon hung vertically across the flight deck. In this crash involving a fighter jet, the American naval pilot on loan to the Navy discovered he could not lower his hook. He touched down as close to the after end of the flight deck, passed through the first barrier, neatly separating the wings from the fuselage, and ended up in the second barrier. The pilot unstrapped himself, climbed out of the cockpit and began to walk towards the island. Then, realising the engine was still running, he returned to the aircraft to switch it off before reporting to the bridge to discuss his arrival with "Wings," the Commander (Air) and the head of the Air Department. It was said that he had told "Wings" there had to be easier ways of making a living, or words to that effect!

The Firebrand was a frequent candidate for the barrier. It was a single-seat, propeller driven torpedo bomber, with a huge in-line piston engine, and a cockpit set well back along the fuselage. It also had a very tall main undercarriage to allow a torpedo to be slung beneath the fuselage, and a tail wheel. This configuration produced a high nose-up attitude when landing, restricting the pilot's view ahead of the aircraft. During the final approach phase it was necessary to fly in a tight banked turn to keep the batsman in view right up to the "cut" signal and, as the wings were levelled for touchdown, the pilot lost sight of the deck.

Human nature being what it is, some would "tweak" the tail down to bring the hook a little closer to the wires. If the aircraft speed was even a fraction higher than ideal, the aircraft would float down the deck and go straight into the barrier! The "goofers" platform, an area on the island superstructure reserved for those of the ship's company who wanted to watch the flying, was generally full whenever the Firebrand featured in the flying programme.

I watched all this with admiration but no envy, and never took the opportunity to fly in the back seat of a Firefly—although we were encouraged to do so. It was during one such joyride from another fleet carrier that Frank Meeks, who had been in my term at Dartmouth, died when the aircraft ditched and he was unable to escape from the rear cockpit. I was still determined to leave the navy and was just searching for the right moment.

I passed the Midshipman's exams by the skin of my teeth. A section of the navigation exams required us to produce several examples of astronavigation and, as usual, we left the production to the last moment. By this time the ship was operating inside the Arctic Circle, just north of Iceland, it was late October, and bitterly cold. We were required to establish the position of the ship by "shooting" the angle of various heavenly bodies in the dawn sky, no easy task as we stood in the open, on top of the bridge, frozen fingers fumbling with the sextant. Then we discovered that it was possible to work out a very accurate star sight backwards.

The first step was to telephone the bridge to find out the actual position of the ship from the Midshipman of the Watch, and from this we could calculate what the various angles would have been if we had actually taken the sight; it took longer, but we could do the whole thing in the warmth of our cabins. All went well until we presented the last of our efforts for the approval of Jimmy Dixon, the Navigating Officer. Later that day he summoned us to the bridge where he congratulated us on producing results that far surpassed anything that he could come up with—especially as there had been total cloud cover at the time we claimed to have taken the sight!

The ship took part in Exercise Mainbrace, a NATO fleet operation involving more than ten aircraft carriers and sixty other assorted war vessels. It was held in the North Atlantic between Iceland and Norway, an area renowned for winter storms and that winter was no exception. At times the wind reached Force eleven, Hurricane force, and the seas were so huge that the exercise came to a halt. At one point an American carrier, the *USS Wright*, which had been converted from the hull of an old passenger liner, requested permission to heave-to as she was rolling to her approved limits. This provoked a reply from the American Admiral: "Permission to heave-to denied. Permission granted to roll further!"

During the storm a Norwegian submarine failed to make her daily position report. It was feared she was in trouble and the fleet was ordered to head for her last known position. Few of the ships were able to increase speed with any safety, and *Eagle*, the Royal Navy's newest carrier, and *Vanguard*, its last battleship, steamed majestically ahead of the fleet. It was impossible to fly off a search aircraft. Even if the crew had been able to see anything on the wind-torn surface, our flight deck, nearly one hundred feet above the water, was being swept regularly by green water as the ship plunged her bows into the waves. It was my first experience of the total power of the sea, and I wondered how it had been possible to operate aircraft from the decks of the tiny Woolworth carriers escorting convoys through these waters to Russia. Thankfully the submarine checked in and we were able to reduce to a more comfortable speed.

At the end of 1952 I was appointed to *HMS Cheerful*, a one thousand ton Algerine class minesweeper based at Harwich. She was ineptly named and was never a happy ship. The Algerines were uncomfortable to live in and were given some unpleasant tasks. During my six months on board we spent weeks on end towing barges up and down the Firth of Forth in an attempt to find a way to sweep pressure activated mines—one of Winston Churchill's brainchildren. As a break from this we were sent to clear the minefields laid in the North Sea by the Germans, a hazardous job since many of the charts of these fields were either inaccurate or missing. We also spent some time in the River Crouch, acting as a floating hotel for the army personnel helping to repair the damage caused by the horrendous flooding of the East Coast that year.

The highlight of our social programme, apart from holding a Coronation Celebration cocktail party for dignitaries from Cromer whilst at anchor off the Norfolk coast during an onshore gale, was the Coronation Review at Spithead, quite the most spectacular naval event of the post war years. Nearly two hundred ships drawn from all the navies of the world, including the U.S.S.R., anchored in Spithead to be inspected by Her Majesty, Queen Elizabeth the Second from the deck of the Royal Yacht. It is unlikely that a similar display of naval might will ever be repeated.

The review excepted, my lasting memory of *Cheerful* is the way she moved in any sea way, I believe she would have rolled on a piece of wet blotting paper. On one occasion we were passing through the Pentland Firth in a comparatively mild westerly gale and a Royal Marine officer, on board for some sea experience, found himself very nearly standing on the door of the radar shack as *Cheerful* rolled her upper deck into the water. He left the imprint of his hob-nailed boot on the door as proof of the event!

On promotion to Acting Sub-Lieutenant I rejoined the remainder of my term, this time at the Royal Naval College at Greenwich. I have never been able to discover a good reason for our presence there, but it may have been a trial by Their Lordships to see whether the years of naval indoctrination could withstand an assault from the attractions of civilian life. We did little or no work, and were required to pass few, if any exams. This was probably fortunate as our nights were a series of parties thrown by the many nurse and teacher training colleges that abounded in London. For those who could afford it, the bright lights of the West End beckoned; my visits there were rare, and depended on how large an overdraft I could squeeze from a reluctant bank manager, for my salary of twenty-one pounds a month would not stretch too often to the high life! This period of lotus eating lasted for nine months and eventually we moved to Portsmouth for more courses. These were designed to train us for service with the fleet, and to discover which of the many specialisations would suit us best.

I had made up my mind that this would be the optimum time to make my break from the Navy. My requests to resign my commission had continued to be frustrated by my inability to purchase my release, so I had decided to fail the first course I attended. I spent four hours in the examination room ensuring this, and then went to the officer-in-charge to explain why there was no need to mark my exam papers. Within minutes I found myself in front of Commodore Godfrey Plaice V.C. R.N., the Commodore of the Naval Barracks, where I discovered that I had sadly miscalculated both the Navy's resolve to keep me, and mine to leave! The Commodore was an impressive person of few words, all of them well chosen. He left me in no doubt as to what would happen if my name came to his attention again. The threat of "Courts-Martial," and "Dismissal-with-Disgrace" frightened the hell out of me, and I passed the rest of the exams, if not with distinction, at least anonymously in the middle orders.

Realising that I was now committed to the Navy, I began to look around to see which specialisation I should choose. Perhaps my time in *Eagle* had left a greater impression on me than I had realised, for before I had completed the Junior Officers Air Course at Lee-on-the-Solent I was totally hooked on flying.

It was there, in 1954, that I became airborne for the first time in my life. We were taken to the squadron crew room to meet our pilots, all of whom were experienced aviators serving in a training squadron between front line operational tours. Mine was Tony "Baron" Crosse, who was to take me up in a De Havilland Vampire, a small, two seater, single-engined jet trainer. I found him sitting in a corner, clasping his right wrist with his left hand, checking his pulse rate. My already minimal enthusiasm took a spectacular dive as I heard him mutter, "I'll never pass my medical!"

His briefing was short and to the point. "Get strapped in, don't touch anything unless I tell you to—and if you throw up, *you* clean up!"

We climbed into the cramped cockpit and I sat with my hands folded in my lap, afraid to move a muscle in case I touched a wrong lever or button. There seemed to be thousands to choose from, and obviously any one of them would spell instant disaster. Lights flashed and needles rotated on the instrument panel as Tony started the engine and taxied out to the runway threshold. I heard a disembodied voice in my headset saying we were cleared for takeoff. At that precise moment I was seized by a frantic desire to tell somebody that it was all a terrible mistake, that the last thing I wanted to do was fly.

It was too late. Tony opened the throttle and we accelerated down the runway. I can remember very little of the next few minutes. I was far too busy helping my stomach catch up with the rest of my body as we climbed, seemingly vertically, into the blue sky above the Hampshire countryside. At twenty thousand feet I was given a few minutes respite to collect my thoughts and view the scenery. The air was gin clear. I could see beyond London to the north, and south across the English Channel to the French coast. There was a sense of freedom that I had never before experienced and I was enthralled.

Tony became bored with straight and level flight and, with a muttered warning about making sure my straps were tight, commenced some mind-bending gyrations. We pulled up into a series of loops, rolls and spins and my stomach was once again left far behind, to be followed shortly by my brain. By the time he had finished I was breathless, dizzy and totally disorientated, but I had not felt sick. When he let me take the controls for a moment or two my conversion was complete. I wanted to be a pilot!

At the end of the course I volunteered to join the Fleet Air Arm, but was told I would have to wait until I had completed all the courses and obtained a bridge watchkeeping certificate before I could be considered.

I was appointed to *HMS Grenville*, an Anti-Submarine frigate of the Portland Training Squadron, whose main task was to take training classes to sea to practice the art of submarine detection. For the most part this entailed steaming in circles around a submerged submarine while the trainees listened to sonar echoes, and was not very exciting. Once I had obtained the watchkeeping certificate I applied again for flying duties.

I was fortunate that my Commanding Officer, Captain G.G. Wilson, despite being a seaman officer of long standing, did not decry my choice of specialisation. Once he had made sure that I was serious he did everything he could to help me. Within weeks I was ordered to go to the RAF base at Hornchurch for an aircrew medical and the flying aptitude tests. For two days I was poked and prodded by doctors, and made to carry out a series of tests to prove I was sufficiently co-ordinated. On completion I returned to *Grenville* to await the results.

These came all too soon. I had passed the aptitude tests, but failed the medical. The RAF doctors had found a scar inside one ear, the legacy of a burst eardrum when I was nine years old, and in their opinion this debarred me from flying. Bitterly disappointed I went to the Senior Naval Medical Officer at Portland to find out whether there was anything that could be done. He passed me on to the Senior Ear, Nose and Throat specialist at Chatham Barracks.

A few days later I went there for a final check-up, and a decision on my future. The specialist noticed a scar above my right eye, the result of a mistimed tackle during a game of rugby at Dartmouth, and for the next fifteen minutes we discussed the forthcoming rugby season and the chances of the Navy in the Inter Service Championships.

"Do you really want to go flying?" he asked me. I assured him it was all I wanted to do. He began to peer inside my ear, grunting in that disconcerting and noncommittal way that doctors must spend hours practising. Then he spoke.

"I can see no reason why you shouldn't. I'll recommend that you be accepted for flying training."

Barely restraining myself from hugging that rather Senior Naval Captain, I returned to Portland. I had made it! Two weeks later I received my appointment to HMS Gamecock, to join Number 58 Naval Flying Training Course at the RAF station at Syerston, in Nottinghamshire.

Chapter Two

In some ways I was sad to leave. *Grenville* had been a very happy ship and for the first time I had been given real responsibility. We had been very much "under training" as Midshipmen and acting Sub-Lieutenants, but in *Grenville* I was treated as a useful member of the ship's company. I had been able to reconcile myself to a life in the Navy and, although the thought of flying certainly changed my outlook, I have no doubt that my short time in the ship had much to do with my new-found peace of mind.

I had a few days leave before I was due to join the course at Syerston, and decided to visit my father and stepmother. On retiring from the Army he had gone to live in Winchester, and had started a new career as an aircraft design draughtsman. At that time he was working on the hydraulic system for a new breed of naval fighter aircraft, the Scimitar. It was only the second time we had met since I was three, but after an initial period of caution we decided we liked each other and were able to strike up a good and lasting relationship.

I drove on to Syerston a few days later. The air station lay astride the A40, a few miles south of Newark—the airfield on one side of the road overlooking the River Trent, the main living quarters on the other. I presented myself to the RAF Corporal guarding the gate leading to the living quarters, expecting to be directed to the Officers Mess.

"You a student?" he enquired. I said I was and he pointed to the air-field. "You lot live over there."

I had visions of spending the next few months living under canvas, but was gratified to find there was a new block inside the airfield perimeter fence in which the students ate and slept. In retrospect I think it was a pity we were segregated in this way from the RAF Officers. There has always been intense rivalry between the Fleet Air Arm and the Royal Air Force—a rivalry that all too frequently boils over into an unhealthy dislike of the other service. Perhaps if we had lived with them from the start we might have not perpetuated the "Them" and "Us" attitude.

One reason for this dislike is not hard to find. The Royal Naval Air Service, the first British military air force, and the Royal Flying Corps, staffed by Army personnel, were formed at the start of the First World War. It was not until 1918 that Lord Trenchard succeeded in having these two amalgamated and renamed the Royal Air Force. The Fleet Air Arm was formed in 1924, but all military flying was conducted by the RAF and, between the wars, they provided the aircrew and maintenance staff for aircraft flying from aircraft carriers. It was hardly surprising that few career-minded RAF officers were prepared to waste time flying with the Navy; equally, the system did little to educate naval officers, long steeped in the traditions of Nelson and the gun, to understand or appreciate the expanded horizons that a naval air force, staffed by the navy, could offer. It was not until 1937 that the Fleet Air Arm came under the sole control of the Admiralty.

Between the wars the RAF held the monopoly for training all British military aircrew. The necessities of war changed the situation, and better weather and the absence of enemy interference made it preferable to send student pilots to the U.S.A. and Canada. For several years after the cessation of hostilities naval pilots continued to be trained at the U.S. Navy airbase at Pensacola, in Florida, but by 1956 the RAF had resumed their monopoly. This was the reason for some thirty naval officers arriving at an RAF air station to be taught to fly. Six, like myself, were regular officers who had volunteered for the specialisation, the remainder, aged between eighteen and twenty six, were Short Service. Our appointment to Gamecock, an old naval air station near Birmingham and about as far from the sea as it is possible to get in Britain, was so that our names could be held on the pay records of a naval establishment.

Syerston was commanded by an RAF Group Captain and staffed mainly by RAF personnel. The navy was represented by the Senior

Naval Officer, Commander Joe Honeywill, and a few naval instructors. This part of the course was to last six months and, during that time, we could expect to fly about one hundred and twenty hours in the Percival Provost; then we would transfer to the RAF station at Valley, in Anglesey, for a further six months of advanced flying training on the jet-engined Vampire.

The Provost was a two-seat, piston-engined, propeller-driven aircraft with a fixed undercarriage and tail wheel. The pupil and instructor sat side by side, each with his own set of controls. It was a very simple aircraft to fly, although a succession of modifications to the Alvis Leonides engine had left it somewhat underpowered. My instructor, Norman Giffin, was as new to instructing as I was to flying. He had only just completed the instructors course and, because I was to be his first pupil, he would not be allowed to send me solo—that dubious privilege was to be given to one of the more experienced instructors. For some thirteen hours Brian sat patiently alongside me as I struggled to master the aircraft. The first few flights were to demonstrate the effects of the various controls; the rest of the time was spent "circuit bashing", going round and round the airfield practising takeoffs and landings until Brian felt I might be competent to do it on my own.

I was handed over to Flight Lieutenant Peters for the great day. We flew down to the grass airfield at Newton, a few miles south of Syerston, where I demonstrated my newly acquired skills, and after a couple of circuits he told me to taxi back to the takeoff point. As I came to a stop, he slid back the canopy and said, "O.K, you're on your own now. Do one circuit and landing and then come and pick me up." He climbed down to the grass and walked away without a backward glance.

My mind went blank. For the first time I was by myself in the cockpit with the engine running, confronted by a battery of instruments and controls that had suddenly become alien to me. There was no way I could fly! I was having trouble with joined-up thinking. Then the repetitive training took effect. I closed the canopy, eased open the throttle and taxied forward, turning the aircraft into the wind. Taking a deep breath, I opened the throttle wide. The aircraft bumped over the rough field, accelerating towards the far fence; then, all of a sudden, the vibration from the undercarriage ceased and I was airborne! I have no other recollections of my first solo, but Flight Lieutenant Peters must have been satisfied since, after another fifteen minutes dual, he sent me off again for three-quarters of an hour solo circuit bashing. I had passed the first hurdle towards becoming a pilot.

The course went swiftly. After each new facet of flying had been demonstrated by the instructor, we were sent out on our own to practice it. Stalls, spinning, gentle aerobatics and navigation were followed by instrument flying, night flying and more advanced aerobatics. I was not entirely an apt pupil, and for some time lived with the spectre of a "scrub-check." If a student's progress was considered to be too slow he was handed over to one of the more experienced instructors, or even the Flight Commander himself, to assess whether it was worth continuing with the very expensive training. I had one such check following an abysmal navigation exercise in which I became "temporarily uncertain of my position" or, in layman's terms, totally lost! I managed to get through it and was allowed to continue.

Our numbers dwindled as the course progressed. Two or three left within the first few weeks, one because he did not achieve his first solo, the others as a result of scrub checks or because they could not cope with service life. We lost another one half way through our time at Syerston. John was, by common consent, the most natural pilot among us; his problem was described by officialdom as a lack of self-discipline. This first surfaced when he was sent to practice forced landings at Ossington.

Ossington had been a wartime airfield, but was now a single disused runway. On either side a farmer was cultivating the land. We were not allowed to continue our forced landing approaches below two hundred feet and the farmer became somewhat irate when John, bored with having to break off his approaches before touchdown, decided to carry out full "dead stick" landings instead. He was taken in front of the Wing Commander (Flying) and warned to watch his step. We started formation flying a few days later, and before long the pilot of an RAF Dragonfly helicopter was surprised to find a Provost in close formation. From the pilot's account of the incident he must have been able to read the name-tag on John's flying overall, but the side number of the aeroplane was sufficient to earn John a final warning.

His ultimate indiscretion would probably have ensured his withdrawal from flying training without the first two incidents. The pilot of an Elizabethan aircraft complained that, whilst flying in a "purple airway" reserved for Royal flights, he had been buzzed by a Provost aircraft near Nottingham. He had been unable to read the side number, but a subsequent investigation revealed that only two Provosts had been airborne at the time—the other one flown by the Wing Commander (Flying) from Syerston. John was grounded and returned to the Navy, where he retrained as a Fleet Air Arm Observer.

We had little time to ourselves. Half of each day was spent flying, the other half in the classroom.. We had to acquire an intimate knowledge of our engines and instruments, and to know how and why an aircraft stayed in the air. We were taught about the weather, navigation, and even a small amount of Civil Air Law, although we would not be required to pass any civil exams. I had little trouble with the class work, leaving me more time to concentrate my attention on the flying. With the patient help of my instructors, Norman had been joined by Flight Sergeant "Jock" Murdoch, I made it to the final handling check, and passed. Then, with twenty-two others who had graduated, I moved to Valley for jet training.

The regime at Valley was very similar to that at Syerston. Only the aircraft had changed, and we were no longer segregated from the staff pilots. Because of the shortage of accommodation we all shared the same prefabricated mess, and slept in converted Nissen huts. Winter was soon to be upon us, the huts were heated by old, pot-bellied, coke-burning stoves and it was always a toss-up whether to open the windows and freeze at night, or risk asphyxiation from the fumes that poured from the cracked chimneys every time the wind blew.

We flew two versions of the De Havilland Vampire, the T11 two-seat trainer and the single-seat FB5. The T11's were comparatively new and in good condition; the FB5's were all old, ex-front line squadron aircraft, and had seen better days even before being relegated to the training role. The Vampire was considerably more complicated than the Provost. The engine had to be handled more delicately because, if the throttle was opened too quickly, the sudden increase in the speed of the engine would cause the compressor to stall; the supply of air to the combustion chambers would drastically decrease and the engine temperature would almost certainly exceed the limits. As a result of such mishandling the engine would probably blow up! We had to remember to raise the undercarriage after takeoff and, much more importantly, to lower it before attempting to land, although Charles Manning, one of our course, discovered very early on that it was possible, if messy, to land a Vampire with the wheels retracted. His nose wheel refused to come down at the end of one of his early solo flights, and he was talked down to a wheels-up landing by the Wing Commander (Flying), from which he walked away totally unscathed.

The aircraft was much faster and needed quicker reactions, while the controls, effective at low altitude, became less so as altitude increased and the air became thinner. We were warned that the FB5 would stall very easily at height, and careful handling was needed to avoid spinning from the stall. Intentional spinning was prohibited because recovery was almost impossible. Greater emphasis was placed on night and instrument flying. I had some difficulty with instruments, not least because one of my instructors delighted in beating me over the head with a rolled up map every time I did anything wrong, and I developed a Pavlovian response of hunching my head into my shoulders every time I entered cloud. My problems were eased when I was turned over to a new instructor, Jim Cabourne, and I made better progress.

All our night flying at Syerston had been done in sight of the ground, and I had taken great comfort from being able to see the lights of the surrounding countryside. At Valley we had to carry out a night climb to the operational ceiling of the aircraft, over thirty-five thousand feet. Jim came with me in the T11 to demonstrate the exercise. There was full cloud cover that night and we had to climb through the overcast, breaking clear at fifteen thousand feet into almost total darkness. The only light came from the canopy of stars above us and the glow of the instrument panel. Jim was a large officer who took up more than his fair share of the cramped cockpit, pushing me into one corner. Yet, as we climbed steadily upwards, I began to experience a feeling of intense loneliness which stayed with me until we returned to the ground. The following night I carried out the same exercise, this time on my own. There was no cloud, and I could see the bright, friendly lights of Anglesey and North Wales beneath me. As I climbed into the night sky the same feeling of loneliness overtook me, and it took a considerable effort to complete the flight.

I had my first experience of losing a close friend in a flying accident at Valley. We had progressed to advanced aerobatics and Ronnie Taylor had flown to an area over the Snowdon mountain range to practice in an FB5. He did not return. An eyewitness saw his aircraft enter a spin from which it never recovered. Only the T11's were fitted with ejection seats and, without one, Ronnie had little chance of baling out and was killed in the crash. He had been very popular and his tragic death hit us all very hard. It affected my flying to the point that my Flight Commander suggested I should seriously consider giving up altogether, and for several days I came close to doing just that. Then, as the initial impact wore off, I realised that sudden death was part and parcel of military flying and, if I was going to continue, I would just have to get used to it. Over the next few months there were more fatal accidents involving people I knew well. The first was one of our naval instructors whom I had known in *Eagle*. He had an engine failure shortly after takeoff and tried to return to the airfield, something that we, as students, had been warned was a recipe for disaster. He crashed just short of the threshold and was killed. Another was a student on the course ahead of ours. He had taken off for a night sortie and, hardly climbing at all or deviating from his takeoff course, had crashed into the hills near Snowdon, nearly forty miles away. I found myself less and less affected after each of these, developing a shell inside which I could hide.

The course finished in March 1957. I was graded proficient and presented with my Wings. I was now a pilot. All that was left to do was to learn how to use an aircraft!

We had been asked to choose between the fighter and antisubmarine worlds for our future employment. Although I was reasonably competent in the Vampire, I had not enjoyed the "fighter" aspects of flying and decided to volunteer for antisubmarine work, a decision I never regretted. I was accepted and, with four others from the course, was appointed to join 737 Squadron, based at Eglinton in Northern Ireland, for the conversion to the Fairey Gannet.

The Gannet was a twin-engine, turboprop monoplane with a crew of three—pilot, observer and telegraphist. As qualified pilots, however ignorant, we were expected to be able to fly an aircraft, and the conversion was short—three or four hours with an instructor in the dual-controlled training version to learn to handle the Double-Mamba turbine engines that drove the in-line, contra-rotating propellers. Once that was completed we turned to the operational aircraft, the Gannet AS2, to continue instrument and formation flying, and to learn about the tactics and weapons we would be using.

The aircraft could carry a wide range of weaponry and we were expected to be able to deliver these accurately, spending hours over the gunnery range on the eastern shores of Loch Foyle. We dropped practice bombs and fired rockets at a fixed target. We practised this by day with both engines running and with one shut down. We practised at night, illuminating the target with flares and went on practising until our instructors were satisfied we could straddle the target, even in our sleep.

It was surprising that some of us did not do it that way. We had left the austere, serious atmosphere of the basic training school far behind and were on the fringe of the real world. We were allowed, almost expected, to play as hard as we worked and were treated as full members of the squadron and air station. The level of social life at naval air stations was in direct proportion to their distance from London. Eglinton, separated from the flesh pots by the Irish Sea, and Lossiemouth, in the far north of Scotland, had the deserved reputation of being two of the liveliest wardrooms in the Fleet Air Arm.

Almost everyone who served at Eglinton will remember "Wardroom Two," or Joe Knox's pub as it should more correctly be known. It owed little of it's popularity to decor or cultural atmosphere, and everything to convenience, situated as it was at the end of the main runway! It was a typical Irish spit-and-sawdust bar, designed for the speedy sale of alcohol and was full to bursting every night, and frequently at lunch time as well. Joe Knox never appeared. It was rumoured that he had sold the pub for the price of a bedroom and a bottle of John Jameson's whisky a day, had retired to the bedroom and never reappeared! The pub was the haunt of both officers and ratings, including the members of the WRNS, and was the breeding ground for many a naval wedding—and some divorces!

The I.R.A. were active at this time, although their targets were restricted to the occasional boy scout hut and secluded water pumping station. Despite the "Troubles" we were able to cross the border into Donegal, and the hotels in Muff and Buncrana were favourite weekend retreats. There were plenty of good golf courses, and for those who enjoyed it, excellent rough shooting—we were even allowed to keep shotguns on the station. That concession lasted until one of the pilots, returning late one night, decided to find out how many of the plaster-board partitions that divided the Nissen huts in which we slept could be penetrated by a twelve bore shotgun. He placed the barrels close to the wall and pulled the trigger. The answer was three, somewhat to the surprise of the occupants sleeping in the rooms in question.

After a couple of months in 737 we were transferred to 719 Squadron, also at Eglinton. We joined up with the observers and telegraphists who had just completed their training, and began to practise our newly learned skills on the submarines based at the naval dockyard at Londonderry. They would wait for us on the surface in the deep-water exercise areas off the north coast of Ireland, submerging once we arrived. After we had dropped a pattern of sonobuoys, passive listening devices fitted with a radio transmitter, around the target, the telegraphist and observer would track the submarine by tuning in to the sound of her propellers. Occasionally we would dive over her presumed position and drop a small explosive charge and a smoke marker. The submarine would respond with a smoke marker of her own, and we could check how accurate our attack had been. Most of the time the pilot was little more than an airborne taxi driver, and I spent many a long hour flying round and round in circles over an apparently empty sea.

By October we were considered ready for operational flying, and Tony Holloway and I were appointed to join 815 Squadron at *HMS Seahawk*, the Naval Air Station at Culdrose near Helston, in Cornwall. The squadron was still embarked in *HMS Ark Royal*, a sister ship to *Eagle*, and was not due to return to home base for a month. As a result we were both loaned to 796 Squadron, the observer-training outfit at Culdrose.

Our task was to fly the trainee observers around the Cornish skies, hopefully ensuring, should they get lost, that we could get them back to the airfield before we ran out of fuel. I had lived in Cornwall for several years and knew it well, but it looked very different from the air. There were occasions when it was a case of the blind leading the blind, compounded by language problems when I flew with the foreign students from Germany or India.

815 disembarked from the Ark to Culdrose for Christmas leave, and Tony and I made the short journey across the main runway to our new home. We both believed we were reasonably competent pilots, but were soon disabused of this idea. It was pointed out that, although we could fly the Gannet, neither of us had flown to the deck of an aircraft carrier and once more we found ourselves on a course of concentrated training. We were fortunate in one respect: the days of straight decks, batsmen and crash barriers were long gone.

By 1957 all our carriers had the angled deck and stabilised mirror landing sight, both facilities invented by members of the Fleet Air Arm. The flight deck was still split into two separate areas, with the deck park at the front end, but there were no barriers between it and the landing area. Instead, an extension had been built on to the flight deck sticking out halfway along the port side, and the approach and landing was now made at a slight angle to the fore-and-aft line of the ship; if the aircraft missed the wires all the pilot had to do was open up the throttle and go around for another try.

There was no longer a need for the batsman. He had been replaced by the mirror sight, consisting of a beam of light projected into a concave mirror, and reflected back up the correct glide path. A horizontal line of green lights was fixed on either side of, and level with, the centre of the mirror and the whole device was stabilised to counteract the movement of the ship. The pilot only needed to keep the reflection of the light—the "meatball"—in line with the bars of green lights, maintain the approved approach speed and then, in theory, the aircraft would touch down on the correct spot and pick up a wire. The system was sufficiently accurate for the mirror to be adjusted to allow an aircraft to hook up to a specific wire out of the five available.

One of these mirror sights had been set up alongside the runway at Culdrose, exactly as we could expect to find it on board the *Ark* but without the arrester wires. During the next month Tony and I each flew a total of over one hundred approaches, by day and by night, until we could almost guarantee to keep the meatball in the middle every time. During the same period we flew normal exercises with our crews; my observer was Danny Ferguson, a young Sub-Lieutenant with as little experience as an Observer as I had as a pilot, and we were both kept extremely busy.

In the middle of all this came Christmas leave and marriage. I had met Jane, my wife-to-be, in Northern Ireland, where she had been on tour with the Colchester Repertory Company at Portstewart. We were married in London and, after a short honeymoon, returned to Cornwall. Three weeks later we bade each other a temporary farewell as I left to embark in *Ark Royal*.

Despite all our practice Tony and I joined the ship in Devonport Dockyard with the maintenance personnel and squadron heavy baggage. Our aircraft were to be flown on board by the more experienced pilots as the ship steamed down-Channel, heading for the Bay of Biscay and then the Mediterranean. At the same time the remainder of the Air Group, consisting of Seahawk day fighters, Sea Venom night fighters and four Skyraider, American built, piston-engined early-warning radar (A.E.W.) aircraft, would fly on board. The search and rescue helicopter flight, two Sikorsky S55's Whirlwinds, had landed on the ship while she was still alongside in the dockyard so that they would be available for their duties when the fixed-wing arrived.

This time I watched the fixed-wing arrival with a mixture of interest and envy. It was a very slick affair, seldom more than thirty seconds elapsing between each aircraft touching down. As soon as it was clear of the wires the pilot would taxi the aircraft up the deck, folding the wings as he was marshalled into the deck park. Within seconds the next aircraft would be thumping down among the wires, and so on until they were all on board.

It was to be several days before the new pilots were allowed to fly. The Bay of Biscay lived up to its reputation for rough weather, and we had to wait until we were off the coast of Portugal before the seas were calm enough and the ship had stopped moving too much. The first morning was given over to the "jet jockeys." I did not watch them; we were all very nervous, and I felt it was a more friendly gesture to stay below deck and not witness their first, tentative passes. Our turn came all too soon. Tony and I went to the briefing room where our Squadron C.O., Johnny Mortimer, ran through the programme for the afternoon. We were to carry out a series of "roller" landings, keeping the hook retracted and clear of the deck until he was satisfied with our performance; then he would tell us to lower the hook for an arrested landing.

We sat in the briefing room until the order came over the tannoy for us to man our aircraft. I climbed the ladder to the flight deck, and walked out to my aircraft in what I hoped was a nonchalant and experienced manner. I was barely settled in the cockpit before the order to start our engines came from "Flyco," the Flying Control position on the wing of the island superstructure. I pressed the starter button and, with a huge cloud of black smoke, the cartridge fired and the first of the big propellers began to spin. As soon as the engine was up to speed I started the second engine and ran through the cockpit checks for takeoff. Before I had finished Tony was taxiing up the deck towards the catapult and a marshaller was signalling for me to move forward and unfold my wings.

Once again there seemed far too much to do, leaving little time to feel nervous. I arrived on the catapult and felt the aircraft move sideways as the powered rollers centred it on the track. Aircraft handlers ran under the nose, and after a couple of seconds I felt the aircraft squat down as the tension was taken up on the wire bridle connecting the nose wheel to the catapult shuttle. I looked over my right shoulder to where the

Flight Deck Officer (F.D.O.) had just launched Tony's aircraft. He started to wave his green flag, the signal to open up my engines. A final check inside the cockpit, engines at full power, flaps down, elevator trim setting correct—I was as ready as I ever would be. Setting my head back against the padded head rest I gave the thumbs up to initiate my very first catapult launch.

The F.D.O. dropped his flag with a flourish, and for what seemed like an eternity nothing happened. Then, with smooth acceleration, I was rushed towards the bow and was airborne. By the time I had collected my thoughts I was climbing through three hundred feet. I had made it safely into the air. Now all I had to do was get myself back to the deck in one piece!

We circled while the ship prepared the flight deck for the training detail. From one thousand feet it looked no bigger than a postage stamp and far too small to make a safe landing. The C.O. spoke to us on the radio: it was time for us to make our first approach. Entering the circuit, I turned downwind about a mile off the port bow of the carrier. A final check in the cockpit, wheels down and locked, full flap, trim in the right position; as I turned on to finals I could see the meatball, just as it had appeared so often at Culdrose, and right in the middle of the bars. There it stayed the whole way down to the deck and my wheels touched down in the middle of the wires. I was so pleased with myself I almost forgot to open up my engines again.

We carried out several more rollers. Each one seemed easier than the last and my confidence grew. Johnny came back on the radio: it was time to lower the hook for the arrested landing. Again, as I turned on to finals, the meatball appeared in the middle of the mirror and I thumped the wheels down among the wires. The hook caught and I was thrown forward, almost hitting my head on the instrument panel—I had forgotten to lock my seat harness. As I taxied up the deck I did not know whether to laugh or cry. I was told I climbed down from the cockpit wearing a smile like a Cheshire cat: indeed, I couldn't but help it! Two years to the day that I had started flying training I had made it—I was a Fleet Air Arm pilot.

Ark put into Gibraltar for two days because, by some quirk of bureaucracy, we had actually to visit a Mediterranean port before the ship's company could draw foreign service pay allowances. Once clear of Gibraltar, the ship continued eastwards towards Malta so that we could use the naval air station at Halfar as a diversion. This was not strictly necessary for, as a last resort, if the plane could not be landed safely on board the aircrew could ditch or eject and be picked up by a rescue helicopter or the ship. In peacetime, however, it was considered a wise precaution to have an airfield within comfortable range, so that an aircraft that could still fly could divert to a shore base.

When we did restart flying, much of the antisubmarine work for 815 was pure make-believe. With no submarine to play with we were reduced to practising search patterns for a non-existent target, or investigating any surface shipping we picked up on our radar. At the end of March we disembarked to Halfar, in the southeast corner of Malta. This allowed us to continue flying while the ship was in Grand Harbour for a maintenance period. When we rejoined her the cruise became very repetitive, two or three weeks at sea carrying out flying exercises followed by a visit to a suitable harbour, and in the months that followed we visited Genoa, Palermo and Naples.

It was during this period that 815 had their excitement for the cruise. Tony Holloway was coming in to land at night and missed the wires. He appeared to be a little late in opening up the throttles and disappeared over the edge of the angle. Tom Kinna, our Senior Pilot who was watching from the deck, told us later that Tony's aircraft reappeared, engines screaming at full power, climbing vertically away from the sea, before subsiding tail first into the water. The crew were rescued, unhurt, by the planeguard destroyer.

A few nights later Vic Sirett, another of our pilots, was out on patrol when he realised his aircraft was not responding to elevator control. He discovered that he could maintain a semblance of level flight by using the elevator trim control, but there was no way he would be able to make a safe landing back on board. He warned the crew that they should be prepared to bail out, and then asked his observer for a course to take them to Halfar, feeling there was a chance he might be able to land the aircraft on the runway there. Before his observer had a chance to speak, Terry Peet, the telegraphist, told Vic over the intercom there was a rod running through his cockpit that was moving, but did not appear to be connected to anything. They established that it was, indeed, the elevator control and that a bolt connecting two sections was missing. Terry pulled the two ends together and stuck his pencil through the hole, effectively, if only temporarily, permitting control of the aircraft. Vic then repeated his request for a course to Halfar. His observer, rather sheepishly, admitted that when he had heard the words "bail out," he had ejected his cockpit canopy and thrown away all his navigation equipment to clear his exit! There was a happy ending and they made it back to Halfar.

It was during a NATO exercise that, for the first and only time during my fixed-wing career, I sighted an "enemy" submarine. We were carrying out a patrol in front of the fleet when, about two miles immediately ahead of me, a periscope popped to the surface. Opening the bomb doors, I dived in to attack. I don't know who was more surprised, myself at actually seeing a submarine, or the submarine skipper when two small charges exploded on either side of him! At the subsequent exercise debriefing we were credited with a "kill."

After a further period at Halfar the airgroup rejoined the ship as she moved east across the Mediterranean. She was to relieve Eagle, and take over the patrol of the waters around Cyprus in an attempt to prevent gunrunners supplying the EOKA terrorists. However, one of our Gannets had become unserviceable at Halfar and the station maintenance team was carrying out repairs. We were promised it would be ready to fly within hours of the ship sailing, and I was left behind to ferry it to the ship. It was ten hours before I was able to get airborne, by which time the ship was nearly two hundred miles from Halfar.

I was not totally happy with the prospect before me. The *Ark* was steaming away from me at twenty knots and under radio silence, while her high-powered beacon, which would have enabled me to home directly to her, had been switched off. I had no observer to navigate for me and I was going to have to rely on my own, limited, expertise. I had been given her course and speed and plotted her likely position, allowing for the fact that she would be moving further east all the time. What concerned me most was whether I would have enough fuel to return to Malta if I failed to find the ship! Once I reached cruising height, I engaged the autopilot and busied myself with the map. It was of small comfort! Apart from Malta it showed little but sea. Running through the radio frequencies was not much better. Within thirty minutes radio contact with Halfar had faded and there was no one else I could talk to. I was well and truly alone. I found the ship after two of the longest hours of my life and landed. I felt rather proud of myself and reckoned I had done a full days work. Tom Kinna disagreed and scheduled me for a navigation exercise that night.

The ship stayed in the Cyprus area for several weeks, during which time 815 flew many sorties looking for gun runners but found none. Then we turned westwards for the journey home. It was with regret that we heard the Gannet was to be phased out as the navy's antisubmarine aircraft. I had enjoyed flying it immensely. It was a gentleman's aircraft with few vices, although ponderous in comparison with the Seahawks and Sea Venoms. If it never performed quite as well on one engine as had been intended by the designers, it was very forgiving. The landing speed of a mere eighty-five knots gave plenty of time to correct any mistakes on final approach, and during the entire embarked period only once did I fail to pick up a wire first time. On that occasion the *Ark* was operating in fairly heavy weather and, despite keeping the meatball in the middle, at the last moment the ship dropped her stern into a large hole in the waves and I was forced to go round again. There was a limit to the weather in which we operated, and we stopped before reaching conditions that might have been considered acceptable in wartime. The equipment we had, both in the aircraft and on board the ship, was far superior to anything available during the 1939-1945 war. Even so, I was able to appreciate some of the problems faced by Fleet Air Arm aircrew of that period, and am still amazed at how they coped.

The Gannet was to be replaced by helicopters. The Americans had been using them in the antisubmarine role for some years with considerable success, and the Royal Navy had decided to follow suit. Gannet pilots were to be given the option of retraining to fly helicopters or transferring to night-fighters. I opted for helicopters. I had not wanted to fly day fighters and night fighters presented an even less attractive prospect, especially as several friends, including Rodney Carne from my training course, had already died flying them.

Once the *Ark* had returned to home waters, 815 disembarked to Culdrose. Ten days later the squadron was formally disbanded. My last service fixed-wing flight as a pilot was the sad one of taking the aircraft to the Naval Holding Yard at Abbotsinch, near Glasgow, where they were to be put into mothballs.

Chapter Three

On the 1st September 1958 I joined 705 Squadron at Lee-on-the-Solent, and Jane, now more than eight months pregnant, joined me. Helicopters were not new to the Royal Navy. The American-built R4, one of the first true helicopters, had been used in the Search and Rescue role towards the end of the Second World War, while in the early 1950's a Royal Navy squadron of Sikorsky S55's (again American built), had supported the ground forces in the Malaysian campaign against the communist terrorists. However, flying these machines was not highly regarded by many fixed-wing pilots and, quite unfairly, it was considered to be the last resting place for ageing aircrew before they were put out to pasture, or for those people who could not make it in the fixed-wing world.

Despite a claim by the RAF that the Fleet Air Arm was infringing their prerogative, we had set up our own pipeline for helicopter pilot training. We claimed that the pilots had their wings, the helicopter was just another form of aircraft and that we were not breaching their monopoly. To an extent that was true since all but one of the course were ex-Gannet pilots, but we had been joined by Peter Deller. Peter had completed the basic training with the RAF, but had been transferred before the award of his wings. The RAF suggested we were not entitled to continue his training, but he stayed and became, I believe, the first pilot to be awarded his wings by the Royal Navy since the end of the Second World War.

Our instructors were all naval pilots. Mine was Geoff Bagnall who had, for a time, been one of my instructors at Syerston. He introduced me to the Hiller HT1, an American helicopter since there were no suitable British machines. It was a two-seat piston-engined aircraft in which the instructor and pupil sat side-by-side.

A helicopter is kept in the air by the same forces that sustain a fixed-wing aircraft. When an aerofoil shape (a wing), moves through the air, an upwards force is produced. This force, known as lift, can be changed, increasing and decreasing with speed and with the angle at which the wing passes through the air (the angle of attack). A conventional aircraft generates this lift by moving the wing forward; if it reduces below a certain speed (the stalling speed), insufficient lift is produced and it stops flying. A helicopter generates lift by rotating the wings (the rotor blades) through the air, and can do so while hovering over a spot.

To control a helicopter in the hover the pilot must maintain a balance between several forces. Gravity is opposed by the lift from the rotor blades. There is a tendency for the fuselage to rotate underneath the blades, instead of the blades rotating, and this is balanced by a sideways force exerted by the tail rotor. If the machine is hovering close to the ground, an increase in upwards force is derived from the cushion of air that builds up under the fuselage, known as the ground cushion, and can also be increased by any natural wind, which may speed up the passage of air over the blades but also tends to destroy the ground cushion!

Contrary to some expectations, especially from writers of fiction, film directors and film sound men, the speed of rotation of the blades in flight must be held within a small band at all times, in most cases no more than about two percent of the optimum. If this speed is too low the blade tips will rise, pivoting around the blade root, until they "clap hands" above the helicopter. If they rotate too fast, the centrifugal force will increase to the point at which the blade will be pulled out from the root; in both cases the helicopter ceases to fly.

A helicopter is manoeuvred using three main controls. The first is the cyclic, which is the equivalent of the control column in a conventional aircraft. Movement of the cyclic in any direction causes the rotor disc, the path which all the main rotor blades follow, to tilt in the direction of the movement and pull the helicopter in that direction. The second control is the rudder pedals, used to increase or decrease the angle of attack of the tail rotor blades, altering as necessary the force holding the aircraft straight. The third is the collective lever. This is moved in the vertical plane by the pilot's left hand, and alters the angle of attack of all the main rotor blades together and by the same amount, increasing or decreasing the total amount of vertical lift.

There is a further complication. Increasing the angle of attack on the rotors also increases the drag of the blades through the air, which in turn requires more power to maintain the rotor speed. To achieve this the collective is linked to the engine, and raising or lowering the collective broadly compensates for the change in power requirement. In helicopters not fitted with a full engine speed governor, the fine tuning is controlled by a twist grip throttle attached to the end of the collective.

The interaction between the controls is considerable. Any change to the flight path by an external force or an input by the pilot, requires an alteration to all the controls to keep the helicopter in balance. When I first tried to hover the Hiller I found myself skittering across the airfield like a demented dragonfly; it was like trying to stand on top of a partially deflated rubber ball, while at the same time rubbing my stomach with one hand and patting the top of my head with the other.

A major difference between fixed-wing and helicopters was immediately apparent as I stepped in to the cockpit. In fixed-wing the Captain, or a student under training, sits in the left seat, in a helicopter he sits on the right. No one has ever given me a truly satisfactory reason for this. As with so much in aviation, if you ask six pilots the same question you will get seven or even eight different answers. The probable reason is that most people are naturally right handed, and by placing the Captain in the right hand seat he has the cyclic which, without some form of autopilot must be held at all times, in his right hand. This leaves his left hand free to operate the collective and the remainder of the controls, radios and switches which are normally placed in the centre of the cockpit. It has also been suggested that it is easier to escape from the right hand seat should there be an emergency!

There was yet another hazard in the Hiller. There was no automatic engine speed control and rotor speed had to be continuously adjusted using the twist grip throttle. The collective was linked directly to the rotors by a system of rods that transmitted all the rotor head vibration to the pilot's left hand. A firm grip, convulsive in the case of many student pilots, had to be maintained on the collective as it was raised and lowered, while at the same time the wrist was flexed to rotate the throttle. By the end of a training sortie which could last up to an hour or more, the student's left hand could be bent into a deathlike claw, known as "Hiller wrist," which took several minutes to relax at the end of the flight.

Once we had mastered the hover our instructors moved us on to forward flight. Apart from the problems of maintaining balanced flight there was little difference between the helicopter and the aircraft we had been flying before; what was changed was that we had to remember to slow down and stop before attempting a landing. Unlike the fixed-wing aircraft, the helicopter would not stall and fall out of the sky.

Once he was satisfied that I would not come to too much harm on my own, Geoff carried out the final stage of the dual training and showed me that the sudden loss of the engine was not catastrophic. The demonstration was simple and effective—at one thousand feet above the airfield he switched off the engine!

The silence was deafening, the result startling. The rotor revolutions sagged and Geoff had to lower the collective swiftly to prevent them dropping any further. Although the helicopter seemed to me to descend with all the aerodynamic qualities of a brick-built toilet, the rotors kept going around, driven by the updraught of air through them, and it also flew under full control. This is known as an autorotation.

As we approached the ground, moving forward at about sixty knots, Geoff eased back on the cyclic, bringing up the nose of the helicopter and converting our forward speed to higher rotor speed. We came to a full stop about ten feet above the ground and, as we sank towards the grass, Geoff pulled up on the collective and used the remaining energy in the system to cushion the touch down. We landed, light as a feather, no damage to the helicopter and no requirement for the high forward speed needed for a forced landing in a fixed-wing aircraft. Once we were safely on the ground I recommended breathing!

We were not allowed to practice autorotations to a full landing when solo. If mishandled they could be as disastrous as any other form of emergency. We were required to initiate an autorotation by closing the throttle fully, which separated the rotors from the engine; and then stop the descent and come to a hover several feet above the ground by opening up the throttle and reconnecting the engine and rotors.

Over the next two hours, with Geoff alongside me to take the blame if I fouled-up, I carried out fifteen or twenty autorotations to the ground until he was satisfied that I would probably walk away from a real engine failure. Then I was sent up for my first solo. I had eight hours dual experience at this stage, about average for the conversion of a fixed-wing pilot who did not need to be taught basic airmanship. The time taken to go solo for someone with no flying experience of any kind depends on the aptitude of the student, but would seldom be less than twelve or fourteen hours.

Ground school was not neglected. One afternoon, when the weather was too bad for flying, we were shown three films. These had been produced by the British, Americans and Dutch respectively, and were supposed to explain the theory of helicopter aerodynamics. As the lights went on at the end of the show our instructor informed us we now knew as much as he did on the subject. I was confused; the films gave divergent opinions on the hows and whys; they even used different technical terms! I decided I would accept that the helicopter could fly—after all I had been doing it for several weeks—but would not enquire too deeply into why.

The Hiller was used only for the basic conversion, and after twenty hours on it, we moved to the American Sikorsky S55, known in Britain as the Whirlwind. It had a big, rotary piston engine and a three-bladed main rotor system, was much bigger than the Hiller and had a main cabin that could seat eight people. Once we got used to the size it was easier to fly. There was far less vibration and the controls were hydraulically assisted, making for far more precise control. The throttle was still manually operated, and we had to use it continuously to maintain the rotor speed between 205 and 213 RPM. Less than two hours sufficed to bring us to solo standard, then we progressed to learning how to use the aircraft. Although we were all destined to end up in antisubmarine squadrons, training for that role would be given after we left 705; at Lee we concentrated on Search and Rescue (SAR) techniques.

In the SAR role the Whirlwind carried a crew of three, a pilot and two crewmen, and was fitted with an hydraulic winch that could lift a survivor from the water. This was normally controlled by one of the crewmen although the pilot could use it in an emergency. In the early stages of training we practised over the airfield. One of the crewmen remained on the ground, simulating a survivor, and the helicopter would be brought to a hover about twenty feet above him. Because the pilot could not see directly underneath his aircraft he had to hold an accurate hover over the "body" by following the instructions given to him by the winch operator. This required close co-operation and total confidence between all members of the crew.

Once we had become proficient over land we were allowed to pick someone out of the water. The "survivors" for this exercise were meant to be volunteers, but they also had to be stupid enough to jump into the cold, October waters of the Solent and swim around until they were rescued. There were seldom enough, and frequently the pilots-under-training were "volunteered." This provided us with an excellent incentive to improve our techniques; if we took too long to carry out the rescue or dragged the body at high speed through the water on the end of the wire, we could guarantee we would receive the same treatment when we went swimming at a later date!

Early in October I went to the Naval Air Station to play in the trials for the Fleet Air Arm rugby team and over a period of two days played several games, mostly in the pouring rain. Whether it was this, or my immersion in the Solent I have no idea, but shortly after my return to Lee I began to feel very ill, shivering and sweating at the same time. It could not have come at a worse moment. Jane went in to the nursing home to give birth to our first son, Sean, and I had my final handling check within a matter of days. I waited until both events had been successfully completed before going to see the doctor who, after a short examination, informed me I was recovering from pneumonia and sent me on convalescent leave!

The helicopter conversion completed, we went to *HMS Vernon*, the Torpedo and Antisubmarine school at Portsmouth, and then to the naval base at Portland, for Antisubmarine courses. These were to introduce us to the sonar equipment fitted in helicopters, and the tactics we would use when operating with surface ships. We were joined by some Aircrew Observers and the seaman ratings trained to operate the sonar, the submarine-tracking device.

Our welcome at Vernon was warm and friendly, in stark contrast to that at Portland where our reception was frosty in the extreme. Plans to add a helicopter base to the dockyard facilities were well in hand, and we appeared to be regarded as the advance guard of a most unwelcome invasion, more evidence of the distrust of aviators by the seaman branch. When we left Portland to go on Christmas leave, and then to Eglinton in the New Year to join 815 squadron and recommence flying, it seemed that the pleasure at our departure was entirely mutual. My pleasure was greater than most, since I had managed to rent one half of an old farmhouse close by the air station, and Jane and Sean were to join me there.

815, despite it's frontline number, was a training squadron and again we were faced by a conversion to a new type. The majority of the squadron aircraft were Westland Whirlwind MkVIIs, a copy of the

American S55, but with an Alvis Leonides Major, a British engine, replacing the American Pratt and Whitney or Wright engines. The Whirlwind VII was fitted with a cartridge starter instead of the American electric system, and the Alvis engine was a reluctant starter at the best of times, more so in the cold Northern Ireland winter. We had a couple of American aircraft that, after a few asthmatic grunts and wheezes, would burst into life, leaving the MkVIIs firing salvoes of cartridges. Sometimes the rotary container containing the cartridges would jam, and when shut down away from base it was not uncommon to see the pilot climb from his cockpit, walk to the front of the aircraft, open the clamshell doors and give the starter a hefty kick.

All the helicopters were fitted with sonar, the modern name for the wartime ASDIC. It consisted of a dome containing a sound transmitter, which could be lowered into the water on the end of a long, electrical cable. Unlike the sonobuoys carried by the Gannet, sonar is active, pushing out pulses of sound and then listening for the echoes that return when the sound pulse strikes a submerged object. By measuring the time taken between the transmission of the pulse and the reception of the echo, an accurate estimate of the range of the object can be made. By adding a bearing to the range, the position of the object can be pinpointed. It sounds easy, but is complicated by the fact that almost any object in the water will return an echo—rocks, shoals of fish, even a patch of water at a different temperature to the rest.

The observer and sonar operator, sitting in the main cabin, had the task of finding the submarine and distinguishing it from other echoes. They then had to maintain contact with it, plotting the position, course and speed, so that an attack could be made with some form of antisubmarine torpedo or depth charge. While the sonar was in the water the pilot had to hold an accurate hover at thirty feet above the surface. There was no autopilot, no governor to maintain the engine and rotor speed, and no means of estimating the height above the water apart from the Mk I eyeball. The aircraft were always operated at close to maximum all up weight, requiring the engine to run at near maximum power and leaving little margin for error. The pilot could not see the cable beneath the belly of the aircraft and had to follow the gyrations of a small cockpit indicator which showed the angle the cable was making with the vertical. A loss of concentration could have several results, all of them bad. Failure to keep the cable close to the vertical produced inaccurate sonar information; too high a hover and the dome would break clear of the water, too low and the helicopter would be covered with corrosive salt water from the spray kicked up by the rotor down-wash. In strong winds and bad weather, although the power require-ment was reduced, the pilot had to follow the wave pattern to maintain an accurate height. It was possible to get out of phase with the troughs and crests: one minute the dome would be swinging wildly in the air, the next, the crest of a wave would approach at eye level and there was a danger of the aircraft being swamped and ditching. The days of the antisubmarine pilot being little more than a taxi driver were long gone; now we worked like one-armed paper hangers, and the effort required was both mentally and physically tiring.

The course had its lighter side. There were members of the Women's Royal Naval Service still stationed at Eglinton. During a long and rather boring sortie, we eavesdropped on a conversation between an observer and his pilot in one of the aircraft in the training area. It centred around his desires and designs on one of the Wrens, but he was totally unaware that his radio transmitter had temporarily stuck on and that his inten-tions were being broadcast to the world in general, and to the Wrens in the Eglinton control tower in particular. He was made aware of the radio fault when, on his return to base, the pilot was ordered to land in front of the tower where they were met by several senior officers—and the Chief Wren!

Eglinton, despite only recently having been considerably refurbished, was soon to close as a Naval Air Station and, at the end of March 1959, very sadly we moved the aircraft to Portland. Despite the isolation from the rest of the UK, Eglinton had always been a popular appointment and we had some reservations about our reception at our new home. Our concern was not far from the truth, but fortunately we had only three weeks to go to the end of the course. This was just long enough to cross swords with "The Establishment," but not long enough for it to have a lasting effect on our futures.

At the end of the course most of us were sent to 815, disbanded as a training squadron and reformed, at Culdrose, as a front-line antisubmarine outfit. However, before we had a chance to start flying, the Whirlwind VII was grounded. For some time the aircraft had been plagued by failures of the clutch, the mechanical linkage between the engine and the rotors, and until a "fix" was found for the problem the aircraft was not to be allowed to fly operationally. As an immediate measure a Gannet squadron, 810, was formed at Culdrose to fill the antisubmarine gap left in the Far East Fleet. Most ex-Gannet pilots were now flying helicopters, so some of them had to be transferred back to fixed-wing. At least one was seen attempting to bring his Gannet to a hover over the threshold of the main runway at Culdrose!

The rest of us were sent on leave to await the supply of modification kits for the Whirlwind. When they arrived, 815 was renumbered 700H and became a trials squadron. Our task was to fly the new clutches, to destruction if necessary, and prove one way or another whether the modification would work. For the next two months we all flew up to six hours a day; never going outside the airfield boundary but simulating the rigours of antisubmarine flying by hovering for fifteen minutes and then flying a circuit back to the hover. To strain the clutch even further we carried out several autorotations during the ninety-minute flights. It was incredibly monotonous. We flew throughout daylight hours, even over the lunch hour when we were provided with sandwiches which we ate while airborne. In the afternoon it was quite normal to see two or three helicopters hovering close to one another over the hardstanding, performing what appeared to be a tribal dance. In fact we were playing blow-football, using the downwash from our rotors to move the screwed-up paper bag that had contained our sandwiches from one end of the dispersal to the other.

The trial was a success, and in September 815 reformed and began a workup programme before embarking in HMS Albion in January 1960. The nearest submarines were at Portland, and since it would have been impossible to exercise with them using Culdrose as a base, we moved the whole squadron to Dorset. There had been many changes there. The old Fleet Canteen had been converted to squadron offices, and the sports fields were now a helicopter landing area; best of all it was obvious there had been a radical change of heart, and we were no longer regarded as interlopers.

For two months we operated daily with both submarines and surface ships. The transit distances to the exercise areas, unlike that at Eglinton, were quite short and the limited endurance of our aircraft was less of a problem. Everything went well until we lost our first aircraft. Four of our machines were operating off Portland Bill when one of them, with John Arbuthnot as pilot, failed to answer a radio call. The other three, myself among them, broke hover and went to start a search of the area. It was not long before we found the crew, sitting unhurt in their dinghies. Our aircraft were not fitted with winches; the weight penalty would have cut our endurance by an unacceptable margin, and instead we carried a "heave-ho" hoist, a lightweight system of ropes and pulleys that could be attached to a fuselage strongpoint and used to pull a survivor up to the cabin by muscle power. We each lifted one cold, wet body—all the extra weight we could manage—and returned to Portland.

The crew had received no warning of the failure. One moment they were sitting happily in the hover, the next the engine had quit and they ditched. As the rotor blades hit the water the aircraft rolled on to it's left hand side and sank like a stone. The sonar operator had been carried some way down inside the aircraft before he was able to struggle clear.

He reported that he had great difficulty in getting out through his window with the bulky dinghy pack strapped to his back, but had managed to pull himself to the main cabin door. Even then his troubles were not at an end since he had become disorientated, and had no idea of which way was up. This was not the first engine failure in the Whirlwind VII, nor by any means the last. We were to be plagued by the problem for many years to come.

At the end of 1959 we returned to Culdrose. After a short period in rented accommodation, Jane and I had bought a cottage in Mullion, once lived in by Group Captain Cheshire when he was starting his "home" at the old Predannack airfield on the Lizard peninsular. It was very small, two tiny bedrooms, bathroom, living room and kitchen, but it suited us well, especially the price of just over two thousand pounds. We felt it was reasonable to expect that I would spend the next few years working from Culdrose, and that it would be sensible to obtain a foothold in the house market there. We never regretted our decision, even if I never spent much time living in the cottage.

Albion was due to sail for the Mediterranean at the end of January 1960, and 815 embarked while the ship was still alongside the South Railway Jetty in Portsmouth Dockyard. The majority of the personnel went by road. Once they had settled in, we flew the aircraft to the ship, refuelling at Exeter civil airport on the way—even with full fuel we could not make the journey non-stop. Three days later the ship sailed southwest down the Channel for the start of a year away from home waters.

Chapter Four

815 squadron had two main tasks when embarked, the first to protect the carrier and any other accompanying vessels from attack by submarine; the second was to provide the search and rescue cover for the carrier airgroup. As a bonus we could take mail and small loads of stores around the fleet, and carry passengers when necessary.

The pilots had to become deck qualified before being allowed to operate from the carrier. Only "Nob" Cornabe, our Commanding Officer, and John Brigham, the Senior Pilot, had flown a helicopter from a ship at sea; the rest of us would have to carry out a minimum of four takeoffs and landings, without passengers and with the ship under way, to become qualified, and this had to happen before the fixed wing arrived so that we could provide the SAR cover.

There is no black art to deck operations in a helicopter and the techniques are very similar to those employed onshore. What art there is lies in concentrating on the deck for a hover reference on takeoff, and not looking at the sea rushing past until you are about to move into forward flight. On returning to the deck the aircraft is flown close to the ship and facing into the combination of the natural wind and the ship's forward movement—the relative wind. Once there, the pilot comes to a hover using a spot on the deck as a reference to maintain a position in formation with the ship. When the marshaller signals that the deck is ready, the pilot manoeuvres in over the deck edge and lands. As long as he doesn't allow his concentration to slip away from the deck to the sea, all should be well. Whether it be at sea or on land, the actual touchdown is the same, although if the ship is pitching and rolling it may be necessary to hover in the ground cushion and wait until there is the inevitable period of calm in the wave pattern.

We maintained two aircraft in the SAR role throughout our stay in the ship, with the sonar gear removed and the hydraulic winch fitted. The SAR crew, a pilot and two crewmen, was available throughout daylight hours, sometimes even when the ship was in harbour. If we were at sea the SAR was at thirty minutes notice, and when the ship was at flying stations the helicopter was ranged on deck with the crew at immediate notice in the briefing room. When fixed wing operations to or from the deck are in progress the SAR aircraft, or Planeguard as it is more often known, would be airborne, taking off before the ship turns into wind for the launch or recovery. During the launch the SAR pilot takes up a position about fifty yards out from the port bow, level with the catapults, and hovers there while the planes are boosted off. As soon as the last one has been launched the Planeguard lands back on board or, if there are fixed wings to be recovered, slips back to a position abeam the after end of the deck. There it stays until the last plane has landed, before itself returning to the deck.

The first crewman operates the winch, the second, fully equipped in shallow water diving gear, stands by in case a pilot has a problem during his takeoff or landing, and ditches. If necessary the diver can go down with the aircraft as it sinks and help the crew escape. There have been all too many occasions when planes have crashed alongside the ship with the aircrew unable to extricate themselves, and the crew of the carrier have had to stand by, helpless, and watch a man drown. Hopefully this need never happen again.

I had a grandstand view of the arrival of the airgroup from the cockpit of the "Planeguard." I had been a willing enough volunteer for helicopters, but I could not help wondering whether I might not have furthered my career more by staying in fixed wing. Helicopters were still regarded as a backwater, and at that time there was no talk of a rundown of the Fleet Air Arm.

Since the end of the Second World War the Fleet Air Arm had provided most of the air cover in almost every sphere of Britain's wartime operations, from Korea to Suez, and later on even in the abortive attempt to prevent Rhodesia from declaring UDI, when an aircraft carrier was kept on almost constant standby on the "Beira Patrol" in the Indian Ocean. It appeared to us in 1960 that the need for the fully mobile air arm we represented was obvious. Six years later, with Mr Healey as Defence Minister, and not a little support from some people in our own service, our optimism was to prove unfounded. Subsequently, our concern at the loss of the conventional fixed wing force was to be proved correct. Apart from the bombing of the Stanley runway, all air cover during the recovery of the Falklands was provided by ship-based aircraft, and the lack of Airborne Early Warning Radar (AEW) aircraft was to have a significant bearing on the losses of ships. Shortly after that campaign a programme was instituted to fit helicopters with AEW radar!

While it may be argued that the Cold War, and confrontation with the Eastern Bloc, required a land-based airforce, history and the United States of America have proved that the true fixed-wing aircraft carrier is almost the only way of providing air cover to the flash points, especially when overflying or operating rights to allow land-based aircraft access to the scene of conflict may not be granted by less belligerent countries. At the time of writing, at the start of the new Millennium, even the Labour Government seems to have hoisted in that fact, and is contemplating a return to larger aircraft carriers for the Royal Navy.

Our antisubmarine duties in Albion involved the remaining eight squadron aircraft. Unlike submarines in World War Two, the nuclear submarine has most of the advantages as it lurks beneath the waves. It seldom has a problem getting in to an attacking position, since the submerged speed of modern nuclear submarines exceeds that of most surface ships, nor does it have to surface to replenish its batteries or air. The modern torpedo can be fired in the general direction of the target and then homes on to it; the submarine need not even come to periscope depth to aim the weapon. Long range detection of both submarines and surface ships is carried out by listening to the propeller and other noises; surface ships are inherently noisy while submarines can be made almost noiseless when submerged.

Although massive improvements have been made in active detection methods since the early days of ASDIC, there are still layers in the sea which prevent the sonar "seeing" through them, and even at close range it is possible for a submarine to hang beneath a layer unobserved. There are more difficulties for the Task Force Commander. The elements seldom cooperate and the wind always seems to blow from any direction other than that in which he wishes to steam. When the time comes to launch fixed-wing aircraft, a surface screen of ships must be reoriented, inevitably leaving gaps as it does so. It is these gaps that the modern antisubmarine helicopter is designed to fill. Their speed and endurance allow them to range far ahead; they can lower their sonar dome to considerable depths to detect targets beneath the layers and, since only the sonar dome is immersed in the water, they are a difficult target for the submarine.

In 1960 we had few of the advantages of the modern helicopter. Our Whirlwinds were underpowered, overloaded and of very limited endurance. Our sonar was short range, and the length of sonar cable we were able to carry allowed the dome to be lowered beneath only the shallowest layers. We could not operate at night; we could transit as long as we had some visual references but, without an autohover device, we were unable to maintain an accurate enough hover for either antisubmarine or SAR work. At night both these duties reverted to surface ships.

Albion was scheduled to take over the duties of Far East Carrier from *HMS Centaur*, but first we were going to spend a couple of months in the Mediterranean. After the obligatory stop at Gibraltar the ship left harbour and sailed east, our helicopters providing a leaving-harbour screen. Within minutes of takeoff we lost another aircraft. Three of our helicopters were in an arc a few miles ahead of the ship, sweeping the depths with their sonar before leaping into forward flight to prevent the carrier overrunning them, when one of them failed to answer the radio and disappeared off the ship's radar.

The SAR was scrambled and a search commenced. We were fortunate that the weather was good with a calm sea. The crew were found without difficulty, sitting in their dinghies and apparently unharmed, and they were back on board *Albion* being debriefed within fifteen minutes of ditching. It seemed to be a repetition of the Portland accident. They had been decelerating to enter a hover when the engine had failed without any warning, leaving the pilot no option but to ditch; and also, as at Portland, the moment the rotors touched the water the aircraft rolled on it's side and sank. The loss of a second helicopter from engine failure, coupled with reports from other squadrons of similar failures, caused us considerable concern. We had proved the clutch could take the strain, but had we just transferred the problem further down the drive train? Westlands and Alvis' were already working to find an answer and we had to live with the risks involved, for to ground the Whirlwind yet again was deemed unacceptable. We continued flying as the carrier continued eastwards to Malta, where the airgroup disembarked to Halfar.

Within twenty-four hours of disembarking, it was my turn to have an incident. I had just taken off on a maintenance test flight, and was climbing out over Marsaslokk harbour, when the engine coughed and lost power. Instinctively I lowered the collective and entered autorotation; then, realising that the engine had not actually stopped, I gently re-engaged the rotors to check whether I had enough power to get back to the airfield. There was not enough to maintain height, but in a slow descent I was able to make it back to our dispersal. A full strip of the engine revealed that I had suffered a malfunction of the fuel system—a relief in some ways, but we were no closer to a solution to the main problem.

The atmosphere in Malta had changed, even in the short time that had elapsed since I had been there in the *Ark Royal*. It was obvious that the British were no longer popular, and in comparison to the heyday of the pre-war Mediterranean Fleet the change was radical. The population still relied heavily on the money brought in by the military, but the winds of change were blowing as strongly here as in Africa, and local politicians were making noises about independence. There were still a few signs of the old naval way of life. The "Gut," the bar and nightclub area in Valetta, still catered for naval tastes, and the polo club was still operating. A polo match was arranged between 815 and the Sea Venom squadron, although of the ten people involved only two had ever ridden before, and neither of us had played polo. This was not allowed to interfere, but it was debatable who suffered most, the ponies or us!

The airgroup lost its first two fixed-wing aircraft while we were disembarked. The Sea Venoms, a navalised version of the Vampire, were carrying out night interception exercises from Halfar when two of them had a mid-air collision. Despite an exhaustive search only splintered fragments of the wooden fuselages were found. Two of the aircrew managed to eject and survived, but the other two were killed.

We left Malta and steamed further east towards Suez, but before actually entering the canal we were to suffer an Admiral's inspection. This was designed to ensure the ship and airgroup were, in all respects, ready to assume the mantle of "Far East Carrier," and for any other contingency that might befall us. The staff of Flag Officer (Aircraft Carriers) put the entire ship's company through their paces. The airgroup flew constantly, by day and by night, the ship was "struck" by torpedoes and the damage control parties proved that they could keep the ship afloat; the guns were fired and the engine room staff steamed the ship with some of the boilers shut down. Even the Supply and Secretariat branch were involved, although I do not believe they were required to fry the proverbial egg at the masthead. I say I believe, because my part in the inspection was less than glorious. A couple of nights before the start, while retiring to bed after a somewhat high spirited wardroom mess dinner, I had fallen up a ladder and bruised my shin. By the following morning my leg had turned a delicate shade of purple and the Medical Officer grabbed me with glee, putting me to bed in the sick bay. He said I was the first real casualty he had seen since leaving the UK, and that it made a change from doling out aspirin and treating VD; by the time the broken blood vessels had mended, and my leg had resumed its normal colour and size, the inspection was over.

I was up and about in time for the passage through the canal. It was all new country to me since I had never been "East of Suez." We joined a southbound convoy, *Albion* and her attendant frigate being the only warships. It was obvious that we were less than popular with the Egyptians—hardly surprising since the abortive 1956 Suez campaign must have been reasonably fresh in their minds. They lined the banks of the canal as we passed, whistling and jeering; several of them turned their backs on us and, raising their nightshirts, revealed bare backsides—not a pretty sight! We had travelled only a few miles when an Egyptian tugboat tried to savage us. It came at high speed and against the flow of traffic, displaying every intention of trying to ram, and forced us to take avoiding action. The speed of ships in the canal is limited to prevent their wake damaging the banks, and at low speed our rudder was not very effective. We missed the tug but plugged our bows into the canal bank.

The reaction of our captain, Captain Torrens-Spence, was quick and decisive, but in one way somewhat unusual. The engines were put full astern, and then the entire ship's company, apart from those on essential duty, was summoned to the flight deck. We were marshalled to one side of the deck and, at the given order, we ran from side to side in an attempt to rock the ship clear of the clinging sand. I have no idea whether the movement of over one thousand men had an effect, but we broke clear and continued on our way.

We passed several Egyptian Air Force bases, still littered with the wrecks of aircraft destroyed by the British and French during the Suez campaign. We saw some Russian-built helicopters, although from intelligence sources we gathered they were mostly unserviceable due to both lack of spares and the expertise to maintain them. As we transited the Bitter Lakes we had to thread our way through a fleet of salvage ships removing the freighters that had been sunk by the Egyptians to block the canal. Ironically, many of the salvage teams came from either Britain or France.

Once clear of the canal and into the Red Sea, we were able to stop to investigate the damage caused by our grounding. We were taking water into some of the bow compartments, and an external examination by the ship's divers revealed we had bent the lower section of the bow. It was obvious we would need the services of a dry dock to make repairs and, since the nearest one was in Singapore, it was decided we should curtail our stay in Aden.

This decision did not worry the ship's company unduly. It was to be another seven years before the British garrison forces were pulled out, but Aden, once an important fuelling station on the route between Europe and the Orient, was dying. From the smell that drifted across the harbour it seemed that Aden was actually dead and decomposing! The heat was intense. The cabin I shared with Peter Deller, immediately beneath the after end of the steel flight deck, had no air conditioning and the temperature never dropped below ninety-five degrees Fahrenheit. We were forced to choose between sleeping in a sauna bath, or on the stern gun deck. Peter chose the gun deck and I stayed in the sauna!

We left after two days and began a fast passage across the Indian Ocean. Our destination was *HMS Terror*, the naval base and dockyard on the northern shore of Singapore Island. During the voyage we received a signal from the Ministry of Defence (Navy) grounding the Whirlwind again. The engine problems had been caused by failure of the main crankshaft bearing and, until these had been replaced, we were not to be allowed to fly, except for one short journey from the Johore Straits to the Naval Air Station at Sembawang.

Sembawang was a grass airfield carved out of the jungle in the centre of Singapore Island. There was little activity there, the only full time residents being a small naval holding party who coped with the helicopter squadrons that disembarked from time to time, and a detachment of the Army Air Corps. The army was operating Auster communications aircraft from a perforated steel-planking runway left over from the war.

In 1942 the air station had been one of the last places to surrender to the Japanese, and still bore signs of their occupation. They had tried to build a second runway using prisoner of war slave labour, and had started to excavate a hill to make way for it. Using all the delaying tactics they could devise, the POWs had ensured that the job was never completed, and the excavation stood out like a huge red scar against the surrounding jungle. The officers mess, a long, single-storied building built before the war, was perched on top of a small hill overlooking the field. Inside the mess the air was stirred, but not cooled, by huge fans hanging from the ceiling. We lay at night, sweating under mosquito nets in what appeared to be permanent, one hundred percent humidity. A single, unshaded light bulb burned continuously in the wardrobe; without it our clothes would have been covered by green mould within twenty four hours. We were warned to keep anything of value under lock and key, especially at night; it was then that the "grease monkeys" appeared—local thieves who covered their naked bodies with grease to make capture more difficult.

We worked tropical routine, starting at six in the morning, pausing for breakfast and finishing by one in the afternoon; by then it was considered too hot and humid to work, even for the English. After a leisurely lunch we were free to retire to our beds or the swimming pool. This system also allowed us to avoid flying during the daily downpour, which arrived like clockwork towards the end of the afternoon. By four o'clock the thunderclouds would start to build, rearing their heads over the island, and by five o'clock it would be raining. This was no gentle dew from heaven—it came down in solid sheets of water, sufficient at times to force cars to stop, their windscreen wipers unable to cope. The only sensible action for a pilot caught flying a helicopter in such a storm was to land or, if this was not possible, to come to a hover in contact with the surface until it ceased. Within minutes of the start of the storm the monsoon ditches that drained the airfield, some of them eight to ten feet deep, would be filled with fast-flowing, muddy, red coloured water. Then, almost as quickly as it had begun, the rain ceased, the clouds disappeared, and the sun and humidity would reappear.

We cooled our heels at Sembawang for a fortnight, awaiting the arrival of the new engine bearings. Once they had been fitted we started a trial similar to the one at Culdrose—endless hovering over the airfield at high power in an attempt to break the engines. When we had completed about thirty hours on each engine without mishap they were declared serviceable, and 815 became operational again. We stayed on at Sembawang however, *Albion* was still in dry dock having a new section of bow welded on to the hull and it was to be another two weeks before she would be ready for sea. It was during this period that I received the news that I had a second son, Anthony, born in the cottage at Mullion.

Once the dockyard had finished with *Albion*, she slipped and sailed for the next stage of the commission, 815 flying on board as she steamed down the Johore Straits. The remainder of the airgroup, which had disembarked to various airfields scattered around the island, returned once the ship reached open water. In company with a frigate and a small Fleet Train of Royal Fleet Auxiliaries—merchant ships built for and owned by the Royal Navy, but manned by the Merchant Navy—we were to sail north-east along the coast of Asia. Our destination was South Korea, where we were to take part in an exercise with the American navy.

As we sailed up the east coast of Malaysia we stopped for a while over the wrecks of the *Prince of Wales* and *Repulse*, and held a memorial service for those members of their crews who had been killed. In December 1941 these two ships, regarded as among the most powerful in the world, had been sent to try to prevent the Japanese landings on the Malaysian coast. They had been escorted by a small destroyer force, but had no air cover. They were attacked by Japanese torpedo carrying aircraft and both were sunk within minutes with the loss of over one thousand lives. This action, among others, heralded the coming-of-age of naval aircraft, and the demise of the battleship.

The temperature began to drop as we approached more northerly latitudes, bringing a welcome relief to the crew, and the return of Peter Deller to our cabin. I retrieved a couple of blankets from the cupboard to supplement the sheets under which I had been sleeping. One day on passage was much like another for the aircrew, although the fixed wing pilots were luckier than those of 815. They could polish their skills by using each other as camera-gun targets, or by firing live ammunition at a splash target towed astern of the ship; we, on the other hand, needed a real submarine to obtain maximum benefit from our flying, and these were scarce. We spent most of our time in the hover, tracking non-existent targets and carrying out attacks with make-believe torpedoes. It was a soul destroying occupation that reduced one of our pilots to request permission to return to the carrier on the grounds that he had destroyed the paper submarine with his cardboard depth charge. Our Commander (Air), Joe Honeywill, my ex-Senior Naval Officer from Syerston days, was less than amused.

In the evenings we could relax over a drink in the wardroom, and reread old newspapers and magazines. I discovered that *Hansard*, the report of parliamentary proceedings, was frequently more amusing than *Punch*, and read them from cover to cover. I also discovered, to my cost, that Roman Catholic padres are often very good poker players. Father John Sheehy explained that he felt his prowess was a necessary part of his vocation, saying, "If you are going to beat the devil, you must know where he lives!"

Our stay in Korean waters was short. After a few days exercising with the Americans, during which time we got to play with a real submarine for the first time since leaving the Mediterranean, we anchored off Inchon for the exercise debriefing, and 815 aircraft were used to ferry debriefing officers around the fleet, and also ashore to the American base at Yong Son. Shore leave was granted to the ship's company, but few people took advantage of it. Korea seemed a very depressed country, still suffering from the aftermath of the war, and anyway, most of us were saving our money for the first "social" visit of the cruise, Yokohama. We were scheduled to spend three weeks in Japan, the first five days in Yokohama "Showing the Flag," the remainder of the time at Yokosuka, the main American naval base on the east coast of the country, for a self-maintenance period.

As is usual for any Royal Navy warship on a social visit, the first evening in Yokohama was given over to the Official Cocktail Party, probably the single most important event as far as the Wardroom was concerned. A liaison officer had been sent ahead before the ship left Inchon to organise and co-ordinate both "Official" and "Social" events for the visit. These included the formal call by our captain on the mayor of Yokohama, the mayor's return call to the ship, sports fixtures, cultural visits to temples and a host of other details. He was also held responsible by his fellow officers for ensuring that, as well as the lengthy list of official guests, there were as many young, unattached females as possible invited to the official cocktail party.

This was held on the quarterdeck and attendance was compulsory for all officers not on duty. The ship's executive officer prowled the area to make sure that we were not only there, but also entertaining all the guests. This is not always easy, and was not helped in Yokohama by the fact that many of the guests spoke nothing but Japanese. However there are ways around most problems and, after about half an hour and as the over-strength drinks began to take their toll, faces became redder, voices were raised several decibels and the starch began to disappear. There was also a less than subtle change in the shape of the party, for it was during the second half that we hastened to finalise our social arrangements for the rest of the visit. Then, as the guests moved from the quarterdeck to the flight deck to watch our Royal Marine band "Beat the Retreat," a military extravaganza at which they are unexcelled, those officers who had managed to achieve their aim, whatever form it might have taken, slipped away to their cabins. Within minutes they had changed into civilian clothes and were ready to proceed ashore with their newfound friends or hosts.

For those who failed there was always the alternative of the "Run Ashore." It is a sad fact that, despite the golden opportunities given to a Royal Navy ship's company for worldwide travel at public expense, a run ashore seems to follow a set pattern. It starts with a meal at a suitable restaurant, then deteriorates into visits to a succession of bars and night-clubs which get sleazier and more expensive as the night progresses. Once money, or stamina, or both are exhausted, the weary reveller returns to the ship. I have found it very impressive, as Officer of the Watch in the early hours of the morning, to see the return of the ship's company. There will always be the "all-fall-down" drunks among them, and they will be suitably reproved at a later date. Many, however, seen at a distance to be obviously well in their cups manage to stiffen themselves, climb the gangway silently and unaided, salute the officer of the watch in an exemplary fashion and proceed out of sight. Although as soon as they are out of sight their resolve may fail and they may fall head first down the nearest ladder, this does not matter: the name of the game is to get back on board without bringing one's self to the attention of authority, and most members of the Royal Navy are masters of the game.

Yokohama was very little different to any other visit, although the proximity of the Ginza, the famed nightclub district of Tokyo, ensured that many ventured further afield than the normal two-mile radius from the ship. By day, cultural visits to the many temples were well patronised but, fascinating as they were, one temple soon began to look like any other, and before long it became obvious that many of the visits were being used as an excuse to get out of the ship. Equally, many of the sports fixtures were little more than a way to work up a thirst for the run ashore. Five days was enough for most of us, and I was quite glad when the ship sailed for Yokosuka.

It is strange that a country like the United States, which prides itself on its ideals of freedom, initiative and self-help, produces military bases abroad that are run on some of the finest socialist principles. Most of the personnel live within the base, families and all. The camp contains everything that they could possibly find in America, much of it supplied by the Post Exchange (PX), the American answer to the British NAAFI but on a much larger scale. At Yokosuka there were Officers clubs, Enlisted mens clubs, swimming pools, laundries, football pitches and baseball parks, almost anything that was needed to turn a piece of Japan into little America. It was not unknown for some servicemen posted there to complete their entire hitch without leaving the base!

They were incredibly hospitable. *Albion's* crew were made honorary members of all the facilities, and given free run of the PX, an Aladdin's cave filled with everything we needed in the way of presents for our families. There was a fair return, and the traffic between the *USS Hancock*, an American aircraft carrier tied up close by, and *Albion* was heavy, especially at lunchtime and in the evening. The *Hancock*, like all American warships, was dry while the *Albion* wardroom had a well stocked bar. I heard one young American navy pilot declare, after a long, liquid lunch, that his ambition was to return to the States and urinate on the grave of Josephus Daniels, the Secretary of the Navy at the time of prohibition, who had banned alcohol from their ships.

It was not only their ways that were different, but also the potential of their navy. The Commanding Officer of the bomber squadron on the

Hancock invited me to look over their facilities. One of his squadron aircraft was positioned on the catapult, wisps of steam from the track showing that the catapult was operational. He told me that the crew was at readiness in the briefing room and that the aircraft could be launched in harbour, no matter what the wind direction. This was in stark contrast to *Albion* where in light wind conditions our catapults were only just able to launch a Sea Venom at maximum all up weight, and then only with the ship steaming at full speed. There was another of his aircraft further down the deck, surrounded by a rope barrier and guarded by two US Marines. As we passed by, I made to climb over the rope to take a closer look, but was forcibly restrained by my host.

"Don't even think about it," he said. "I am the CO of the squadron, but if I try to cross that barrier without proper authority those marines would shoot me!" I did not need to be a genius to realise that the aircraft must be fully armed, or to guess what weapons it might be carrying.

Our visit to Japan at an end, we sailed and wandered through Far Eastern waters, stopping for a weekend in Hong Kong and ending up in Singapore. Once more the airgroup dispersed to shore bases, 815 again to Sembawang. This time we had been allocated a submarine to play with, but we ran into trouble almost immediately. The submarine exercise areas lay well to the east of the island, and the transit time from Sembawang ate deeply into our endurance. In an attempt to maximise our fuel loads, we had stripped the aircraft of everything that was not essential, including the soundproofing from the cabins. We had weighed the aircrew, the heaviest pilot flying with the lightest observer and vice versa; even the observer's navigation bags had been weighed and everything that was considered excess to requirements had been removed, including the novels they read during the paper exercises that were so much part of our lives. Finally we were forced to use the RAF airfield at Changi, at the eastern end of the island, as a staging and refuelling point and to change crews, and by doing so we nearly doubled our time on task with the submarines.

It was now September. We were over half way through the commission and *Albion* sailed once more, this time to take part in a major exercise with the South East Asia Treaty Organisation (SEATO) navies. The forces included units from the USA, Australia, New Zealand and Thailand, and we were to escort a convoy from the Gulf of Thailand to the American naval base at Subic Bay, in the Philippines. For once 815 would be gainfully employed since there were to be submarines ranged against us, and we would also be kept very busy ferrying stores and personnel around the fleet, even to the "enemy." It was during one such transfer to *HM Submarine Teredo* that Alan Hulme, my observer on the Planeguard, managed to drop some mail into the water. We were lowering it to the conning tower when the knot securing the mailbag to a long line came undone. With the possible exception of rum—now history in the navy—and leave, mail is the most important item for a ship's company when abroad. We had to devise a method of rescue since, by the time the submarine could launch her rubber dinghy, a difficult task in the swell that was running, the bag would have disappeared.

There was only Alan in the back of the helicopter, and he was going to have to go down into the sea while I operated the winch from my cockpit. He put on the harness as I manoeuvred into position close to the mailbag. When he was ready, he swung himself out on the end of the wire and I lowered away. I lost sight of him under the aircraft before he reached the water, and had to judge when he splashed down by monitoring the hover power—as his weight came off the winch, less power was required to maintain height; then I moved sideways to watch his progress. He had very wisely remained in the harness with the wire attached and was swimming the few yards to the bag, towing the wire as I reeled it out. He retrieved the mail and gave me a triumphant thumbs-up, my signal to start moving the helicopter back over his position and hoist him on board, reeling him in like a large fish until he appeared alongside my door, dripping wet but grasping the all important bag. *Teredo* got their mail and Alan deserved a medal.

It was his fault the knot had come undone, but then he was a Short Service Officer and had not had the advantage of being trained in such essentials at Dartmouth. I confess I would not have agreed to be lowered into the shark-infested South China Sea knowing that if the winch wire broke, or my pilot had any problems, there would be no way I could get back into the helicopter!

Subic Bay was much like any other American naval base, with all the usual facilities, this time including an eighteen-hole golf course carved out of the jungle. Once again we were made honorary members of all the base facilities, but although there was no green fee it was the most expensive golf I have ever played. The fairways were narrow and the rough was reputed to contain many varieties of highly venomous snakes. Nothing would have induced me to leave the fairway and as far as I was concerned any ball that entered the rough was lost!

Our first night in harbour was given over to the cocktail party, less formal than usual since our guests were all serving US Navy officers and their families. It was followed later that evening by a return match at the Base Officers club. The highlight there was a magnificent display of Filipino dances. One of these was very traditional, involving two pairs of long bamboo poles laid at right angles to each other, leaving a square in the middle. The pairs of poles were moved so that the square opened and closed, while the dancers stepped in and out in time to the music. No doubt inspired by the congenial company, Joe Honeywill decided to join in. His performance, while nowhere near as graceful as the lovely, lissome Filipina ladies, was greeted with rapturous applause. This proved his undoing and, instead of bowing out while he was ahead, Joe opted to continue as the pace of the music increased. The result was inevitable—he stepped in when he should have been stepping out, the poles came together with a resounding crack and Joe retired with a badly damaged ankle.

Subic had other forms of entertainment that were possibly more dangerous than either golf or dancing. Immediately outside the base lay the town of Alongapo, with more bars, nightclubs and brothels than any comparable small town I know. They dispensed alcohol and VD with equal abandon, but little else. The VD was a particularly nasty species that had, we were warned, defeated the efforts of medical science to find a cure; it was even rumoured that it was standard practice for shore-bound American sailors to be given a shot of antibiotics before they left the base, rather than on return from a night on the town!

From Subic to Hong Kong was a three day trip, enlivened for me by a transfer of one of our doctors to a freighter. The SS *Twin Horse* had broadcast a distress message, requesting medical assistance for one of her seamen injured during a storm. Alan and I, as Planeguard crew, flew to the freighter and commenced lowering the doctor on the winch. From the confident way he went down I think it may have been his first airborne transfer; Alan had felt it wiser not to tell him that the drop area was smaller than we could have wished, and that the operation was made more difficult because the *Twin Horse* was rolling heavily in the swell, her mast moving to and fro across my windscreen like a huge wiper.

I flew twice during this, our last, visit to Hong Kong, both times to ferry spares to Kai Tak airport where one of our Sea Venoms had made an emergency landing the day before we entered harbour. The main purpose of the visit was "Rest and Recreation," and this took precedence over almost everything else. Hong Kong never sleeps, and both sides of the harbour were ablaze with neon signs advertising the many restaurants and nightclubs; the recreation part was easy, though whether the ship's company achieved any rest was doubtful.

After a night ashore saying farewell to friends, I returned on board early on the morning the ship was due to sail, along with what seemed like at least half the ship's company. The cable party was already preparing to weigh anchor and the ship was bustling with activity. 815 were providing a leaving harbour screen, but my name had not appeared on the flying programme until the afternoon and I planned to retire to our crew room, the only air conditioned space we could use, and catch up on some sleep.

No sooner had I closed my eyes than I was rudely awakened and told I was needed to fly. John Brigham had somehow ricked his back as he walked out to his aircraft and had decided I should replace him. It seemed an unlikely tale, but he was senior to me and I had been fool enough to be available so I had no other option. By the time I arrived at my aircraft all the others had started and were ready to lift-off. I clambered in to the cockpit and started my engine. It was not until I was airborne that I realised I had little idea of what we were meant to be doing, and this was followed immediately by dismay when I remembered John's observer had returned on board with me! My worst fears were realised when he tried to explain the briefing and it became apparent we did not have a common language to converse in. We stayed out of trouble by orbiting out of sight of the carrier, and making all the right radio calls until it was time to return to the ship and land!

Our destination was Singapore, the last stop before we began the journey home. The airgroup flew most days, the jets carrying out high level interception exercises while 815 tracked imaginary submarines. Forty-eight hours out from Hong Kong I took over the Planeguard duties. It was a miserable day, the sun losing the battle as it tried to pierce the unseasonable cloud. My crew and I were on deck waiting for the next fixed wing launch, vainly trying to repair the damage done to our suntans by the Hong Kong nights, when a broadcast from Flyco broke into our contemplation.

"Scramble the SAR!"

We manned the aircraft and I started the engine. It was still warm from the last flight and I was able to engage the rotors without having to wait for the engine to reach operating temperatures. In less than a minute we were airborne and, as we climbed away, I was able to do up my seat straps. Flyco came up on the radio. One of the Seahawk pilots, Mickey Styles, had broadcast a Mayday call: it appeared his aircraft was on fire and he was about to eject. I turned towards his last known position, about thirty miles from the ship, and pulled in full power. Twenty minutes later we were in the area. The fixed wing aircraft already airborne had been searching for Mickey but had found nothing and, by the time we got there, they were running low on fuel and had to return to the carrier.

There was a strong wind blowing, kicking up a lumpy, grey sea that made the search difficult. We flew at five-hundred feet and could see no more than a mile on either side of the helicopter. If we had flown any higher it would have been only too easy to miss the tiny one-man dinghy in which we hoped Mickey would be sitting. Thirty minutes later Alan gave a yell! He had spotted a yellow object on the surface in an area we had covered only minutes before. I headed directly for it, but even so we found it difficult to maintain visual contact: each time the object dipped into a trough we lost sight of it, and on several occasions failed to see it immediately as it rose on the next crest. When we arrived on top we found Mickey sitting in his dinghy like a waterlogged Buddha, winched him up into the helicopter, wet but uninjured, and returned him to the ship. During the debrief we discovered we had flown almost over the top of him, bringing home to us all just how difficult it was to see even a bright yellow dinghy in any sort of sea.

The airgroup stayed on board during the stay in Singapore, thoughts firmly fixed on the forthcoming visit to Mombasa and the journey home. Those who had been to Kenya before were loud in their praises of the hospitality we could expect. From the number of invitations received in the ship before we sailed it appeared Kenya was looking forward to our visit as much as we were. By the time we arrived at Mombasa it was obvious we did not have a large enough crew to take up the hospitality offered. We had eighteen hundred souls on board and at least half of them would have to be available in the port area at any one time. I was one of the lucky ones, and with Bob Hilditch, one of the Sea Venom pilots, joined the party on the night train to Nairobi. Most of the crew were going to stay there, but Bob and I had accepted an invitation to visit a cattle ranch about one hundred miles further north. After a night spent in a hotel in Nanyuki we were collected by our hostess, Irralie Murray, and driven the final miles to their home, a newly built ranch house nine thousand feet up the northern slopes of Mount Kenya.

This was the period between the end of the Mau Mau Emergency and *Uhuru*, Kenyan independence. The Murray's lifestyle was superb, but they worked hard to maintain it. Bob and I were given a free run of the ranch by day, while George and Irralie were working. The evenings were spent sitting around the table after the evening meal, either at their ranch or on neighbouring properties. The conversation ranged far and wide, frequently over their immediate future in Kenya and the prospects generally for white Africans. I fell in love with the country. I believe few people who have visited the area fail to be impressed with it, and it was with some regret that we returned to Nairobi to join up again with the rest of the *Albion's* party for the journey back to Mombasa. They were much changed. Gone were the fit, sun-tanned young men we had left, and in their place were some haggard wrecks. Talking to those who were able to stay awake we discovered that the party they attended had started as soon as they arrived in Nairobi, and had continued unabated until they boarded the night train to return to Mombasa. They had also been left with the impression that the question "Are you married, or do you come from Kenya?" was less a question and more a way of life!

We had two more ports of call, Karachi and Aden, before the final stretch home. On arrival off the coast near Karachi we joined up with units from the Pakistani and American navies for a fleet exercise. For once 815 was not used for antisubmarine work. Instead, our sonar gear was stripped out and we joined the military support role, ferrying our detachment of Royal Marines and their weapons to assault a beach. After the exercise, the ship anchored off Karachi and we were used to ferry the debriefing teams from the fleet to the Pakistani naval base at

Karsaz. Karachi seemed a smart modern town but I saw little of it, and the visit suffered in comparison with Kenya. Our route to Karsaz lay over the shantytown areas, and my abiding impression was of the stench of dirt and sewage that rose on the hot, foetid air. Initially, we transited at five hundred feet. Soon we were climbing to three thousand feet to avoid the smell.

Our departure from Aden was delayed by the late arrival of the relief carrier, allowing those of us who still had Christmas presents to buy for our families a chance to make these last minute purchases. From there we headed through the Suez Canal and the Mediterranean on a fast passage home. Instead of returning to our home base at Culdrose, 815 continued with the ship and disembarked just before *Albion* entered Portsmouth harbour. Our aircraft were to be delivered to the Royal Naval Repair Yard at Fleetlands, where they would be stripped and completely rebuilt. Even on this last flight the Whirlwind managed to let us down. As John Brigham crossed the coast his aircraft was wracked by heavy vibration from the rotor head, and he had to make an emergency landing at the old naval airbase at Gosport.

I didn't bother to find out what the problem had been. My new appointment had already arrived, and I felt it was safe to assume I would not have to fly the Whirlwind VII again. I was to join 700(H) Squadron at Culdrose in the New Year, and assist in the proving trials of the latest addition to the Fleet Air Arm. This was an all-weather, turbine powered antisubmarine helicopter, the Westland Wessex MkI.

Chapter Five

I returned to Mullion where I was introduced to Anthony and reintroduced to Sean to whom, after nearly a year abroad, I was a virtual stranger. 700(H) was based at Culdrose and, since any front line Wessex squadron would almost certainly be formed up there, we felt I could look forward to almost a year of living at home. The first half dozen production aircraft had already been delivered and the trial was well under way.

The airframe was a copy of the American Sikorsky S58 built under licence by Westlands, but there the similarity ended. The piston engine fitted to the American aircraft had been replaced by a turbine engine, the Napier Gazelle, and the flight control system (FCS) had been designed by another British firm, Louis Newmark.. From a pilot's point of view the Wessex was light years ahead of the old Whirlwind. The engine and airframe gave us a smoother and more powerful vehicle, while an automatic engine and rotor speed governor released us from the constant and tiring concentration on throttle movements. The FCS was divided into two separate, but linked, sections. The first gave us an autopilot capable of maintaining the helicopter on a set course, height and speed. The second gave us a capability of descending from cruising height, and then holding an accurate hover over the sonar dome without necessarily seeing a horizon, or even the water itself.

The Wessex was considerably more complicated than the Whirlwind, but many of the complications were taken care of by the black boxes themselves and much of the conversion could be carried out in the classroom. Once the technical systems had been mastered, learning to fly the aircraft took a very short time and consisted mainly of an appreciation of the considerable increase in size compared to the Whirlwind. My instructor was, yet again, Geoff Bagnall, and when he was satisfied with my progress, he put me on a concentrated course of instrument flying. It was not enough that for most of the time I would be wheeled about the sky by black boxes; I had to be able to take control and continue the flight when they malfunctioned. A fixed wing machine is basically stable and, left to its own devices, will try to stay in the air. A helicopter is inherently unstable and is not a good platform for instrument flying. Fortunately the techniques for flying by reference to instruments are the same for both, although it needed a higher level of concentration in the Wessex when the autopilot was switched off.

The progression to using the full FCS followed the instrument flying. We started by flying by day and in clear weather with a crew of four, two pilots, an observer and a sonar operator, and used Falmouth Bay for our training. Once we were down to our antisubmarine operational transit height of one hundred and twenty five feet above the water, we started to punch the buttons that controlled the autohover device. The black boxes decreased our height and speed until we reached a rough hover at thirty feet above the surface; the sonar operator then wound down the sonar dome on the end of the cable. As soon as it was submerged the control of the hover was switched to the sonar cable, any deviation from a position directly above the dome being translated into corrections and fed to the controls via the autopilot..

The aircraft captain monitored the height at all times, taking over control and flying the aircraft up to a safe height should any of the black boxes malfunction. The FCS was not foolproof, having an occasional, and very alarming, habit of feeding spurious signals to the controls. It could happen in any of six directions, up, down, left, right, forwards or backwards, and was known as a 'hard over,' as the controls were driven to the full extent of the autopilot's authority. If you were really unlucky, a hard over could be a combination of movements in any direction. It happened without warning and, if immediate action was not taken to counteract it, led inevitably to disaster.

I was happy to let the electronics have their way as long as I could see where I was going, but when I carried out the same exercises "under the ambers" I found it quite unnerving for the first few occasions. The ambers were a system of amber coloured, perspex screens fitted to the cockpit windows, and were used in conjunction with a pair of blue tinted goggles worn by the pilot. The combination of colours prevented a sight of the outside world, but left the pilot able to see his instruments, while the second, or safety, pilot had an unrestricted, if somewhat amber coloured, view outside the aircraft. That was the theory; but all too frequently the blend of concentration and adrenaline caused us to sweat and fog up the goggles, leaving us totally blind! Even though my co-pilot could see everything, I had the thought that there was only a thirty-foot margin between establishing a safe hover and a long, cold swim to shore, and it was always a relief when the power surged back at the end of the descent.

At night it was even worse. Except on rare, clear moonlit nights, all either of us could see was the glow from the instrument panel and the flickering of the navigation lights on the underside of the rotor blades or on the water. Total faith had to be placed on the instruments and the temptation to look outside resisted; false horizons could appear, accentuated by the reflection of the cockpit lighting on the windscreen, and distorted by raindrops clinging to the outside of the screen. As we settled in to a night hover I could see the glow of the navigation lights reflected from the water, and hear a disembodied voice from the rear cockpit intoning, "Lowering the ball." The pattern of lights in the cockpit would change as my co-pilot punched the buttons to activate the hover control, and there we would sit, locked into our confined little world until it was time to break hover and move to a new position. It was always a relief to be able to take control and fly the helicopter myself. Science was wonderful, but there was something to be said for being in charge of one's own destiny!

We lost our first aircraft at night. Geoff Bagnall, with Arnie Lewis, one of the pilots we had on loan from the Canadian navy, had been practising in Falmouth Bay when the aircraft went berserk and they ditched. It appeared that the aircraft had inverted in flight before ditching, but miraculously all the crew survived unharmed. The wreck was recovered within twenty-four hours and the cause of the accident investigated. It was discovered that the rotor brake, a device used to stop the rotors after the engine was shut down, had come on in flight and caused the loss of control. A "fix" was introduced and the trial continued without any further major mishaps.

The first front line squadron of Wessex formed up in the middle of 1961, and for the third time in my career I found myself serving in 815 Squadron. We were to work up at Culdrose. The additional range and endurance of the aircraft allowed us to play with submarines in the deep water of the Western Approaches, and we no longer had to detach the squadron to Portland. When the workup was completed we were to embark in *Ark Royal* in November for a cruise in the Mediterranean.

We had not been together long when the first rumours of an "Escape and Evasion" exercise began to surface. The authorities were said to be concerned that aircrew forced down behind enemy lines were ill equipped to cope with the problems they would undoubtedly encounter. It had been decided to remedy this, and we were to be given training in the techniques for evading capture. We did not find it very encouraging to be told we were also to be taught methods of resisting interrogation; some of us were left with the feeling that perhaps the training in evasion would be less than adequate, and that it was anticipated that we would be captured! As rumour turned to fact and the date for the exercise came closer, the aircrew at Culdrose began to be struck down with all manner of rare and crippling diseases. It was to no avail, and we were told that if we were breathing we would have to take part. Bets were laid as to where the exercise would be held, and it came as rather an anticlimax to find it was to be the Cambrian hills in Wales and not Spitzbergen.

We were driven by bus to the naval air station at Yeovilton very early one October morning, where we joined up with the remainder of the potential escapees from the Naval Air Command. We were briefed on what we could expect during "Exercise Yakidar," as the event was to be known, and in most cases it exceeded our worst fears. We were to be driven to Wales that night, and dropped in parties of three or four on the A470 road near Rhyader. We were then to proceed several miles further west to the Birmingham reservoirs and, after making contact with some exercise umpires, were to continue westward towards the safety line, the A492 south of Lampeter.

We were dressed in "Goon suits," a two piece, rubberised overall, designed, not entirely successfully, to prevent the ingress of sea water in the event of a ditching, but very good at preventing the escape of sweat as we tramped the Welsh hills. We were placed on our honour that we were not carrying anything that could be used to evade the rigours of the exercise, like the price of a hotel room, and were issued with the emergency ration packs that we could expect to be carrying on flights in wartime. Troops from the Guards Regiments, some Royal Marines and the local police were arrayed against us; their job was to capture us before we crossed the safety line and to hand us over to the interrogation centre; ours was to evade them if possible, and to resist the interrogation if we failed.

With three others from 815, I was dropped off as planned just before midnight. It was bitterly cold, a thin layer of frost crunching underfoot as we walked along the verge towards a gate leading to a field. We met an old shepherd returning from the pub, and enquired of him for the most direct way to the reservoirs. Wordlessly, he pointed into the field and down the hill from where we could hear the sound of a fast flowing river. As we moved towards the gate he spoke.

"I wouldn't go if I was you. We lose shepherds up there each winter, and they know the area!"

With those words of encouragement ringing in our ears we stumbled into the dark. After fording the river we continued to stumble for the rest of the night, reaching the rendezvous at daybreak. The umpires did not seem particularly interested in us and, having taken our names, sent us on our way while they continued to eat their hot breakfast. We learned later that almost their only duty was to ensure that the escapees had marched west into the exercise area, rather than east and to safety.

By now we were down to three, one of our party having sprained his ankle too badly to continue. Had I known what the future held for me, I might have happily broken my leg there and then! We spent a second sleepless night in a small wooded valley where the trees kept the worst of the frost off us but, mindful of the risk of capture, we did not light a fire and ate our rations cold, washed down with water from a nearby stream. We need not have worried about our enemies: they were all congregated much closer to the safety line and had no intention of stopping us until we were well and truly tired. It worked against them in one respect. A group drawn from the SAS reached the safety line before anyone thought it was possible, and well before the enemy had set up their defences. The senior member of this group, wishing to experience the rigours of the interrogation centre, returned into the exercise area to give himself up. His offer of surrender was refused on the grounds that no one in his or her right senses would do this, and that he therefore had to be an "agent provocateur" from the press!

The third night, too weary to care any more, we dossed down in a ruined farmhouse, covering the broken windows with sacking to keep out the chill wind. Before long we were joined by another group of escapees who were very much out of breath. They told us they had just escaped from an army patrol, using a certain amount of force to do so. We could not have been thinking clearly! If we had, we would have legged it away from the farmhouse. As it was, we just finished our meal and settled down to sleep. The result was inevitable. The sacking was pushed aside and the barrel of a rifle appeared through the window. It was the same patrol, and this time they were taking no chances. Tying our hands behind our backs with baling wire and linking us together with a rope around our necks, they towed us behind their vehicle at a fast trot until we reached the "Prisoner of War cage." This was the mouth of some old mine workings that had been sealed off with barbed wire. We spent the rest of the night standing in our stockinged feet, and ankle deep in freezing water; if we moved or spoke, the guards threw a bucket of water over us.

Next morning we were driven, hooded with a pillow case and lying face down in the back of an army lorry, to the interrogation centre which, I discovered later, was at the naval air station at Brawdy, in Pembrokeshire. On arrival we were ordered to lean against a wall, still hooded, with only our fingers supporting our weight and our feet spread wide apart. We remained in that position for what seemed like hours; my hands went numb, followed by my mind and the rest of my body. I can just remember one of our guards coming up behind me and saying, "Have a look at this one, his hands are all blue!"

Eventually I was led into a warm room, unhooded, and subjected to a full medical examination that left little to the imagination. At the same time my captors removed my meagre possessions and ordered me to sign a receipt for them. We had been warned about this; if we signed anything it was possible for them to use this on any other document they wished, especially a "confession," so I refused. I was immediately rehooded and taken out to resume my position against the wall.

The memory of the next few hours of my life remains with me as a series of tableaux, but happily distanced from the discomfort. We had been told there was a limit to the time we could remain in captivity, but I lost all sense of time and have no idea how long my ordeal actually lasted. I found it difficult to remember it was only an exercise, especially as I lay on the bare springs of an iron bed in an open-sided bell tent, my hands manacled to the bed head. Just as unnerving was to find myself in what appeared to be a wooden sentry box, my hands manacled this time to the walls; to add to the discomfort, they had installed a loudspeaker just in front of my face, through which came a recording of the chimes of Big Ben, the speed of the tape being varied to make the sound even more intimidating.

The interrogators were experts. I was made to sit on a one-legged stool, a red haze in front of my eyes after three days with no proper sleep. Initially I resisted the desire to talk, but became irritated at being able to give only my name, rank, service number and date of birth. A benevolent gentleman offered me a cup of tea, and began to talk about music. I answered him, realising too late it was a trick, and found myself unable to stop. A few minutes later the interrogation was taken over by the "Bad guy," who played me a tape of myself giving away classified information. I was just sufficiently aware of what was happening to realise it was probably a fake and managed to remain silent again.

Shortly afterwards I was released from custody and, for me, the exercise finished. I do not think any of us enjoyed the experience. At times it was very unpleasant, at others terrifying, but there were few, if any, real complaints, and personally I believe this type of exercise should be undergone by all members of the Armed Services. I was never physically assaulted. Torture and interrogation are regarded as being counterproductive and the interrogation team had other, far more subtle, ways of extracting information. Many of us, myself included, discovered just how unprepared we were, and perhaps at some future date would have been able to resist more effectively. I hope that I would have had no hesitation at taking part in another such affair, but fortunately the chance never materialised!

815 embarked in Ark Royal in November as planned but the cruise was short-lived. We had only just passed Gibraltar when a signal was received on board, grounding the Wessex again. There had been more problems with the rotor brake. We were ordered to cease flying and

return to the UK on board *HMS Victorious*, transferring our aircraft and personnel to her in Grand Harbour in Malta. We were allowed one more flight, off-loading to Culdrose as the ship steamed up the Channel, and there we stayed until modification kits were available.

In the New Year, our aircraft once again serviceable, we continued to use Culdrose as our base until the *Ark* returned to home waters. It was on a cold, February night that three of our aircraft were following each other around a navigation exercise. Not far from Falmouth we encountered a large snow squall; three aircraft went into it, but only two came out. There was nothing we could do. Our fuel was running low and we could not have seen anything on the ground in the prevailing weather conditions anyhow. We returned to Culdrose to await further news. It was not long in coming. Gordon Fraser, the Canadian pilot of the missing aircraft, telephoned the base to say all four of his crew were safe, but the aircraft was badly damaged. Shortly after entering the squall his engine had flamed out, but he had managed to autorotate and put the aircraft on the ground in one piece. Unfortunately he had landed on the side of a hill; his brakes had failed to hold the aircraft and it had rolled backwards down the hill and turned over on its side.

The full extent of the accident became apparent in daylight. It had been a magnificent piece of flying by Gordon, autorotating completely blind and using his radio altimeter to judge the right moment to flare and kill his rate of descent. He had also been incredibly lucky. He had landed in a steep-sided valley and his flight path had taken him very close to some high power cables; if he had hit them his chances of survival would have been minimal.. It was decided the engine failure had been caused by snow blocking the air intake, and we were warned not to fly in snow squalls!

I left 815 a month later and joined 737 Squadron at Portland. This was an operational training squadron, and my job was to teach newly qualified pilots the art of antisubmarine flying. Jane and the boys stayed at Mullion. The Dorset summer season was about to start and accommodation was hard to find, landlords preferring to take vast sums from holidaymakers rather than the pittance we could offer.

The squadron was still equipped with Whirlwind VIIs, since all the Wessex were required for front line outfits. Most of my flying was now done from the left hand seat, seldom touching the controls, but monitoring the trainees as they practised sonar hovers and instrument flying. The Whirlwind was still giving us problems and we had several ditchings, but I seemed to bear a charmed life. The closest I came to one was when I had returned early on a Monday morning after a weekend in Cornwall, and overslept. By the time I reached the crew room I was late for my scheduled flight, but found Peter Deller already preparing to take it while I was to take over his flight later in the day. He had been airborne for a couple of minutes and was just passing the Portland harbour breakwater when his engine coughed and died, and he had to ditch. From then on there was a strange reluctance among the other instructors to swap flights with me.

By the end of the summer we had managed to find a small bungalow, and Jane and the boys joined me. The flying was also more interesting, the Wessex was becoming available for training squadrons, and we had received the first few of our allocation. They were delivered direct from Westland's at Yeovil, and required an acceptance test flight before we could use them. I was one of the few Wessex trained pilots on the squadron, and the job of accepting them frequently fell to me. One such aircraft had just arrived, and it was flying so well I decided to use it for a training sortie that very night. It was dark and windless with no horizon, definitely a night for full instrument procedures as we moved from hover to hover in Weymouth Bay. All was going well as we commenced the seventh approach towards the glassy sea beneath us. The aircraft came to a hover and Pat Gunning, my observer for the night, lowered the dome. As it entered the water and my co-pilot, Chris Hodgkinson, punched the buttons, the aircraft lurched and the nose dropped savagely and swiftly. The rotor blades hit the water and we rolled into the sea.

I was flying with my sliding cockpit door open, and was hit by a wall of cold water as the aircraft began to sink. I struggled to get out, but found I could not move. Only then did I remember to release my safety harness, dragged myself out of the cockpit and floated to the surface. Pat and the sonar operator were already in their dinghies and, since neither my lifejacket nor my dinghy seemed to be properly inflated, I swam across to Pat's dinghy, and lay across his feet. There was no sign of Chris and we began to fear the worst until he popped to the surface quite suddenly, coughing and spluttering. Once he had inflated his dinghy and climbed into it, he explained he had considerable difficulty in finding his door jettison handle in the darkness, and had gone down a long way with the aircraft before managing to get clear. He also said that I had used his face as a step in my efforts to exit the aircraft, and that he had the imprint of my boot on his forehead to prove it!

We were not long in the water. The radar operator in the safety boat had noticed our disappearance from his screen, the ship had come at full speed to find us, and within an hour we were back at Portland. After a medical check and a quick debrief from Peter Bailey, our CO, we were allowed home. It was gone midnight and Jane was asleep when I arrived. I stood by the bed, wondering whether I should wake her and tell her what had happened. Sleepily, she stretched out her hand, felt my wet trousers and said, "Oh, you've been swimming," turned over and went back to sleep.

Next morning there was a full debrief on the accident. It seemed only too straightforward. Chris had been checking the flight instruments at the time and had seen the attitude indicator register a sudden, twenty-five degree nose down movement. We had experienced the dreaded hard over and I had not been quick enough to pick it up. The wreck was recovered from the sea a couple of days later and brought back to the heliport, the magnesium alloy fuselage smoking after its immersion in salt water. The accident investigation team stripped it, confirmed that the FCS had malfunctioned, and the case was closed.

I returned to flying, but found the accident had affected me more than I cared to admit. Frequently at night the sensation that the aircraft was in a continuous climbing turn was very strong; although I was experienced enough to realise I was suffering from disorientation, and was able to concentrate on the instruments and not the sensation. I was also experienced enough to know I could not continue that way. Peter Bailey suggested I should go to the newly formed Wessex conversion squadron for a refresher course in instrument and FCS related flying. On my return to Portland all seemed to be well, but before long the sensations returned. Peter recommended I should be given a rest from flying, and in March 1963 I was appointed to join *HMS Hermes* in the Far East as a Flight Deck Officer. This was not the most popular job in the Fleet Air Arm, but at least meant I was not likely to be grounded permanently.

It was at this point that Jane and I were struck by a personal tragedy. Sean, our elder son, then aged four, was killed in an accident. As a result I was not thinking very clearly and, believing my appointment would be delayed, if not changed, did nothing to ensure that this actually happened. All too soon I found myself flying out to join *Hermes* in Singapore. I was at an all time low on my arrival there, and to find that the ship was still in Japan and not scheduled to arrive in Singapore for at least a fortnight did little to improve my outlook.

On our return to the UK a few months later we took part in a "Shopwindow" exercise, a week spent cruising up and down the English Channel displaying our expertise to senior officers from all the services and from many nations, British members of parliament and members of the world press. Flight operations were very much to the fore and it was during a 'land on' by the jets that John Rawlins, another of the Flight Deck Officers, went for an involuntary swim.

A Sea Vixen, one of the big, twin-engined jet night fighters, failed to disengage its hook at the end of its landing run. Johnny rushed out to try to lift the hook clear, but at this point the snarlup cleared itself and the marshaller signalled the pilot to open up his engines and taxi forward. John got caught in the jet blast. He took three strides, each covering about fifteen feet, before executing an immaculate swallow dive over the deck edge, just aft of the mirror platform on which I was sitting. He cleared the wire aerials, some twenty feet outboard from the deck edge, and landed in the sea sixty feet below.

The Planeguard helicopter, already airborne near the stern of the ship for the fixed wing land on, hardly had to move. The pilot came to a hover, lowered the crewman on the winch and brought John out of the water and back to the flight deck. I had been passing a commentary on the rescue to the bridge, using the flight deck communications system that we all wore. John told me afterwards he could hear me tell Flyco that he appeared to be all right, and was swimming strongly. He tried to tell us he was *not* all right. He had just fallen sixty feet into the water and, although undamaged, was unhappy! As a footnote to the incident, a very senior army officer congratulated our captain on a superb demonstration of search and rescue techniques, and enquired whether it was included on a daily basis!

On completion of a year in *Hermes* I had hoped to be sent back to flying. This was not to be, and instead my newfound expertise as a flight deck officer was put to use in the School of Aircraft Handling at Culdrose, teaching the trade to newly appointed officers and ratings. It was to be another six months before I was sent to 706 Squadron for a Wessex refresher course, and I remained with them for several months as a spare instructor. I found that the problems of vertigo and disorientation had gone, and began to look forward to a spell of front-line flying.

On the 6th February our third son, Roger, was born at the cottage at Mullion. Within ten days I was on my way out to the Far East again, this time to join 814 Squadron, which was embarked in *HMS Victorious*.

The major problems with the Wessex were now a thing of the past, and the squadron, with Peter Lynn in command, was both efficient and happy. The flying was exacting. The engine was somewhat underpowered in the high ambient temperatures of the Far East, while the FCS, relying as it did for the initial descent and hover on Doppler echoes from the surface, did not respond very accurately over the often glassy-calm sea. This did not matter too much by day when, if the Doppler did not function we used manual techniques to enter the hover, and once the ball was in the water switched in the FCS.

It was a different matter at night. Seldom did we have a horizon, and even on bright moonlight nights the lack of any apparent movement from the sea destroyed our depth perception. It was almost impossible to gauge visually how high we were. Fighting the temptation to maintain that comforting cushion of space between us and the sea, we would enter a cautious, semi-manual descent, one pilot locked on to the flight instruments, the other monitoring the engine and keeping a visual lookout. With no echoes from the surface, we had to wash off the forward speed ourselves, while maintaining a reasonable rate of descent. The power required to hover at the weight at which we flew was perilously close to the maximum available, leaving little to kill a high rate of descent. Even at thirty feet, and hopefully in sight of the surface, we had to rely implicitly on the radio altimeter to assure ourselves we were not too close to the water. Once the rotor downwash began to ruffle the surface we could allow the FCS to take charge and revert to the auto hover mode. All-weather flying was now a reality. The antisubmarine helicopter had come of age.

By the time I joined her, *Victorious* was already more than halfway through her Far East tour. We visited most of the places I had seen from *Albion*, and by the middle of the year we were back in Britain. Pete Lynn left us, and Neil Whitwam, our Senior Pilot, took over as temporary Commanding Officer of the squadron. Pete, before he left, had asked me to become the Squadron Instrument Training and Examining pilot, requiring me to both teach and examine the squadron pilots in the art of blind flying. It became a job in which I took immense satisfaction.

It was with great regret that I left 814 just before they re-embarked in *Victorious* for another tour of the Far East. I stayed at Culdrose, once more as spare instructor for 706, while I waited for the start of my new job. I had been appointed to *HMS Fife* as the Commander of the single Wessex MkI aircraft embarked in this, the latest of the navy's guided missile equipped destroyers. Most of my flying in 706 was as an instrument instructor, and it was with one of the students, Stuart Pendrich, that I had another incident.

We were flying above cloud to the north of Culdrose, Stuart under the amber screens, when a high frequency vibration suggested something was wrong. As I took over control there was a loud explosion. Huge flames appeared from the engine exhausts just beneath the cockpit coaming and the engine lost all power. I lowered the collective and went into autorotation. Stuart busied himself with the shutdown procedures for the engine. I put out a Mayday call, which was somewhat strangled owing to the clouds of choking smoke filling the cockpit and obscuring the instrument panel. Sideslipping the aircraft to clear the smoke, I checked around us for a landing site. It was obvious we were too far away to make it to the airfield so, selecting a convenient cornfield, I put the aircraft down in one piece.

Our troubles were far from over. The parking brake in the Wessex required the pilot to apply the toe brakes, and then lean forward to reach the parking lever. Stuart was very short in the leg, and each time he leaned forward the pressure came off the toe brakes and the aircraft rolled a few more feet down the hill on which we had come to rest. I leaned across the cockpit to help and, as I did so, noticed there were flames licking up the cyclic between my legs. It was definitely time to leave!

We jumped from the cockpit and stood in the knee-deep corn as the machine, its nose enveloped in flame, trundled down the hill towards a stone wall. It hit the wall, there was another explosion and the whole aircraft caught fire. A few moments later the SAR helicopter from

Culdrose landed alongside us and took us back to base. Apart from twisting my ankle when I jumped the eight feet from the cockpit, neither of us was hurt.

I wondered whether there would be enough of the aircraft left for the accident investigators to examine. There was, and they were able to pinpoint the cause of the failure. The main drive shaft connecting the compressor to the free power turbine had sheared, allowing the turbine to over-speed; this in turn had caused the turbine blades to detach. One of these blades must have fractured a fuel line which had caused the engine bay fire. A few months later a Wessex of 814 squadron, flown by Neil Whitwam, was lost as he was approaching the ship at night. All that was seen was a massive explosion. Little wreckage was found, apart from a wheel and a pilot's helmet, and all four crew were killed. There was much speculation as to what had caused the explosion; it was possible it had been a similar failure to mine and perhaps the fuel had reached the engine fire in greater quantities. In any event I felt my guardian angel must have been with me.

My stay in *Fife* was short. She was carrying out extensive radar trials and the aircraft was seldom used, least of all in it's correct role. Before long I was transferred to the Ministry of Defence, taking over a desk from Tony "Baron" Crosse, who was about to retire from the navy for a career in civilian aviation. I enjoyed the job, but the idea of retiring from the navy had crossed my mind as well. The chances of my becoming a Squadron Commanding Officer were receding, and my past would probably preclude any hope of promotion to Commander. The future appeared bleak: there was little expectation of any flying and the probability of a succession of desk jobs as a Lieutenant-Commander. With little idea of what I would do, I opted for retirement at the first possible break point—my thirty-eighth birthday—when I could leave with a small pension.

My father died while I was at the Ministry and left me a small legacy, insufficient to live on, but enough to start a small business. When I received my final appointment, as Lieutenant Commander (Flying) of the carrier, HMS *Albion*, we sold the house we had bought near Esher and, for the first time, moved into naval married quarters. I would be spending two years in *Albion*, and we decided to leave Portsmouth at a convenient moment and to move to the Plymouth area where I intended to set up a power boat charter business. To provide us with a background income while this was in its infancy, we began negotiations to buy a small laundrette in Plympton.

For the third time in my career I flew out to the Far East to join my new ship. *Albion* was in Singapore, just about to commence the return trip to the UK at the end of her commission. Since I had last served in her she had been converted to a commando carrier. Her airgroup now consisted solely of helicopters—almost exclusively the twin-engined Wessex Mk V, used for carrying the Royal Marine Commando from ship to shore.

On board I was known as "Little F," to distinguish me from the Commander (Air), "Tubby" Leonard who, I would hasten to add, was not referred to as "Big F"! He was an excellent boss who, once he had established that I could be left on my own to cope with the job, did just that. As a result I revelled in the work. My days, and many nights as well, were spent in "Flyco," the flying control position perched high above the flight deck, from where I controlled the activities of the helicopters on board, and in the vicinity of the carrier. I had to ensure that they took off and landed at the right time, with the correct loads, and that they did not run out of fuel as they carried the troops and their equipment to and from the shore.

In the Fleet Air Arm aircraft carriers have always had the reputation of being either happy or unhappy ships; *Ark Royal*, *Victorious* and *Albion* were always renowned as happy ships, *Eagle* and *Bulwark* less so. It could have been that I joined her at the right time, and that after a fortnight in Singapore she was due to make stops at Perth in Western Australia, Mauritius and Durban to break up an otherwise fast passage home; but, for whatever reason, *Albion* maintained her reputation to the end.

We did little flying on passage, arriving home in time for Christmas, and for the next six months the ship's company stood by her in Portsmouth Dockyard while she was given a refit. When we sailed again and re-embarked the Airgroup and Commando, it was to go up to the Shetland Isles for a work-up and an Admiral's Inspection. The inspection went well and my Commanding Officer, Captain Henry Leach, was kind enough to suggest I should reconsider my decision to resign. I had already agreed to stay on to the end of the year and, during the next few weeks as we sailed to the Mediterranean, I began to wonder whether I should take his advice.

While the ship was in Malta for a self refit period I took the opportunity to fly back to England to talk the matter over with Jane. Some of my friends decided they would see me off from Luqa airport, since the bar there was still open. They left me feeling very happy, at about five in the morning. My next recollection was of being wakened by a stewardess and looking out of the window to see snow-covered mountains beneath us. I was horror struck! I could not remember any mountains on the route to London and was convinced I must be on the wrong aircraft.

The stewardess noticed my panic and, smiling, said, "You're on the right aircraft, sir. Would you like your black coffee with, or without aspirin?"

After much heart searching, Jane and I decided the plans for retirement were too far advanced and that my resignation should stand. In retrospect, since Captain Leach later became the First Sea Lord, perhaps I should have paid more attention to him.

I attended a resettlement course in London just before I left the navy. It was run by several well-respected businessmen who, after a long interview with each candidate, gave them an assessment of their chances of succeeding in civilian life. My interview over, I awaited the result of their deliberations. They were not very encouraging; it was their opinion that I was qualified to do but one thing—fly helicopters in the navy!

Chapter Six

Life in the Royal Navy had been well ordered, and from one day to the next I had always known what was expected of me. The transition to the freedom of being a civilian, totally my own boss and solely responsible for the result of any decision I made, was not easy. The laundrette very nearly ran itself, with the help of the lady we had acquired with the business. She supervised during the day, sorting out problems and keeping vandalism to a minimum. Jane or I went down most evenings to remind the local kids of our existence, and to ensure that they could not run riot without some risk of retribution. Even so, I arrived down there one evening about nine o'clock to find a small girl, perhaps ten years old, doing the family washing. She was accompanied by her younger brother, and to keep him amused she had put him in one of the gas fired tumble dryers where he was happily revolving. For once I was pleased that the dryers broke down with monotonous regularity; on this one the gas supply had failed.

We emptied the coin boxes and cashed up weekly, and when a machine broke down I attempted to repair it myself, since to employ a professional repair man cost an arm and a leg as soon as he came through the door. I learned to tolerate electric shocks as I lay on my back, frequently in a pool of water, the repair manual in one hand, the other groping in the innards. It might have been sensible to switch off the electricity, but leaving it on made fault finding easier!

I had plenty of time to set up the powerboat business. I was convinced that, as the only person in Plymouth with such a venture, I could not fail. I had bought a 23-foot fast cabin cruiser and advertised it for hire. Throughout the summer, despite it being one of the hottest for years, I obtained only three charters. One was to take a party up the Yealm River. The other two were for BBC television. The first of the

BBC trips was to go and film the Eddystone lighthouse for a documentary, the last to film the final stages of the Fastnet yacht race.

We found the leading boats about twenty miles offshore and began filming. It was a little difficult; there was a strong westerly wind blowing and the yachts were able to sail as fast, if not faster than my somewhat overloaded boat. For a while we managed to stay with *Morning Cloud*, the Prime Minister's yacht, but not wanting to interfere with the race, I kept a respectful distance. The TV producer had other, more left wing, ideas and insisted that I went much closer so that he could have a political argument with Mr Heath. I refused, until it was made clear in a somewhat forcible way that I was being paid for the hire of the boat. The Prime Minister did not appear impressed with being harassed in this way and at least one person on board *Morning Cloud* made it quite clear, in most unparliamentary language, that our presence was unwelcome: references were made concerning the marital status of my parents, and to what would happen if we did not leave the area. I took the point and sheered out of earshot!

The long, hot summer played havoc with the laundrette. Few of the local residents made any use of it, hanging their washing out in their garden rather than paying to use my machines. When my bank manager mentioned that he preferred the more traditional form of banking, whereby I put my money in his bank rather than him putting the bank's money in my business, I did not need to be a genius to know that I had to find more gainful employment.

The advice of the resettlement board was still fresh in my mind. I could hardly rejoin the navy, but at least I could still fly a helicopter. The difficulty was that no civilian company would employ me until I had a civilian licence, and to obtain this I would have to go back to school and sit the Civil Aviation Authority (CAA) exams. I was saved by an advertisement in the *Daily Telegraph*. Airworks, a firm specialising in worldwide aviation contracts, was looking for ex-military pilots to fly helicopters "somewhere in the Middle East," and no licences were required. I rang them, and was invited to go to their headquarters at Hurn Airport, near Bournemouth, the next day.

My interviewer seemed interested only in confirming from my log-book that I had the helicopter experience I claimed, and almost immediately asked me if I wanted the job. At this point all I really knew was that it entailed flying for the Sultan of Oman's Airforce. I asked a few questions and discovered that I would be flying the Bell 205 and 206 in support of the Sultan's Armed Forces. Their main base was near Muscat, in the north of the country; the leave cycle was six months unaccompanied service followed by one month leave, and airline tickets to and from Oman were provided free. The salary was very acceptable, more than I had been receiving in the Navy, and when he asked me again whether I wanted the job, I said yes.

I was instructed to go up to London, pass a medical with the Central Air Medical Board, and then go to Kendalls, the Omani agents, who would organise my travel documents, obtain an Omani visa for me, and give me more detailed joining instructions. As I left his office he said, almost as a throwaway line,

"I believe there are some bullets flying around in the south of Oman, in Dhofar. But you don't have to worry. You'll be spending all your time in the north."

With what seemed like uneccessary haste, Kendalls progressed my visa. The joining instructions gave little away, containing little more than a short description of the country and some of its customs, a suggestion that I should take plenty of suntan lotion and, somewhat incongruously, both black and white dinner jackets. Exactly a fortnight after reading the advertisement I was flying eastwards on a British Airways VC10 bound for Bahrein, leaving Jane to keep the laundrette going and sell the boat.

We landed at Bahrein in the early hours of the morning. It was oppressively hot and humid and I had several hours to wait for my onward connection to Muscat with the local airline, Gulf Air. The terminal buildings seemed little better than old, wooden shacks, and I became increasingly disillusioned with my surroundings. The journey to Muscat, via such exotically named places as Doha, Abu Dhabi and Dubai, did nothing to help. I had successfully avoided going up the Gulf while I was in the navy and the names meant little to me. I had heard the horror stories about the temperature there, and how it was possible to fry an egg on the steel flight deck of an aircraft carrier, but nothing had prepared me for the wall of heat that entered the cabin of the Fokker Friendship each time we landed and the cabin door was opened.

Leaving Dubai behind we flew on eastwards towards Oman. Seen from our cruising height, the ground beneath seemed to be desert, but where the land met the sea, small villages and patches of green appeared. On our right were the Hajar mountains, a range stretching across the north of Oman and separating the coastal plain from the central desert area. As the aircraft descended towards Bait al Falaj, the international airport for Muscat, the mountains drew closer until we let down into one of the wadis. A rock wall materialised, barely feet from the wing tip on my side of the plane; another appeared equally close on the opposite side. Looking forward through the open flight deck door I was horrified to see that the valley in which we were flying appeared to come to an abrupt end. Suddenly the aircraft banked to the right and there was the airport, the single runway stretched out in front of us. I was intrigued by what appeared to be a bend in the middle of the runway. I was told later that two contractors had built it, each starting from opposite ends, and that they had refused to speak to each other during the construction period. I never found out whether the story was true but now, after many years in the Gulf, I can believe it might have happened that way.

The aircraft taxied in to a concrete apron and came to a stop. The cabin doors were opened and we disembarked. It was late September but the heat at Bait al Falaj was a physical force. From a cloudless sky the sun beat down into a dry, dusty bowl, the heat bouncing off the brown hills and reflecting up off the concrete. I contemplated climbing back into the aircraft and returning to Britain, but was prevented from doing so by a hand placed on my arm. I turned to see an officer in khaki shirt and shorts, on his head a blue RAF-style cap with crossed daggers on the badge.

"You must be Mike Tuson," he said. "I'm Bill White, the SOAF duty officer."

He led me across the dusty apron to a scruffy, single-story white building. As we arrived at the door, he went on.

"This is the immigration office. Have your passport and visa ready."

We entered a room filled with bodies. I looked for a queue to join, but Bill pulled me through the crowd to the desk. It was my first lesson in local etiquette. In the countries of the Arabian Gulf, to be part of a queue infers that you're a person of absolutely no importance; people of any stature go straight to the front and it was obvious everyone there considered themselves to be important. Bill's uniform seemed to set him apart from the rest, however. The immigration officer took my papers first and within minutes I was through the formalities. As we moved on to the customs area, Bill asked me whether I had any prohibited items in my baggage. I must have looked bemused so he ran through a short list, mainly pork, alcohol and pornography. I had none, and we were passed through and out into the blinding sun to where my bags were being loaded into a Mini-Moke.

Bill drove about a mile before pulling up outside the Officers' Mess, a white-painted, concrete building forming one side of a rectangular parade ground. He took me into the bar, bought me a beer and introduced me to the assembled company. For the next two hours, I learned about Oman and the job for which I had been recruited.

After lunch Bill took me across the parade ground to my quarters, one of a series of mud block rooms with palm leaf roofs. Mine was a stark affair, a twelve foot by twelve foot space with a shower cubicle at the back, sparsely furnished with a truckle bed, wardrobe and chest of drawers. An air conditioner, loosely fitted into a hole in one wall, was rattling itself to pieces as it tried vainly to cool the hot, dusty air that blew in through the gaps in the walls and ceiling. I tried the shower and was greeted by a trickle of tepid, brown water.

I lay on the bed and mulled over all I had been told. Oman had a turbulent history. Wracked by internal jealousy and tribal wars, it had always been split between the more outward-looking, coastal tribes and the fiercely independent and mistrustful inhabitants of the interior. The rulers of the country, the Imams, were elected, but seemed unable to unite the tribes except when they were threatened with invasion by either their neighbours in the Middle East, or from Europe, which seemed to have happened with monotonous regularity.

In the fifteenth century Muscat town and the coastal areas fell prey to the Portuguese. They held sway until the middle of the seventeenth century when the Imam, Nasr al Yaarubah, drove them out. He harried them down the east coast of Africa, and in so doing, laid the foundations of the Omani Empire. At its peak this spread from Zanzibar to what is now Pakistan, with much of Oman's wealth coming from the lucrative slave trade. The Al bu Said family came to power in the mideighteenth century and have ruled the country ever since. It was they who, at the turn of the nineteenth century, concluded a treaty with the British East India Company. This friendship has continued to the present day, although the British involvement in the successful abolition of the slave trade effectively ruined the finances of Muscat and Oman, as it was known at the time.

The Sultan moved the centre of government to Zanzibar in the nineteenth century, and by doing so allowed his influence in Oman to wane. Also by this time he had obtained a foothold in the province of Dhofar, a backwater of the Arabian Peninsular situated some eight hundred miles south of Muscat, but even there the Sultan was little more than an absentee landlord. The country continued to be torn by internal strife, the tribes from the interior being held at bay by the coastal tribes only with the assistance of the British. The Omani empire contracted, the Sultan returned to Muscat leaving a relative as Sultan of Zanzibar, and the situation was little changed until 1920, when the Treaty of Seeb regularised what had been, in effect, the situation throughout the period.

Said bin Taimur, who succeeded to power in 1932, inherited a debt-ridden country. His actual authority extended over little more than the coastal strip north of the Hajar range, from the mountainous Musendam peninsular, past Muscat, to the little port of Sur close to the easterly point of Oman at Ras al Hadd, and even in this area his authority was tenuous. He also still held sway over the province of Dhofar. The interior, known as Oman, was controlled by an Imam from the old city of Nizwa which nestled in the foothills on the south side of the Jebel Akhdar, a lightly inhabited plateau six thousand feet up in the Hajar mountains.

Towards the end of his reign, Sultan Said retired to his palace at Salalah, the capital of Dhofar, and ruled, often by radiotelephone, through a number of mainly British advisors. He isolated himself from his people and treated the inhabitants of Dhofar as little more than serfs, to be punished whenever they offended him. Two uprisings took place in the north, both with the active help of Saudi Arabia. These were led by the Imam from Nizwa, and other tribal authorities. They were suppressed by the Sultan, but not without the help of his mercenary army of Baluch tribesmen who were led by regular officers from the British Army. On another occasion the Saudi Arabians invaded Buraimi, the desert oasis that gave Hammond Innes the background to *The Doomed Oasis*. Buraimi lies on the border between Oman and what was then known as the Trucial Oman, now called the United Arab Emirates. It was, once again, the intervention of the British that defused what could have become a bloody war. In the revolt that started in 1957 there was the active involvement of a squadron of the Special Air Services, diverted to Oman while on their return to Britain from Malaya, and RAF strike aircraft from Sharjah in the Trucial Oman. The

SAS climbed up the Jebel Akhdar by a hitherto unknown route, surprised the defenders who had considered their positions unassailable, and effectively ended the revolt.

The discovery of oil in the 1960s produced an increase in Oman's income, but little change in the lifestyle of the people. Pressure applied by the British Government, aimed at persuading the Sultan to institute a programme of major reforms in return for their continued help, failed to move him. His reasoning, actively encouraged by some of his advisors, was that the pace of any improvements should be slow and measured to avoid the traumas of a sudden transition to wealth and prosperity. His plan failed to impress his people.

He began a small programme of building hospitals and schools, but in 1971, when I arrived, there were less than a dozen miles of tarmac road in the north of Oman. This, in fact, had not been much of a drawback under the old Sultan, since only members of his family, the Government and the military were allowed to possess motor cars. It was also less than a year since the rescinding of the laws requiring the inhabitants of Muscat town to carry an oil lantern when walking the streets at night, and to have a pass signed by the Chief of Police to leave the city after dark. I was also told, but was never able to confirm the fact, that at one time the people of Oman were allowed to have a bicycle or a battery powered radio, but not both!

Omanis were forbidden to leave the country to seek work, and those who succeeded risked imprisonment if they returned. In 1964 militant Dhofaris, following an illegal stay in Iraq where they had been trained and armed, crossed the desert through Saudi Arabia and began a guerrilla movement against the Sultan. He retaliated by taking oppressive measures against all Dhofaris, including cutting off most of the life-giving water from the Jebel to the Salalah plain. By 1965, the Dhofar Liberation Front (DLF) had been formed. Two years later the pullout by the British from Aden left a vacuum, quickly filled by the communist powers, and their influence began to spread across the border into

Dhofar and Oman. The DLF was infiltrated and became the Peoples Front for the Liberation of the Arabian Gulf (PFLOAG), although the details of which people, and from whom they were to be liberated, always seemed to be left conveniently vague. The armed conflict increased, action by PFLOAG being met with harsher punitive measures by the Sultan, to be followed by more support for the guerrillas from Aden, which had now changed it's name to The Peoples Republic of South Yemen (PDRY). By 1970 it was a stalemate; PFLOAG was not strong enough to throw the Sultan out of Dhofar but had almost total control of the hill country; the Sultan's forces held the town of Salalah and the plains area, but could not defeat the rebels.

The Sultan's son, Qaboos bin Said, born of a Dhofari mother, had been educated at an English public school, trained by the British army at Sandhurst and had served for a short time as an officer in the Cameronians. He was brought back to Oman by his father, and promptly placed under house arrest in the royal palace at Salalah to prevent him from becoming a focal point for a coup. Despite this, as the problems grew in Dhofar, he became the centre of a plot to overthrow his father. It was made known from London that the British serving in Oman should do nothing, either to help or hinder the attempt. Some seconded and contract personnel disregarded these instructions and actively helped the organisation. On the 23rd July 1970, Sheikh Baraik al Ghafari, the Wali (headman) of Salalah, went to the Sultan and demanded his abdication. In the firefight that followed, Sheik Baraik was wounded by the Sultan. The Sultan was wounded in the foot and stomach, and one of his servants was killed. He then surrendered. Once the abdication papers had been signed, the Sultan was flown to Britain in an aircraft of RAF Transport Command that just happened, conveniently, to be at the airfield at Salalah. He lived for another two years in London before he died.

For the next year His Highness, Sultan Qaboos, organised the build-up of his forces to enable them, in the autumn of 1971, to take the offensive against the adoo, as the guerrillas were known. More Baluch mercenaries were recruited; the Sultan's request for additional British army and RAF personnel to be seconded to Oman was granted, and nothing was put in his way to prevent him recruiting contract pilots from Britain for his fledgling airforce.

The Sultan of Oman's Air Force (SOAF) had its HQ at Bait al Falaj and was commanded by a seconded Wing Commander from the RAF. It consisted of a fighter ground-attack squadron of fourteen Strikemasters, the armed version of the jet-engined Provost trainer, ten Agusta Bell 205 troop-carrying helicopters, four Agusta Bell 206 communication helicopters, and an assortment of Short Skyvans, De Havilland Caribou and Vickers Viscount transport planes. All but a few of the pilots were British, about forty percent seconded from the RAF, the remainder, like myself, ex-military pilots from Britain. The few were dyed-in-the-wool mercenaries, who had come to us from such places as Biafra and the Congo. The maintenance engineers were, almost to a man, drawn from the ranks of retired personnel from the RAF or Fleet Air Arm. They were employed by Airworks and considered to be civilians. I learned almost immediately that we should not use the term "mercenary" as it offended the delicate sensibilities of some elderly and long serving ex-British officers on contract to the Sultan's army. As far as I could see, mercenaries was exactly what we were, military personnel in the service of a foreign country, for reward. It is possibly the second oldest profession, and I can still see nothing wrong with the term.

The army was still largely a mercenary force. Some of the officers were seconded from the British Army, the rest drawn from the ranks of ex-officers and NCOs of many nations. The rank and file were mainly Baluch from the enclave of Gwadur on the borders of Pakistan and Iran. The Sultans of Oman had also been Sultans of Gwadur and, when they relinquished control, retained the right to recruit soldiers from the area.

Two things were certain; I was not going to have much time to wear either of my dinner jackets, nor was I going to spend much time in

Muscat. My immediate task was to convert to the two types of helicopter and, on completion of this, to go down to Salalah and join the sharp end of SOAF, known as SOAF(Tactical), SOAFTAC for short. As it happened I had flown no more than a couple of hours on the 205 with John Atkinson, an RAF instructor on secondment to SOAF, when an urgent signal was received from Salalah: one of their 205s had been struck by several of the bullets that were flying around in Dhofar, and they needed a replacement as soon as possible.

Adam Carter, an ex-Army Air Corps pilot, had just returned from leave and was awaiting a Viscount flight to take him to Salalah. It was decided he should ferry one of our two 205s south, and that I should go with him on the six hour flight to gain experience, and to assist him on the controls as necessary. Even with long range tanks fitted we could not carry enough fuel to fly direct to Dhofar. Our route would take us first to Masirah, an island off the east coast of Oman where the RAF maintained an airbase, and which they used as a refuelling stop for trooping aircraft on their runs to and from the Far East. This was part of a deal between Britain and Oman, whereby the RAF could use Masirah in return for providing the ground staff to run the airfield at Salalah.

We took off at first light and climbed steadily southwards to ten thousand feet, partly to avoid the severe turbulence that could occur over the eastern Hajar, but mostly because at that height it would be relatively cool. It was also higher than I had ever been in a helicopter; as an antisubmarine pilot most of my flying had been well below one thousand feet. I had expected to be able to see for miles but was disappointed. We became enveloped in the dust and heat haze that covered the area, and all we could see was the ground directly beneath us. Soon the southern foothills of the jebel and the last of the bright green oases slipped behind us, and we were over the rolling sand hills of the Wahiba Sands, the eastern extremity of the Empty Quarter.

Adam was army trained and could read a map, but it has been said that there are few things as dangerous as an army officer with a map! I was used to having an observer to tell me where we were, and in which direction to point the nose. I could tell the difference between sea and land on a chart—the sea was a pretty blue colour, the land various shades of green or brown! There was little on the maps we had been given to help either of us; they were covered with such reassuring information as "Unexplored," "Height Unknown" and "Position Approximate." (I half expected to find a notation, "Here be dragons!")

I busied myself with the only piece of radio navigation equipment we had, the radio direction finder (RDF). We were out of range of the beacon at Bait al Falaj within half an hour of takeoff, and were left with only the BBC World Service transmitter at Masirah until we came within range of the airfield beacon at the RAF station. I prayed that the BBC would keep transmitting so that we could follow the RDF pointer in the aircraft. Science triumphed, but I was still glad when the strip of ocean between the mainland and Masirah appeared, and the airfield came into view.

Our time on the ground was short and, after refuelling the aircraft and grabbing a quick sandwich in the mess, we were airborne again for the longer sector, a flight of three-and-a-half hours to Salalah. Although we crossed the coast back to the mainland a mere forty miles south of our track into Masirah, the landscape was much changed. The sand hills had been replaced by a flat, dusty, stone covered plain, criss-crossed by the wheel tracks of countless oil prospecting vehicles. The haze cleared after a couple of hours and we could see the northern edge of the Jebel Samhan and the Qarra mountains, beyond which lay Salalah. Our track took us by way of a dogleg over the Jebel Samhan, almost fifty miles east of Salalah. I had queried this with Adam before takeoff, and he had explained that although the monsoon was over, and the cloud associated with it normally cleared fully by the first week in September, there was always the chance that Salalah could be obscured. There was only a low-powered beacon there, and he didn't fancy letting down blind to the airfield; it would be only too easy to meet a hill, the enemy, or even both, suddenly and with very unpleasant consequences.

The Jebel Samhan, marked on our map as "about three thousand feet," dropped an almost sheer five thousand feet to the Selha Plain, near the little fishing village of Marbat. There, we descended to sea level and took a wide sweep out to sea to avoid the Wadi Darbat, an enemy stronghold where the hills came to within half a mile of the coast. Rejoining the coast to the west of Taqa, another fishing village on the Salalah plain some thirty miles east of the airfield, we followed it until we could see the green fields and trees that surrounded the town of Salalah and, just inland, the airbase with it's two dirt runways. Within minutes of landing I was taken to the "civilian" terminal, a tent on the south side of the base, and climbed aboard a Viscount for the return journey to Muscat.

Life at Muscat became very relaxed. With only one 205 at our disposal, and that one heavily committed to supporting the army in the north, my attention was transferred to the 206, the Jetranger. It was sadly underpowered for the high temperatures and mountains in which we operated. It was once suggested, rather rudely, that the total lift capacity was the pilot and a verbal message, and that if the pilot was overweight you could forget the message. I learned to calculate the available weight very carefully; it was necessary to avoid carrying too much fuel, thereby being able to offer the army only a small payload, or conversely too little, with the subsequent embarrassment of an involuntary landing some miles short of the destination.

The 206 was a typical Bell product, even if ours had been built at the Agusta factory in Italy and not Fort Worth, Texas. At almost any speed it developed a vertical vibration once every rotor revolution, known as a "Whumper," while in the hover it acquired a mind of it's own. As it entered the ground cushion the Jetranger skated in any direction other than the one required, and I found myself fighting the controls several movements behind that of the aircraft. John Atkinson sat beside me, patiently watching my efforts until he could stand it no longer; then he took over control and made a perfect landing. Before handing back the controls, he gave me some advice that took the sting out of the aircraft.

"Don't grasp the cyclic with your whole hand. Just use your finger and thumb. Try to imagine how an elderly dowager duchess might hold a dirty old tramp's private parts!"

It worked like a charm, and before long I was converted to the Jetranger.

Much of the flying in the 206 was done in support of the Oman Gendarmerie, a paramilitary force that policed the many outlying towns and villages. I covered the whole of the north of Oman, from Sohar in the north-west, reputed to be the birthplace of Sinbad the Sailor, to Sur. Sur had been one of the main harbours for the slave trade but was now very run down. Apart from being an entry point for much of the weaponry smuggled in to support the uprisings, the only activity was centred around fishing and a small boatyard. It was in this yard, in 1980, that the "Sohar" was built, the dhow used by Tim Severin to retrace the fabled footsteps of Sinbad on his journey from Muscat to Canton.

I took an army officer to visit the garrison at Saiq, a village six-thousand feet up on a plateau in the Jebel Akhdar, near the scene of the SAS victory in 1957. To reach it we had to fly down the Wadi Sumail, a wide valley that carved a route through the jebel from north to south, leading to the desert beyond. On the eastern side the slopes of the wadi climbed fairly gently to three and four thousand foot peaks; on the western side there was an almost vertical, scree-covered cliff rising to the plateau that was my destination, cut by narrow clefts that would become waterfalls in the winter rains. Halfway down the wadi I began a spiral climb, for there was no way the 206 could climb the cliffs in a straight line. After ten minutes I had reached six thousand feet and was able to turn towards my destination. The temperature had dropped to a cool twenty-five degrees centigrade, a relief from the thirty-five plus of the wadi floor. My passenger told me that at night it was sometimes necessary to wear a wooly pullover, and sit in front of a fire to keep warm.

Having dropped my passenger at the army garrison, I started the return flight to Bait al Falaj. It was much easier, even exhilarating, as I flew with my skids brushing the small thorn trees that scrabbled for an existence in the sparse soil. I headed for the cliff edge; one moment I was less than ten feet from the ground, the next a four thousand foot chasm yawned beneath me and, for a moment, I became disorientated. Locking on to the flight instruments, I lowered the collective and took the quick way down to the wadi bottom in autorotation. When I got back to Bait al Falaj I spoke to John about the problem. He apologised, saying he had meant to warn me about it. Apparently a newly joined pilot had experienced the same disorientation a few months before and had quit the job on his return to the airfield!

Whenever possible I flew as John's co-pilot in the remaining 205 on army co-operation sorties. It was not formal training, but at least I was gaining valuable experience. One of these flights was in aid of the army and the civil medical service. A patrol had been visiting a village four thousand feet up the jebel, and had been asked by the villagers to transport three injured women to the local medical centre at Rostaq, the nearest town of any size. There were only rough tracks in the area and the journey would have taken nearly a day in a Land Rover, with the additional danger of further injuring the women by bouncing them around in the back of the vehicle. By helicopter it was little more than a fifteen-minute flight!

Nick Holbrook, another ex-Army Air Corps pilot, flew ahead in a 206 to reconnoitre a suitable landing site, while John and I followed in the 205. We landed in a wadi about four hundred feet below the village which hung precariously on the mountain side, and the officer in charge of the patrol put us in the picture. It was not a pretty tale. One of the village men had accused his wife of infidelity and had started to beat her. The woman's mother had tried to intervene and the enraged husband had shot her in the shoulder with his rifle; for good measure he had then stabbed his wife with his khunjar, a wickedly curved dagger that all Omani men carry at their waist, slitting her open across the stomach. At this point his daughter had tried to help her mother, so he stabbed her as well, opening her up from kidney to belly button. The husband had been shot dead by his brother-in-law who then, quite literally, took to the hills. This was regarded as justice by the villagers and they had lost interest in him; their concern was how to get the casualties to Rostaq.

The three women walked down the steep path to the wadi, disdaining the offer of the stretchers we had provided. They arrived at the helicopter and, only then and very reluctantly, allowed themselves to be placed on the stretchers and lifted into the cabin. I was amazed at the stoicism with which they bore their wounds, and the calm, matter-of-fact way they accepted the machine. Saud, our Omani crewman, assured me we were probably the first white people the villagers had seen, and it was absolutely certain that the women had never before ridden in a helicopter. The youngest was unveiled and seemed little more than a teenager. She lay on the stretcher without making a sound and making little effort to brush away the hordes of flies that gathered on her face, her huge, dark, doe eyes gazing at the unfamiliar surroundings. Saud spoke a few words to her and told me later that he had asked her age; she had replied that she was not sure, but thought she was nine years old.

We left the wadi heavily loaded, taking with us not only the casualties, but also most of their relatives. They had to come; although the treatment the injured would receive would be given by a fully qualified doctor, the aftercare had to be provided by the family and they would remain at Rostaq until the patients were fit enough to return to their village.

The following day I was walking through the hangar at Bait al Falaj when one of the helicopter engineers called me over to the 205. He pointed to a small hole in the belly, and told me he had just removed a bullet from the honeycombing near the fuel tank. He assured me it had not been there the previous morning and that we must have been hit during the casualty evacuation. There was no way of finding out who had fired at us; at that time all Omani males between the ages of puberty and death carried a gun of some form, ranging from aged blunderbusses firing homemade bullets, through nineteenth-century Martini Henry rifles to modern automatic weapons supplied by the Russians and Chinese. I had served in the navy for twenty-five years without hearing a shot fired in anger; three weeks after arriving in Oman I had received my baptism of fire, and had not even realised it!

Back at Bait al Falaj we worked tropical routine, starting at six in the morning and working through to one o'clock. Later we could sleep away the heat of the day, or drive along the stony track, through the Wadi Ruwi, to the oil company compound and "Blackpool Beach." This was a secluded sandy cove the Sultan had ordained should be for Europeans only, so that the white women could sunbathe in their bikinis without their semi-nudity offending the strict Islamic customs of the Omanis. The beach was always packed since, although only the very senior officers in SAF had their families with them, almost all the oil company personnel were accompanied.

By mid-October, still without having completed the 205 conversion, it was time for me to pack my bags and move south to Salalah. The post-monsoon push on to the jebel was well under way, the helicopter pilots were at full stretch, and it had been decided the rest of my conversion should take the form of "on-the-job" training.

Chapter Seven

Dhofar is an area of incredible contrasts—ethnically, geographically and climatically. Legend has it that the Queen of Sheba once ruled it. Certainly it was, for a long time, a centre of the rich frankincense trade. The Salalah plain had been immensely fertile as recently as the First World War, and was reputed to have produced enough vegetables to sustain the British Mesopotamian army. In 1971, from the air, it was possible to see the outline of the fields, the irrigation courses that watered them and the foundations of many villages, but little else of that bygone glory remained.

In the east, on the Selha Plain, only the fishing villages of Sudh and Marbat remained, both garrisoned by askars, the locally recruited militia. At the eastern end of the Salalah Plain Taqa, another small fishing village was constantly under threat from the adoo based in the Wadi Darbat. A Royal palace and garden, fed by water from the Wadi Arzat, stood in the middle of the plain at Marmoura and, apart from Salalah town, it was the only splash of green in an otherwise drab brown countryside. When the old Sultan had ordered the destruction of the falaj, the man-made courses bringing water from the jebel, he had spared the one originating in the Wadi Arzat. The wadi was now an adoo stronghold and they regularly blocked the source of the falaj. Equally regularly the army sent a patrol to unblock it.

Halfway along the coast was the capital of Dhofar, Salalah, a barbed wire fence surrounding both it and the village of Auqat. Um al Gwarif, the main army camp, was three miles northeast of the town, while the airbase lay in the dust, halfway between the edge of town and the foothills. The wire fence surrounding the airfield was no more than six thousand metres from the jebel, almost exactly the maximum range of the man-packed 75mm recoilless gun, the heaviest weapon possessed by the enemy, while the airfield defensive perimeter with its mortar pits and machine guns was even closer.

Mugshayl, a small and almost uninhabited village, lay at the western end of the plain, where the Qarra hills came down to the sea. Between there and Salalah was Rizut, with an army camp, a dirt airstrip and a bay where Taylor Woodrow was building a deep-water port. About twenty miles from the northern edge of the jebel and almost due north of Salalah, lay Midway, later renamed as Thumrait. This had been the site of an oil drilling camp, but in 1971 it was a military airbase and, being in open desert, reasonably safe from adoo attack. These areas were all in the hands of the Sultan's forces. The hills, stretching from the border with the PDRY in the west to the eastern end of the jebel Samhan, were adoo country.

The adoo were a very mixed force, some Arabic speaking Dhofaris, some incomers from the north of Oman or from other Arabic countries, and a few advisers who had little in common with any known Arab nation. The rest were jebali, the true inhabitants of the Dhofar hill country. Ethnically, the jebali belonged to the tribes which had occupied the Hadrahmaut from very early times, with looks akin to the Somalis and who speak a language of their own, somewhat removed from Arabic. There were probably three or four hundred hard-core communists. The majority of the jebali were devout Muslims, and Islam and communism make strange bedfellows. Most of them would have preferred to be left alone to get on with their cattle herding, interspersed with the occasional bloodletting of inter-village or inter-tribal warfare. However, if they could not understand the communist denial of the existence of any god, they were aware that the old Sultan had not lavished much of the newfound oil wealth on them. They were also left in no doubt that those who were not active supporters of PFLOAG would find their lives made very unpleasant.

The core of PFLOAG were communist trained guerrillas. We had captured training manuals and many pictures of the adoo leaders taken while they were on training courses in Russia, China and North Korea, and they had all read Chairman Mao's little red book from cover to cover. The adoo were all hard men, fighting mostly in their own back-yards, but well capable of travelling great distances at high speed, on foot and on minimum rations. They were well armed, predominantly with Russian and Chinese weapons including the AK47, arguably the finest assault rifle of its time. They had mortars, some of which were believed to be of British origin left in Aden at the time of the pullout, and 50mm Spargen heavy machine guns. They were resupplied through the PDRY, supplemented by whatever they could confiscate or steal. Their main problem was a lack of transport, other than donkeys, camels or the backs of men, and the geographical split in their areas of operation.

The hills to the north of Rizut and Mugshayl marked the line between the eastern and western sectors. To the west, right up to the border with the PDRY, lay "Moon country," an area made up partly of a gravel plain and partly of deep, sandy bottomed wadis that made labyrinthine patterns as they twisted their way north to the desert. Apart from small patches of land near the coast, where the hills in places dropped nearly vertically two thousand feet into the sea, the western sector was barren and inhospitable. In the eastern sector, the fertile Qarra hills towered above the Salalah plain, touching the sea at either end and cutting the plain off from the rest of Dhofar. It was on the Qarra hills where, apart from during the monsoon, the jebali grazed their herds of cattle and their womenfolk tilled small patches of ground.

The climatic split was as marked as the geographical one, and lay effectively along the same line that divided the two sectors. It rained only infrequently in the west and clouds seldom interfered with air operations. The eastern portion, bordered by the coastline between Mugshayl and Marbat in the south and the northern edge of the Qarra hills was affected by the monsoon. From the beginning of June to the end of August each year, the moist winds from the Indian monsoon are funnelled in across the plain and forced up by the high escarpment; the moisture condenses and the result is cloud. For three months the climate is reminiscent of an English summer—a three hundred foot cloud base over the plain, and steady drizzle. The cloud is three or four thousand feet thick, the jebel wreathed in thick fog and the ground underfoot turns into a quagmire. Even the hardy jebali bring their cattle to the foothills below the cloud line, leaving the high ground to the blackfly.

During the early months of 1971 the Sultan's forces in Dhofar were reinforced. Two regular regiments were based there, one at Um al Gwarif, the other, the Desert Regiment (DR), at Akoot in the western sector where resupply by air was possible throughout the year. SOAF(Tac) received new aircraft, ten Strikemasters, eight 205s, two 206s and an assortment of transport aircraft, mainly Short Skyvans manufactured in Northern Ireland.

One of the first acts of Sultan Qaboos had been to offer an amnesty to the rebels. This had some results and there was a fairly steady, if not spectacular, flow of Surrendered Enemy Personnel, SEPs as they were known. They, with other jebali who had remained loyal to the Sultan, had been formed into militia regiments known as firqats, and were being trained by the British Army Training Team, a pseudonym for a detachment of the SAS from Hereford, known to us all as the Battmen. Probably the best known of the SEPs was Mohammed Suhail. Nick Holbrook had been sent to Taqa to pick up a SEP, and was horrified to find he was still carrying his rifle, with magazine attached. The escort, who would not be travelling with the helicopter, assured Nick that they could not take the gun away since the SEP was allowed to sell it to the Sultan on arrival at Gwarif.

"Well, at least take the magazine out and make sure it's unloaded," said Nick. At this point the SEP intervened and said, in an immaculate English accent:

"It's all right, old boy. I won't give you any trouble!"

Mohammed was a jebali from Suhait, a village in the hills close to the Wadi Darbat. Fleeing from Dhofar during the rule of the old Sultan, he had joined the Trucial Oman Scouts, a British-officered force in what is now the United Arab Emirates. They sent him to the Military College at Mons, in the UK, for officer training where he passed out high in his class but, shortly after returning to the Scouts, he had deserted. He joined the DLF, but became disillusioned with them as the communists took control and deserted yet again, this time to SAF.

As one of the few fluent speakers of the jebali dialects available to us he was welcomed with open arms and spent the next eighteen months interrogating SEPs. It was frequently said that he could extract anything of use from a male jebali in less than an hour; if the SEP was female it could take much longer! Despite his frequent entreaties, he was regarded as far too valuable to risk on general active service, but in 1972 he was allowed to join a fighting patrol that was going into his home area. Shortly before dawn, as the patrol was moving silently into position, Mohammed seemed to lose his cool, stormed into the village with gun blazing, and was killed instantly by an adoo sentry. Mohammed was a truly charming person with a tremendous sense of humour, and his death was a great loss.

Military action in the early part of 1971 was limited to the Desert Regiment at Akoot, which sent out fighting patrols into Moon country to try to make contact with the adoo. The adoo returned the compliment by mortaring the airstrip and DR camp at regular intervals but, following Chairman Mao's advice on guerrilla warfare, never maintained contact for long, and always retired to safety before they could be caught in the open by an air strike or superior force. A major success for them was the destruction of one of our Caribou transport aircraft. The adoo had opened up with mortars just as the Caribou had been landing at Akoot, and the pilot immediately turned on the runway, opening up his throttles to take off again. The aircraft was seen to lift off into a steep climb. The nose continued up, almost vertically, and the aircraft crashed tail first into a shallow wadi, killing the crew. It was thought that the crewman had followed normal procedures, unlashing the cargo while the aircraft was completing the landing run to speed up unloading, and that the load had slid to the tail as the aircraft became airborne again.

The helicopter crews also had their share of excitement at Akoot. Four aircraft were shut down there, the crews enjoying a hot breakfast in the officers mess tent when the adoo opened up on the camp. Mortar bombs began to land nearby and, to a man, the helicopter pilots dived under the nearest cover, the breakfast table. The unmistakable voice of Neville Baker, the helicopter squadron commanding officer, was heard from the bottom of the pile: "If my old Mum could see me now she would have a heart attack. I told her I was out here crop spraying!"

At the end of the monsoon, usually during the last week of August or the first week of September, the rain in Dhofar stops, the cloud disappears and the jebali return to their villages with their cattle. In 1971, SAF also returned to the jebel to start beating hell out of the adoo. Codenamed "Operation Jaguar" the post-monsoon push was, in the words of the army commander Colonel Harvey during a major briefing, "designed to roll up the jebel like a carpet from east to west." It might have helped if the adoo had also been briefed on our plan since, during the coming months, it became obvious that they were not sure of their part in the larger picture and kept unrolling the carpet behind us!

The first troops were airlifted by helicopter to Jib Jat, in the northeastern part of the jebel. This was the site of an old dirt airstrip, and considered to be far enough away from any adoo strongholds for the landing to be unopposed. Once Jib Jat had been secured, the Skyvans were able to land, and they continued the build-up of our forces. Meanwhile, the ground troops moved on foot a few miles southwest to a high point on the jebel. This was codenamed "White City" and, once an airstrip had been constructed within a defensive perimeter, it was to become the main base for all our operations in the eastern sector.

Chapter Eight

I had to complete the conversion before I was allowed to fly the 205, and Roy Bayliss, an ex-Royal Navy helicopter instructor, was to restart the course as soon as he could spare the time from operational flying. Meanwhile, I flew as co-pilot for the experienced captains, both to familiarise myself with the countryside and to gain experience in the tactics used during operations. Although much of the flying was done with a single pilot, we always carried two if the aircraft was to fly anywhere where there were no friendly troops on the ground to cover either an intentional or unintentional landing.

My first operational trip was made on October 25th, 1971, five weeks after my arrival in Oman and just one day after I arrived at Salalah. Our troops had established themselves at White City, and it had been decided to try to prevent the resupply of the adoo in the Eastern Sector. This was to be done by putting in a blockading force in the hills immediately above the eastern end of the plains area, where the more fertile country was at its narrowest, but was cut by deep wadis and covered by scrub vegetation that supplied cover for the camel convoys. If the adoo could be forced to route their convoys further north they would be in open country, and exposed to attack by the airforce.

The helicopter task in *Operation Leopard*, as this phase was designated, was to carry forty troops to Pasadena, an old airstrip which was in open country several miles north of the proposed Leopard Line. We were not allowed to carry them direct into their final locations since the risk of battle damage to our helicopters, should there be any adoo in the area, was not considered acceptable. Once on the ground, the men would have to walk south to their positions on the hilltops.

Four 205s lifted off from Salalah at 0600, bound for Um al Gwarif. I was in the lead aircraft flying as co-pilot for Neville Baker. At Gwarif the soldiers embarked, each one carrying all the ammunition, food and water he would need until we could resupply them at their final location. Even the smallest Baluch soldier weighed over two hundred pounds with his pack and spare ammunition and, heavily overloaded, we were forced to circle over the plain until we reached our transit height of ten thousand feet above sea level. This height would allow us to cross the jebel edge at least five thousand feet above ground level, and hopefully out of small arms range. Neville turned north and the other three aircraft trailed behind us in very loose order. I had been surprised that we had not been briefed to fly in any sort of battle formation; in fact, the briefing had been very sketchy, little more than the time of lift-off and our destination.

I could see few details on the plain, one feature blurring into the next, making map reading difficult. Then, as we crossed the jebel edge and the hills rose up beneath us, I could make out small trees and scrub bushes clinging to the sides of the deep, dark wadis. A few miles further north the hills gave way to uniformly brown-coloured plateaux, cut by broad wadis with bright, sunlit sandy bottoms. Pasadena was on one of the plateaux and had been used in the past by the De Havilland Beaver light communications aircraft, but it was too short even for the Skyvans and had fallen into disuse.

As we arrived over the Landing zone (LZ), we were joined by two Strikemasters, our top cover, who would dive down and strafe the area with rockets and machine-guns should we come under fire from the adoo. This was considered most unlikely since the airstrip was well clear of any known enemy groups but, even so, I felt my stomach muscles tighten as we started the descent. I recalled a lecture I had attended while still in the navy. It had been given by an American Marine Corps Colonel, fresh from the killing fields of Vietnam, who had described a helicopter-borne troop landing, U.S Marine Corps style. He had spoken very casually of twenty or thirty Bell 205 troop carriers, immediately preceded by a similar number of Huey-Cobra gunships flying in "V" formation. Two minutes before touchdown the Cobra pilots would start firing their heavy machine-guns, laying down a carpet of lead into which even the bravest of Viet Cong was unlikely to raise his head. By the time the barrage was over the troops would have disembarked and the helicopters could climb away, now covered by fire from friendly troops on the ground—and all we had was a couple of Strikemasters orbiting above us!

We touched down on the plateau and were immediately enveloped in swirling dust that cut visibility to a few yards. I watched our troops deplane, some throwing themselves onto the ground in a warlike posture; others wandering away, tripping over the bandoliers of ammunition they had draped around their bodies and staggering under the weight of the mortar bombs they carried, seemingly not totally sure what they should do next. Their confusion was not all their fault. Flying hours were at a premium and I gathered they had been given little training in helicopter-borne warfare. As soon as the last of them cleared our aircraft, Neville called on the radio that we were lifting off. We climbed out of our personal dust cloud into bright sunlight, followed shortly by the other three, each one lifting independently as soon as the pilot was ready.

We arrived back at Salalah without mishap and in time for breakfast, but I wondered what would have happened if we had met with any opposition, or if by chance any of the helicopters had gone unserviceable. I discovered this dilemma was occupying the minds of some of the other squadron pilots, especially those who had flown in the army support role before, and who expected a more military outlook on briefing and flying discipline.

Over the next couple of weeks I completed the conversion to the 205 while, at the same time, continuing to fly as co-pilot. Most days, at crack of dawn, two 205s would be sent to White City where the Skyvans would already be delivering the bulk supplies at the airstrip. Our job was to take the individual requirements of food, water and ammunition to the many forward locations. I soon discovered just how sedate my flying had been in the past. Our approach technique was dependent on the length of transit to be flown. For the shorter distances we flew low level, especially if the ground was covered by friendly troops; for longer trips, or where no cover could be provided by our forces, we climbed to five thousand feet over White City, transited at that altitude, and then spiralled down to the LZ, or into dead ground from where we could complete the journey low level.

Low flying over land by military aircraft in the UK, whether by fixed wing or helicopters, has been a subject of controversy for many years. It is an exhilarating form of flight, but requires a high degree of concentration and constant practice to be able to do it safely; without this practice it has the statistical potential for producing accidents which the military cannot afford in war, let alone in peacetime. My low flying training over land had been limited, antisubmarine pilots having little need of the skill. Commando pilots in the navy were restricted to specific areas, and with specific authorisation. Unauthorised low flying could mean the end of even the most promising career. There will always be the idiots who deliberately break the rules, and they receive little sympathy in the military flying services when they get caught, but the training is essential if the pilots are to be able to survive in wartime. The peacetime lower limit of two hundred and fifty feet, except in a few areas where a lower height is allowed for short distances, and at specific training ranges owned by the Ministry of Defence, would hardly be considered low flying in wartime. To remain undetected by radar, or out of sight of the enemy in the front line, the aircraft must be flown much lower, and despite the advance in terrain following aids the pilot's life depends largely upon his skill. I believe that if the military are required to defend the public, the public must be prepared to allow those with that responsibility every chance to acquire the necessary skills.

In Oman we had no such restrictions. Low flying was essential to our survival and we had to be prepared to use each hillock and tree for cover. My first attempts were under the supervision and tuition of Bill Bailey, an ex-Royal Marine pilot who had already been in Oman for several months, and who in later years was to become the first Chief Superintendent of the Royal Oman Police Air Wing. At one point we were resupplying a forward location, the final run being low level up a small wadi. I was flying at what I considered to be a low enough altitude when Bill grabbed the controls and dived the aircraft.

"When I said LOW, I meant LOW. At that height I need oxygen!" he said.

I felt aggrieved at what I considered a slight on my ability, a feeling that lasted only until the first stunted thorn tree flashed past my window at eye level. Before long I too was flying with my skids no more than five feet from the ground, weaving my way between the bushes at one hundred knots and more.

It was Bill who introduced me to the "Salalah Spiral," the descent from high level to an LZ. We flew to the general area at five thousand feet and, when approximately over the LZ, called for the troops at our destination to throw a smoke grenade to pinpoint their location and indicate the wind direction. On seeing the smoke, Bill lowered the collective and rolled off the throttle to flight idle, lowering the nose at the same time. As soon as the autorotation was established, he began to weave the aircraft, rolling into tight turns in either direction. In a straight line, a fully loaded 205 will descend at fifteen hundred to two thousand feet per minute; putting it into a spiral dive can more than double this, and Bill told me he had once sustained a rate of descent of over five thousand feet per minute. We could also create more problems for any adoo who might try to shoot at us by changing the direction of turn at will!

Pressed back into my seat by the "G" force, I had a momentary thought that perhaps I should have opted for night fighters while I had the chance. The ground rushed up to meet us and I had no time to worry about whether we were coming under fire. Bill pulled up on the collective at about four hundred feet above the ground, rolled open the throttle, straightened the aircraft for the final two hundred yard run into the LZ and slid the skids on to the ground between the two oil barrels marking the touchdown point. Before we had come to a stop our Omani crewman was heaving the supplies out into the waiting arms of the troops; thirty seconds later we were airborne again, spiralling above the LZ until we were high enough to set heading for the return journey to White City. Although a spiral climb reduced the rate at which we clawed our way back to safety, it was considered prudent to remain over our troops in case we did get shot down.

I was already flying on operations in the 206. These aircraft were used mainly for communications, but occasionally we were called out by the army for a casualty evacuation or a *Hawkeye*. If a jebali or a SEP brought in information concerning enemy troop movements, perhaps the location of an arms cache, or even the venue for a meeting of the adoo leaders, the army would ask for an air strike. The 206 would be flown to Gwarif to pick up the informant and an interpreter, and then on up to the jebel. It's difficult enough for a trained observer to pinpoint a target from the air. It should have been impossible for an untrained jebali. They seemed to find nothing strange about flying in a helicopter and their eyesight was incredible. Within seconds they would have identified the target; the position would be transferred to a grid reference and passed to the jets. The strike leader would then dive in and fire a single rocket to ensure they had the right position before pressing home the attack. The information we received was always screened to make sure it held some truth, but we could never be totally certain our informant was not using us to pay off an old score against a neighbouring village, and civilian casualties were inevitable. The reports that filtered back from the jebel showed our attacks were having a positive effect on the adoo, and this was considered to outweigh the negative aspects; as General Sherman once said, "War is all hell!"

The helicopter squadron was kept very busy in the eastern sector for most of November. We had several forward locations that needed daily resupply, and North Group, a firqat led by the SAS, were moving steadily forward across the jebel towards the Midway road. This was the only road leading in to Salalah from the north and had been cut by the adoo the year before. North Group seemed to attract more attention from the enemy than any other unit; resupply missions were delayed frequently by firefights and in these circumstances we had to retire to a safe distance and wait until our troops were sure the enemy had pulled back out of range. I spent many hours on the ground at White City waiting for the all clear, which gave me a chance to view the jebel from ground level.

The camp at White City was on the slope of a small hill, almost the highest point in the area, and overlooked the jebel on all sides. The village we had occupied consisted of two huts, no more than low, circular stone walls topped with a roof made from branches and dry grass. Some twenty jebali with their goats and cattle were still living there, carrying on with their normal routine despite being in the middle of a war zone. The stone-walled compounds they had built to corral their cattle had been broken up to provide the material for the "sangars," fortifications for the soldiers, their mortars and artillery. The new airstrip ran through the middle of the camp, a four hundred yard long dirt runway from which the Skyvans and Caribous could operate. Beside the runway was an open area used by the helicopters, but there was no protection for us when we shut down, or for the barrels from which we pumped our fuel.

On one occasion I joined a couple of the Battmen who offered me a cup of thick, black tea and a bacon sandwich. They were sitting in a sangar, sheltered from the hot sun by a khaki canvas sheet stretched over them and their mortar. It was all very peaceful and rural. I could hear the birds singing in a nearby tree and see the cattle grazing quietly a few hundred yards down the slope from our position. It was not easy to remember that, a few thousand yards further down that slope in the Wadi Arzat, there was a group of rebels whose avowed intention was to kill us! The Battmen pointed out one or two of the main features. Southeast of us, perhaps two kilometres away and close to a single, tall tree, was a small group of sangars, a forward position overlooking the Arzat. North Group was about fifteen kilometres to the northwest, on the other side of the wadi and, as if to remind us that they were there, we heard the adoo open up again on the firqat.

Waterhole, a position guarding one of the springs that fed the adoo stronghold in the Wadi Darbat, lay to the north-east, between us and Jib Jat, and was one of the runs that we could do low level, since the ground was well covered by our own troops. The monsoon had lifted a few short weeks before, but already the sun had burnt the grass, and a layer of dust covered the leaves. All around the camp the jebel was pock-marked with craters surrounded by large black circles, the results of mortar fire from both sides, and the fires caused by the explosions.

Once the firefight at North Group had died down we were able to continue their resupply. This was a high level transit, a spiral into dead ground to the north of their position, and an exciting low level run down a shallow wadi to the LZ. The adoo had attacked from the south. No one knew just how far they had retired and we had been advised not to go anywhere south of the location to turn into the strong northerly wind, forcing us to land downwind. The run was further complicated because the wadi, which provided the only safe route into the LZ, was very narrow and the two helicopters kept meeting, each travelling in the opposite direction at a closing speed of two hundred knots!

By late November the war had become static. North Group, the only really mobile unit, had continued their march across the jebel until HQ decided the vacuum they were leaving behind was sure to be filled by the adoo. The firqat were keen to continue because they were entering their own tribal area, but were withdrawn and sent to Midway to await further developments.

The flow of SEPs had increased, and the information they brought with them was encouraging. It appeared that the leaders in the western sector were agitating for some spectacular successes from their brothers in the east. The eastern sector was, however, being squeezed by our presence on the jebel and by the slowing down of supply trains through the Leopard Line. Convoys were still getting through, but not in the quantities that the adoo either wished or needed.

The propaganda reports we picked up through Radio Aden were hilarious. By the end of November PFLOAG claimed to have killed three thousand, eight hundred and eight of our men, shot down fifty-four aircraft and sunk ten of our ships! It was doubtful if we had that number of troops in Dhofar; we would dearly have loved to have had all those aircraft for them to shoot at, and the Sultan's navy consisted of three bums (pronounced *booms* and the Omani name for the Arab dhow!) and the Royal Yacht! We were taking casualties on the ground, but probably never more than two or three a week, and fortunately seldom fatal. We had lost the Caribou at Akoot from enemy action, and a Strikemaster on landing at Salalah; but, apart from these, any battle damage was always repairable. As far as I know, none of our ships had even been fired upon. The adoo admitted to having lost "seventy four martyrs to the cause" and fifty others wounded, but never mentioned those who were surrendering to the Sultan.

The Leopard Line was not a total success, and to augment it, the Desert Regiment under Colonel Knocker began to carry out offensive operations from their base at Akoot. Troops were airlifted into Moon country, where they were to mine the camel trails and harass the convoys if they could find them. These affairs were given codenames such as *Operation Sandcloud*, but to the helicopter squadron they were always known as *Knocker's Follies*. A few days before the first of them Nick and I were sent to Akoot in a 205. There we picked up Colonel Knocker and two of his officers and flew them into Moon country to reconnoitre a suitable LZ. Our maps were not of much use. The area had been fully surveyed, mostly by aerial photography, but the majority of the wadis looked alike from the air, and it was difficult to ensure that the one we chose on the map was the one we found on the ground. We had to pick a site that was sufficiently far away from any signs of adoo activity to ensure we would not be opposed. We also had to look at it from low level to assure ourselves it was large enough and had a suitable surface to accept four 205s on the day of the action. If there had been any adoo in the area at the time it would not have required a genius among them to realise what we were doing, or to prepare a welcome for us.

The great day arrived. Four 205s, fully loaded with troops, took off from Akoot and, with Nick leading us in a 206, we headed for Moon country. On arrival at the LZ, Nick dropped down to low level and threw out a smoke grenade to mark the spot and reveal the wind direction. We followed as a gaggle, deplaned the troops and climbed away for the return to Salalah. It was a repeat of the *Leopard* insertion. Little briefing was given to the pilots and no plans were made for any emergencies. On our return to Salalah the pilots discussed this at great length, and it was apparent that most of us were in agreement —we had been fortunate that nothing had gone wrong! There was little doubt we had been given so little information about what was intended that if the lead helicopter had gone unserviceable, even with a simple radio failure, we would probably have had to abort the operation. Worse still, because we flew to the location, descended to and climbed out from the LZ, and returned to base as individual aircraft rather than a cohesive unit, the chances of a mid-air collision were increased. When we recovered the troops the last aircraft on the ground would be left virtually unprotected.

We decided to insist on full, detailed briefings for these, and any other operations, with all eventualities being covered. We proposed that we should transit in battle formation, and descend and climb away together. This gave individual aircraft freedom of movement within the formation, but ensured that we remained in close contact with each other at all times. As we became used to this more professional outlook, we were even able to use a modified version of the Salalah Spiral.

A few days later we were again involved in another of the *Follies,* this time to airlift thirty-five troops and some artillery to the southern end of the border with the PDRY. With the connivance of the Yemeni government, PFLOAG had set up a base camp and indoctrination centre at Hauf, a few thousand metres inside Yemen, and our troops were to shell it. We returned with little idea of whether we did any damage; the camp was out of sight, but at least it showed the adoo that they were not safe, even in the PDRY. At a much later date, PFLOAG culled the jebel for as many children as possible from the age of about six upwards, and marched them over one hundred kilometres to this camp for "re-education."

By the end of November the strain of almost daily operational flying had begun to take its toll on the helicopter pilots. Minor illnesses that would normally have been shaken off quickly were developing into more serious ailments. Roy Bayliss was quarantined with what the doctors claimed was mumps; Mike Hall developed an ear infection that grounded him for many days. To add to our problems our Lords and Masters in Muscat then saw fit to recall Chris Chambers to fly the 206 in support of the civil authorities in the Musendam peninsular, reducing our numbers even further. John Atkinson was sent south with two new recruits, Steve Watson and Colin Hardie, but neither of them had flown the 205 and would not be operational for at least a couple of weeks; at one point we were reduced to five fit pilots to fly the eight 205s.

This workload was not limited to the helicopter squadron alone. The fixed wing pilots were also at full stretch, but despite this the morale at Salalah remained high. Most of the aircrew who came south to join SOAF(Tac) volunteered to stay there rather than return to the north, preferring the opportunity of putting their years of military training to the test instead of stagnating in the peacetime atmosphere of Muscat. Peter Hulme, the Commander of SOAF(Tac), was an excellent CO, and popular with both the contract and seconded personnel despite being a contract officer himself. He was a Squadron Leader who had served with the Yemeni Airforce after retiring from the RAF, and when the communists had taken over he had moved next door to Oman.

Peter's task was not exactly easy for we had some weird characters in the airforce perhaps best described by Jack Sullivan, a contract intelligence officer from Gwarif. He was leaving Oman for pastures new, and at a farewell dinner we gave for him in the mess at Salalah he prefaced his after dinner speech with the following words:

"In a long military career I have served with many strange outfits, but none more bizarre than the Sultan of Oman's Airforce, which appears to be staffed almost exclusively by drunks, divorcees and debtors!"

The contract pilots tended to be individuals who, while fully committed to maintaining a very high standard of professionalism in their flying, were less inclined to suffer the attempts by Muscat to impose formalised, peacetime RAF discipline. We seldom saw CSOAF, our commander in Muscat, but orders were passed down to us through Peter that we felt sometimes showed a lack of appreciation of the situation. When we were threatened with dire consequences if our haircuts did not conform to RAF standards, Bill Bailey's answer was to allow his hair to curl over his collar and to grow a beard, something which he had never been allowed to do in the Royal Marines; the rest of us ignored the order until it died a natural death.

The seconded helicopter pilots were generally either very junior and inexperienced, or drawn from the ranks of those whose promotion prospects in the RAF were limited. Fortunately this did not detract from their ability and even the most inexperienced swiftly lost their innocence and proved their worth. I often wondered why the RAF did not give pilots who were approaching the time for command responsibility the chance to fly in combat conditions. I was told, and have no reason to doubt what I was told, that there was no shortage of volunteers, but those who did come tended to be still too junior for their opinions and experience to be very highly regarded when they returned to Britain. I also know that the navy would have welcomed the chance to send some more senior pilots to gain valuable experience, but for some reason they were never allowed to join us; traditionally the RAF had always provided the pilots for SOAF and perhaps they felt this would be poaching on their preserves

Waterhole had become the eastern sector hotspot, and for days on end the adoo put in attack after attack in an attempt to dislodge our forces. When we began to find bullet holes in our aircraft we realised they were not always pulling back out of range when the firefight died down. We gave up using the direct, low level approaches in favour of a spiral from high level into what we hoped was dead ground. We also took to flying with two pilots in the helicopter, and the fighter squadron provided us with top cover. The jet pilots had great difficulty in spotting the adoo, but the guerrillas were known to have a healthy respect for them and normally kept their heads down whenever the Strikemasters were in the area.

Our troops began to take casualties at Waterhole, which involved the helicopters in their other duty. There was always one of our machines at Salalah available for casualty evacuation with a crew at immediate readiness. We were under the same restrictions, and were meant to wait for any firefight to die down before we landed, but this rule was ignored by most of us whenever possible. We were fortunate that we never had to face the dangers met by casevac pilots in Vietnam, who went in under withering fire from the Viet Cong to rescue the injured. It seems ironic to me that many of those American pilots were conscientious objectors who chose to fly the unarmed mercy missions, rather than carry a gun and risk killing someone—thus following in the tradition of many field ambulance drivers in both World Wars.

My first casevac was from Waterhole. One of the Battmen had been shot in the head, and although we managed to get him to the Field

Surgical Team (FST) at Salalah within an hour of his being hit, the surgeons were unable to save his life.

Early December brought with it another of the *Follies*. This time I was volunteered to fly the 206, not the most popular duty since it meant going in alone to mark the LZ. I thought I had it pinpointed but, as I led the 205s to the area, I discovered to my horror and embarrassment that it was well nigh impossible to pick out the particular wadi we had selected, and we had to orbit for what seemed like hours, but actually was for a couple of minutes, before I could be sure of the location. By this time any self-respecting adoo would have been fully alerted to what was happening, and it was with some trepidation that I dived down to heave out the smoke marker. To my great relief there was no rattle of small arms fire. The troops marched away and laid their mines and we retrieved them the next day without mishap. We were told later that several explosions had been heard from the area and that some camels had been reported as killed, but it was never confirmed whether they were friendly or enemy camels, or just some poor, unsuspecting strays!

We were still short of pilots. On one day, supposedly my rest day, I flew two resupply flights to Waterhole, and a casevac from White City. Yet another Battman had suffered injury, this time in the form of a chest wound. The surgeons had more success with him, and he made a full recovery. The SAS were supposed to be in Dhofar in a strictly training role, but seemed to take their responsibilities very seriously and obviously believed in "on-the-job" training; certainly they seemed to take more than their fair share of casualties!

The adoo in the east began to run short of ammunition and food. The Leopard Line was squeezing them, and to make their resupply problems even greater we had extended the line by putting in some troops on the coast at Mugshayl. For a few days we were able to sit back and catch our breath before the adoo called our hand. They moved a convoy through the foothills under the noses of our troops, insufficient to make an appreciable difference to their war effort, but enough to encourage them. When seventy-five unattended camels were found in the area, although it could not be established whether they were, in fact, part of another convoy, camels were declared a legitimate target for the strike pilots.

White City, now known as Medina al Hagg, the City of Truth, was being developed not only as a military base but also as part of the hearts and minds campaign on the jebel. The civil authorities erected a small dispensary within the perimeter, and the Sultan himself flew up to open this new facility, the first of its kind in the hills. Soon after the Sultan returned to Salalah, a SEP walked into White City. He told an interpreter he had been a hard-core communist for five years, had served on the planning group for the adoo in the eastern sector, and that the adoo were about to launch a frontal attack on White City from the Wadi Arzat. He was immediately taken up in one of the 205s already at the airstrip, and a call was made to Salalah for the jets to be scrambled. While the jets were attacking the target, return fire was seen from the Arzat, normally a good indication that the report had been accurate. Next morning a woman walked in from the wadi and told us the attack had been a great success. It had caused many casualties among the adoo, several of them being caught, quite literally, with their pants down.

We had hoped that the lull would continue over the Christmas period, but were out of luck. On Christmas Eve I had just returned from an operation with DR when a call came from the troops on the Leopard Line for a casevac. One of their patrols had been ambushed somewhere on the forward edge of the jebel, and they had taken eight casualties from light machine-gun and small arms fire. Steve Hutton, a young New Zealander seconded from the RAF, came as my co-pilot, and with Stan Stanford, an ex-navy air crewman, in the back we flew to the area. Making contact with the patrol by radio, we called for smoke. The reply came that they had been fired upon from less than two hundred yards and, hampered by the casualties, they had been unable to pull back very far from the scene of the fire fight. They were not too sure whether the adoo had retired and were very reluctant to mark their position, either for us or the adoo! They wanted to try to direct us to their position by radio. This would work, but filled me with little pleasure; it was slow and could leave us vulnerable once we began the final run in to their position.

We orbited at a safe height and tried to locate their position. The ground was covered by small trees and scrub which made any sort of identification difficult, but there seemed to be little alternative and I agreed to follow their directions. I did insist that they direct me to an approximate "on top," from where I would descend to the LZ. When their call came we commenced a tight spiral towards the only clearing that appeared big enough for a 205, praying that it was the right one. As our skids touched the ground the patrol broke cover and began to load the injured unceremoniously into our main cabin, one on top of the other. Within seconds we were airborne again.

Steve and I had already discussed our line of retreat. We were now heavily laden and our rate of climb would be painfully slow, leaving us like a sitting duck if the adoo were close. We felt they were unlikely to have retired towards the nearest point on the jebel edge, about half a mile away; this would have exposed them to the risk of being trapped with their backs against a sheer drop if we had brought in reinforcements. We decided that this represented our safest way out, and with skids brushing the bushes we sped towards safety. The jebel edge appeared beneath us and I pushed the nose of the helicopter down, diving for the plains some four thousand feet below. The plan worked. The patrol reported neither enemy fire in our direction, nor any more contact with the adoo, but it was certainly as close to them as I wished to come.

Christmas Day brought no relief. Following another heavy attack on Waterhole, Colin Hardie and I were sent to retrieve a Baluch soldier who had been hit in the back by a bullet. It had become remarkably unpleasant there. The adoo were able to get within small arms range of the LZ, but it seemed they had yet to realise that if they stayed under cover until we landed, we would make an easy target.

Information from SEPs now indicated that the adoo were becoming desperate. We were told that a force of one hundred and sixty adoo from the western sector were to be joined by eighty from the east in an attempt to push a camel convoy through the Leopard Line. This was almost the first time they had gathered together such a large force, and reinforced our belief that if we could stop the supplies to the east, their determination to continue the fight might crumble. The Leopard Line was strengthened and extended more than ten miles north of the tree line to a water hole at Ayun. We sat back to await developments, and did not have long to wait. Under cover of an attack on the outpost at Mugshayl, the adoo pushed a small convoy along the foothills and into the eastern sector without being stopped.

On New Year's Eve, the helicopter squadron carried out its first night casevac, when John Atkinson and Roy Bayliss brought in a wounded man from White City. For reasons we had never been able to fully understand, there had been a marked reluctance to allow us to operate at night. We had already briefed the army on how to mark the LZ, using torches to make a landing "T", and to the surprise of some people the system worked. There was the occasional hiccough. Bill Bailey went to Mugshayl, and was disconcerted to note that the "T" was rather dim and some of the torches kept going out. Once on the ground he asked the officer in charge whether it was beyond his ability to ensure that their torches had new batteries, and was none too pleased to be told that the army at Mugshayl had no torches. The lights he had seen were the patrol-striking matches!

In the middle of January 1972 the army began to push out from its static positions. The helicopters were to be used to move a firqat to an LZ in the hills above the eastern edge of the Wadi Darbat, while regular troops moved to a similar point on the western edge. Once these two groups had settled in, another firqat was supposed to march to Suhait, even closer to the adoo stronghold. Most unseasonably, it began to rain and the firqat refused to move. Twenty-four hours later they took up their positions, about six kilometres southeast of White City, and we began to shuttle in their heavy equipment.

The new locations represented a major threat to the adoo and we had realised that they would react almost immediately. We had taken the precaution of flying with two pilots in each helicopter, and I was acting as co-pilot for Nick Holbrook as we took in the first load. Within seconds of touching down it became unpleasantly obvious that someone was shooting at us since, through the bubble window beneath my feet, I could see the dirt being kicked up on the ground by bullets! Nick dragged the helicopter back into the air, and we beat a hasty retreat to the safety of White City. We landed and shut down to inspect the helicopter for damage but could find not even the smallest scratch. I shall never understand how they missed us.

The firefight at Amatol, as the new location was called, continued for most of the day, and it was not until evening that we were able to complete the shuttle. The army had stirred up a hornet's nest, and for the next few days we were kept very busy supplying them with ammunition whenever there was a break in the battle. The adoo were reported to have lost twenty killed in one action alone—when they became trapped in a wadi and an accurate mortar barrage was laid on top of them.

Then, overnight, the jebel was covered with cloud and our resupply flights into White City became more difficult. We were forced to fly above cloud to reach the area, and hope that we could find a break through which we could descend. Very occasionally, when a break was not available, we called the army at White City to make sure there was still a gap between the cloud base and the ground, and let down blind. There was always a chance we might arrive below cloud in the wrong place, possibly over an adoo group, but we bore charmed lives and everyone made it safely.

For once the cloud extended beyond the normal monsoon line in the west, and our newfound attitude towards operations now paid dividends. *Operation Sandcloud,* the latest of the *Follies,* had to be delayed for twenty-four hours because the proposed LZ was blanketed by cloud. When the time came for the withdrawal, cloud was again covering much of the area, leaving little more than four hundred feet between the cloud base and the hills. Roy Bayliss was leading the four 205s and he spoke with the army at the pickup point, somewhere under the overcast. The grid reference we had been given put them only four miles from our position, but we could not see any of their smoke markers. We were beginning to get low on fuel and the army was running out of smoke; either we were in the wrong position or they had given us a wrong reference. Roy called for us to tighten up the formation and led us under the cloud in a last attempt to find them. Within minutes the soldiers told us they could hear the distinctive beat of our rotors and had thrown their last smoke marker. We saw the smoke drifting across our track, turned as one and headed for the source. We found them, but there was no doubt in anyone's mind that if this had taken place in the bad old days they would either have had to wait until we had returned to Salalah to refuel, or walk out.

The cloud disappeared as quickly as it had arrived and our flying returned to normal. In early February the Battmen at Marbat asked whether we could send a helicopter to the village for a medevac, the civilian version of a casevac. I was on call that morning, and flew the 205 along the coast, past Taqa and the Wadi Darbat, landing alongside the small fort inside the barbed wire fence that surrounded the village. The medevac was a young jebali woman who had walked in from her home in the hills at about three thousand feet above sea level, a gentle stroll of no more than ten or twelve miles, having just given birth prematurely. We collected her and her baby and flew them back to the recently opened civilian hospital at Salalah. It was always a pleasure to be able to help. In a small way it seemed to make up for some of the damage that was being done by our more belligerent operations.

The war continued, however, and we were soon involved in yet another push forward, this time to LZ "B". This was near the village of Tawi Atair, on the eastern side of the Wadi Darbat. It seemed that this time the adoo had understood our orders, for one of our patrols made contact almost immediately and a call came for a casevac. Nick and I were on the " B" shuttle at the time and flew to the forward area. Once again the casualty was a Battman, yet another regular British soldier to be killed or injured in this war of which so few people in Britain were aware.

In fact in Dhofar we never talked about people being killed. The more usual terms were either "banjoed" or "zapped"; nor did the pilots discuss very often the prospect of being shot down. The adoo had declared their intentions towards us quite precisely. If any of us were captured we were to be taken to Aden where, after being handed over to the women for a particularly unpleasant operation on our nether regions, we would be paraded in the streets. We preferred to put the idea firmly in the back of our minds and personally, I had a strong, if ill-founded, belief in my own invulnerability!

All previous flying records were smashed during the LZ "B" push. In under a week each of the pilots flew more than thirty hours, and we were in danger of having to withdraw the helicopters for essential maintenance just when they were most needed. Our eight engineers worked incredibly long hours to keep the ten aircraft in the air, but spares were scarce, and even engineers need sleep! Then, just before the crisis hit, the action died down and we were back to daily milk runs.

This coincided with my last week at Salalah before I went up to Bait al Falaj for a month of "R and R." Jane was coming out to join me, and and at the end of the month we would be returning to the UK for leave. I flew only once, a night casevac from Amatol. One of the Baluch had complained of stomach pains and the medical orderly on the spot feared it might be appendicitis. With Nev Baker as my co-pilot, we took off into the pitch-black night and headed for the jebel. We had arranged for the troops to release a small flare to indicate their position when they heard us, and then they would set up the "T" torch. We saw the flare and circled to make an approach into wind. Suddenly, to my horror, the area was lit up by another flare, followed by another and another. It was like the Fourth of July throughout our approach and we must have presented a magnificent target, silhouetted against the skyline. I thought of aborting the pickup but, since the ado had not opened fire, I presumed they must be having a night off and pressed on. Some very harsh words were spoken when we landed, and tempers were not improved when we returned to Salalah to find that the appendicitis was, in fact, indigestion.

At the end of February I flew to Muscat in one of the Viscounts. I was sorry to be leaving, if only for a couple of months, and would have preferred to be going straight back to England. There had been rather more bullets flying around than my interviewer in Bournemouth had led me to believe, but Dhofar was a military helicopter pilot's dream. We were flying the aircraft to their limits, there were no unnecessary restrictions and I looked forward to my return to Salalah

Chapter Nine

Our contract had specified that we should be unaccompanied, but three prefabricated bungalows had been erected just outside the main gates of the camp at Bait al Falaj, and we were allowed to book these and bring our families to Muscat for short visits. Jane was due to arrive a few days after me so, having made sure the bungalow was ready for occupation, I spent most of my time relaxing at the beach.

The atmosphere at Bait al Falaj was in stark contrast to that at Salalah. I found it difficult to reconcile the realities as we knew them in the south, with the seeming disinterest that was shown by some of the personnel at headquarters. Visiting the SOAF offices to read the daily operations reports sent by SOAF(Tac) to Muscat, I found them, apparently unread, in a pile in a pending tray. In the mess I received the impression that the army in Dhofar was something of a nuisance, generating extra work for Muscat, and overheard a conversation between two long serving staff officers concerning some supplies that had been sent south.

"We've just sent another load of .762 ammunition to Dhofar," said one to the other. "That's the second lot in as many weeks. I just don't know what they do with it there."

I was told later that he had never visited Dhofar, so maybe he was telling the truth.

There was little flying for me in Muscat. New pilots were arriving, and the three helicopters, one 205 and two 206s, were heavily committed to the training role and civil assistance work. I managed to fly only once before Jane arrived. Arms had been smuggled into north Oman over the years, much of it through the port at Sur, and had been cached in the Hajar mountains for use in further uprisings. The Sultan had offered an amnesty to anyone who would reveal any of the hiding places, and the army at Nizwa had received information concerning a cache in the hills above the town. Charlie Parsons, a newly joined RAF pilot, came with me in the 205 to airlift a search party to the area. This was less than a ten-minute flight for a helicopter, or an hour by Landrover followed by a long climb on foot. The search party consisted of five army personnel and the informant, an old man who seemed to be well in to his seventies but, I was assured, was actually fifty-two. He was thin to the point of emaciation, with long, spindly legs that looked as though they would have difficulty in supporting him, let alone climbing the steep slopes of the jebel.

We flew along the southern edge of the mountains. Grey scree covered the slopes and there were few places where we could land. When our guide pointed out a likely place we landed as close as we could, shutting down the engine and leaving the search party to complete the journey on foot. This went on for four or five hours without success; either it was the wrong cave, or no cave at all and we began to wonder whether the informant had just fancied a day out in a helicopter. We were about to return to Nizwa to refuel when he pointed excitedly at a little gully about one thousand feet above us. Landing on an outcrop of rock scarcely big enough for a mountain goat, we shut down yet again. Up to this point I had steadfastly refused to go walkabout, believing, like so many pilots, that my legs were there principally to keep my backside from dragging on the ground; but I had become bored with sitting in the hot sun and, on being told the cave was a mere twenty minutes stroll away, decided to join the search party.

The old man set a killing pace! This was the fifth time he had scrambled up these hills, yet within twenty minutes he had left all but the strongest far behind. The twenty minutes turned into an hour of steady climbing, but we were rewarded at the top by the sight of a small cave tucked under an overhanging rock outcrop, just big enough for two people to crawl into on their hands and knees. Inside we found several AK47 assault rifles, a couple of Chinese made "Burp" guns and some cases of ammunition. There was also a metal box containing Chinese style uniforms, and copies of Chairman Mao's Little Red Book translated into Arabic. The cache had been there for more than two years and I was a little apprehensive when one of the army officers, finding an AK47 with a loaded magazine attached, pointed it into the air and pulled the trigger. He fired a full, thirty round magazine without a jam or misfire, despite the time it had lain there. We had to carry everything down to the helicopter, little more than a thousand yards away, and I wondered at the determination of the people who had carried it, mostly uphill, from Nizwa.

A few days later Jane arrived, and I managed to obtain permission for her to accompany me on a 205 trip into the interior. The Sultan had been persuaded by his British equerry to allow a team from Paris Vogue to photograph the latest collection by Yves St Laurent against an Omani background. Armed with an order from the Sultan authorising us to go wherever we wanted, and to photograph anyone and anything we wished, we set off early one morning. The aircraft was heavily loaded. Charlie Parsons came as co-pilot. Bill Bailey, like me on R and R, insisted that we needed a cabin attendant, although I believe the main attractions for him were the two models, Natalie and Kirsten. We also carried the fashion editress from the magazine, Franco, an Italian fashion photographer, the equerry, Jane and an Omani interpreter. Because we were going to be away for the whole day we also took several cold boxes laden with food and drink to sustain us on the journey.

Our first stop was the little oasis town of Adam, fifty miles south of the mountains. Navigation was easy. We followed the oil pipeline down the Wadi Sumail and on into the desert until it turned right to the oil fields at Fahud. At that point we turned south, out across the desert to where we could see the pass between the Jebels Salakh and Madmar. There, nestling in the pass among many acres of bright green date palms, lay Adam. I was at the controls for this leg, Charlie and I having agreed we would take turn and turn about both at the flying and at the less pleasant duty of standing guard over the helicopter. This was necessary to prevent any light-fingered soul from stripping some vital part as a souvenir. I made two landings at Adam, the first in the local cemetery! I think I might have been forgiven for the error: the whole area was covered in stones and none of them had any inscriptions. Moving quickly to a less irreverent position, I shut down. Almost before the rotors had stopped turning we were surrounded by what appeared to be the entire male population of the town.

Leaving me on guard, the fashion party was led into the town to meet the Wali and to start the photography. On their return they found me performing an imitation of the oozlum bird, running around the helicopter in ever decreasing circles, and threatening the children with an excruciating death if they touched the machine again. Charlie did not improve my temper by pointing out that they spoke only Arabic, and most probably thought I was playing their version of ring-around-the-roses! Those in the fashion team, in contrast, were cool and rested. They had met the wali in the majlis, the room in his house where the elders sat to discuss town matters of great importance; this was a rare honour since the majlis is normally a totally male preserve. They had been given coffee and tea to drink and halwat to eat. Jane had brought me some halwat as a gift from the wali. It is a concoction of nuts and fruit mixed with a pink jelly, made, I was told, from semolina and honey. It was very thoughtful of our hosts but, after the first mouthful, I was glad we were leaving immediately. I found the taste terrible, and was glad to be able to dispose of the rest later without offending them.

We had been told there was a nomad family camped about ten miles deeper into the desert, and this was to be our next stop. We flew down a shallow wadi, really no more than a flatter, sandier area than the rest, and thickly covered with scrub and small thorn trees, a sure sign of underground water in an otherwise almost lifeless desert. Charlie, who was now at the controls, spotted the camp and landed a few hundred yards away from it. Our interpreter cautioned us to remain with the helicopter while he went to speak with the family. We were close to the Sharqiya and, although we had the Sultan's permission, the inhabitants of the area were not renowned for their high regard for either authority or strangers.

In fact the family was incredibly friendly, and before long we were all sitting on rugs placed on the sand. This was no Bedouin camp beloved of Hollywood, no snow white Arab stallion champing at the bit, no camels, not even a traditional Bedouin tent. Their home was a bit of dirty canvas stretched between two thorn bushes, the only animals some scruffy goats that were being tended by the children. Their hospitality was, however, truly Bedouin and totally unreserved; it was with great difficulty that we persuaded them not to slaughter a goat in our honour. Natalie, a petite French model, had changed from her jeans into a flowing French gown, and was soon deep in conversation with the four or five adult Bedu ladies who were heavily veiled and dressed in the all-enshrouding black abbaya. The contrast in their mode of dress was no more dramatic than was the ease with which they appeared to converse. Natalie spoke only French, the Bedu nothing but Arabic—the language of fashion is truly universal! Franco sat well apart from the group making no effort to pose them and ran through film after film, pausing only to change lenses or cameras.

The rest of us were plied with the inevitable thick, sweet, Arabic coffee in tiny cups, and we made conversation as best we could. One of the Bedu, introduced as the grandfather of the family, was a dwarf. He chuckled away to whomever would listen to him, and there was no doubt in which direction lay his interest: Kirsten, a cool Danish blonde, had obviously taken his fancy. Our interpreter, once he had overcome his embarrassment, tactfully translated for us. While they were anatomically correct, the details of what the old man wanted to do with Kirsten were almost a physical impossibility; he was four foot nothing whereas she stood over six feet tall in her bare feet!

We bade them farewell and continued on our way back to Nizwa to refuel. It was now nearly midday and time for lunch. The site chosen for our picnic was by a large pool, tucked under the southern slopes of the Jebel Akhdar. It was a beautiful setting, the water crystal clear, the pool filled from one end by a fast-flowing stream tumbling down from the hills, and emptied from the other by a subterranean channel reputed to surface in one of the desert oases. We lunched on legs of cold turkey and chicken washed down with beer or wine, although Charlie and I had to forego the alcohol since we still had several hours of flying ahead of us. The meal over, Bill decided to go for a swim. Stripping down to his underpants he dived into the pool, much to the amazement of a passing villager. Bill was very brave, and with true Royal Marine stoicism concealed his agony. We were only a few miles from the Empty Quarter and the air temperature was more than thirty degrees centigrade, but the stream came from the high jebel and was icy-cold in comparison!

Our next stop was at Misfah, a tiny village perched high on the southern slopes of the mountain range. It was inaccessible except on foot or by helicopter, and even by helicopter access was not easy. The houses, their flat roofs covered with limes drying in the sun, huddled in a steep-sided wadi, and much of the surrounding countryside was unsuitable for a landing. We found a small hollow surrounded by rocks on the side of the hill above the village. As I approached to land I realised the combination of the height, temperature and our heavy load had made it impossible to hover; but by that time I was committed to land and our arrival turned into a rather undignified, Salalah-style slide. I wondered how we would get airborne again.

We were met once again by the male population, their womenfolk, many of them unveiled, remaining at a respectful distance. Our authorisation from the Sultan was met with indifference; the people of Misfah were cut off from civilisation, with Nizwa at least a day's walk away. The men made it abundantly clear that Natalie, again dressed in a St Laurent creation, might join the ladies, but Franco would under no circumstances be allowed near them with his camera. Unperturbed, Franco fitted a massive telephoto lens and photographed them at long range from the hill, which proved an acceptable alternative to both sides.

When the time came to leave the temperature had dropped considerably, allowing us to achieve a low hover before dropping over the edge of the hill into the valley below. It was getting late and we had to be back in Muscat in time for the social event of the season, the Muscat Regiment's ball at the Bait al Falaj hotel. This was meant to be a formal affair, dress uniform or dinner jackets being *de rigueur*. I had left my dinner jackets at Salalah so they remained unworn, but Jane and I got to the ball despite of this.

We managed to make one more flight together before returning to the UK. The Commander of the Sultan's Forces, a senior British army officer, was leaving and wanted to make a farewell visit to some of the outlying garrisons in the northern half of the country. Our route took us along the Batinah coastline. The groves were very green with date palms, for which the area is famous, and heavy with the dates that represented a major source of income for Oman in the days before oil. We visited Sohar Fort, lunching with the garrison; then, passing the copper mines which were first worked in Sumerian times, we flew through the huge Wadi Jizzi leading to the desert beyond, and the borders between Oman, Abu Dhabi and Dubai. We landed at Buraimi.

From Buraimi we headed south to the border customs post at Qabil. This consisted of a modern fort surrounded by barbed wire, the home of a few customs officers and the garrison of Oman Gendarmerie. Outside the fence was a vast expanse of desert stretching in all directions, no roads, nothing. I discovered later that I had actually landed in Abu Dhabi, the border being rather ill defined, but nobody seemed to care. By the time we reached the border fort at Sumaini, where Oman and Dubai meet, Jane had become dehydrated. It can be difficult for anyone who has not experienced the dry heat of the desert to appreciate just how much liquid is being sucked from the body, sweat drying almost before it breaks the surface. Soon the symptoms of dehydration appear, diarrhoea and vomiting aggravating the liquid loss. Before long the sufferer is past the stage where he or she is concerned about dying or living, for living barely seems a better alternative to death! Fortunately the cure is nearly as quick as the onset of the problem, water and salt bringing almost instant relief; and so Jane was soon back in the land of the living.

We arrived back at Bait al Falaj in time to go to a party given by some friends in the oil company, where our host's sister-in-law, a rather fey, Irish girl, was persuaded to read some of the guests palms. I had never been a great believer in fortune telling but there had been a fair quantity of alcohol consumed, it was late and I was persuaded to offer my hand. I can remember little of what she said except that I would spend some time in hospital in the near future, but would make a full recovery. A few months later I was to recall her prophesy with a vengeance!

Chapter Ten

On my return from leave I managed to avoid spending more than one day in Muscat, and caught the first Viscount south. The situation at Salalah had changed little. The army had moved into the Wadi Darbat but it had been something of a non-event; either the adoo had not been as strong as we had imagined, or they had accepted the inevitability of our occupation and melted away. In the west, a full regiment had been moved to Mainbrace in a further attempt to cut the adoo supply lines. Mainbrace was a new position in Moon Country overlooking the sea, a bare two kilometres from the border with the PDRY and not far from where we had shelled Hauf a few months before. The adoo had reacted with daily attacks, mortaring our positions from strong points well within range of the camp. Diplomatic representations were made to the Yemen in an attempt to persuade them to withdraw their support for the adoo, but these were ignored. Despite the chance of souring relations with the PDRY even further, it was decided to launch an airborne strike on the PFLOAG camp at Hauf.

All the aircrew involved, including the pilots of the SAR helicopters, were drawn from the ranks of contract personnel. This was a move designed to avoid recriminations between the British Government and that of the PDRY in the event of anyone being shot down and captured, but left the seconded pilots somewhat aggrieved at missing the action. The attack was pressed home, and reports that filtered back indicated we had much success. All the aircraft returned safely and only the Strikemaster flown by Peter Hulme was hit; the damage caused by a bullet that came through the fuselage and passed between his legs, fortunately touching nothing vital, even on the aircraft.

As if in a fit of pique, the adoo transferred their attention to the fort at Habarut, a border post about forty kilometres inland from

Mainbrace. Our fort was perched on a rocky outcrop about four hundred metres inside Oman; the border itself ran along the centre of a wadi, and on a similar outcrop about four hundred metres inside the PDRY stood an almost mirror image of our fort, garrisoned by troops from the Yemen. The British had built both forts during their occupation of the area, and their design seemed to owe as much to P.C. Wren and Fort Zinderneuf, as to the dictates of a defensive position.

The adoo, ably assisted by Yemeni regulars, mortared our fort. We responded in truly British spirit by sending an unarmed Beaver aircraft to drop leaflets asking them to desist, and threatening them with dire consequences if they did not. They did not, so we put in another strike. I was flying the SAR this time and had a grandstand view. We could see our bombs and rockets exploding around the fort, and the return fire from the enemy, their tracers showing up brightly against the drab brown hills behind them. Photographic evidence showed we did little damage, a tribute to the strength of the buildings. A few days later we returned to Habarut, this time to evacuate our garrison. The adoo had partially destroyed our fort with what was believed to have been an unexploded bomb left over from our attack.

The rest of May was very quiet, almost as though both sides were preparing for the monsoon. It was believed by many that no operations could take place on the jebel during the rainy season, but the Battmen were not convinced and it was their intention to stay in the hills with some of the firqat. Personally I did not fancy their prospects, the idea of three months enveloped in pea soup fog and being bitten to death by blackfly was not my idea of a summer vacation. The helicopter squadron had been making preparations for their support, and had acquired two portable radar sets of a type more often found on the bridges of luxury yachts. We were not so much interested in the pinpoint accuracy obtained from normal airfield approach radar; what we needed was something that would bring us to the general area of White

City without first meeting a hilltop. To the surprise of many the makeshift system seemed to work.

The monsoon was a few days late arriving, and we continued the daily milk runs to the jebel into early June. We also carried out a trial at night to see whether we could make life unpleasant for the adoo when they came down into the foothills. A 'Nightsun' is a large searchlight normally strapped onto the belly of a helicopter, and from a height of one thousand feet is reputed to turn night into day on the ground in a circle of one thousand yard diameter. We fitted one to point sideways out of the main cabin of a 205, and the plan was to cruise up and down the plain, parallel to the jebel, and light up targets for the gunners at Salalah. Nick and I were volunteered to fly the Nightsun aircraft, while a second 205, its cabin packed with marksmen, would try to discourage any adoo who might have the temerity to shoot at us. The idea of flying within three hundred yards of the hills and shining a dirty great light at the enemy, which would attract bullets like moths to a flame, did not commend itself to either of us. We maintained a far more respectful distance, reducing the illumination on the ground to a pale shadow of its intended glory. The adoo also failed to put in an appearance and, with many sighs of relief from the helicopter pilots, the trial was designated a failure.

Next morning I was on a day off, went to the beach for a swim, and on my return to camp looked in on the operations room to see what had been happening. Bad news had come from Mainbrace. The adoo had mortared the camp during a troop changeover, catching the new men in the open and inflicting many casualties. The casevac helicopters were already on their way, and the Field Surgical Team were gearing themselves up for a long session at the operating table. The siren at Salalah had also been sounding at frequent intervals. This was the signal that the camp radar had picked up movement in the foothills and that all personnel should take cover, which we seldom did.

That evening, it was the turn of the strike squadron to host the monthly mess party. This was a regular feature of the social scene to which many of the European civilian families from Salalah town were invited. Because of the general situation that day, Gerry Honey, the RAF camp commander, had decided that it should be kept to an in-house function, and the civilian guests were asked not to come. By nine o'clock the party was in full swing, floodlights blazing and the hi-fi blaring to drown out the siren, which continued to sound at irregular intervals. The cooks were preparing the barbecue and there were twenty or thirty people on the patio, a ten yard by four concrete area immediately outside the bar; the rest were in the bar. I had just returned to the patio after refreshing my drink and was in conversation with Taff Hinchliffe, Red Vine and Russ Peart. Over and above the voice of Mick Jagger we heard the siren again, and yet again ignored it.

The next moment I found myself flat on my back, but several feet away from where I had been standing. My glass was clamped to my chest and, as far as I could see, was still full. I could not think what I was doing there. I knew I was 'drink taken' but could not believe I was 'all-fall-down' drunk. I tried to get to my feet but failed. There seemed to be a total lack of communication between my brain and my legs!

Steve Hutton leaned over me and asked me if I was all right. Then I heard him call out to someone.

"Quick, over here. Mike's been hit!"

He and one of the army officers picked me up and carried me, feet dragging in the dust, to the FST. My right leg now felt as though it was on fire, and I was glad when one of the medical attendants gave me a shot of morphine and the fire slowly dulled to an ember. I was lying on what appeared to be a mortuary slab that, apart from being very cold and doing little for my state of mind, allowed me to survey the carnage in the hospital. There were bodies everywhere, some on stretchers, others, including Taff, lying on the bare floor. At the time I found it rather amusing that whenever a medical orderly came to obtain more drugs,

Taff had to move to avoid his head being hit by the refrigerator door. I drifted in and out of full consciousness until it was my turn to be taken to the operating table. My last recollection was of the anaesthetist looking down at me.

"Oh no, not another one!" he exclaimed. "Do we give him plasma or whisky?"

I woke in a small ward in the camp sickbay, the six beds occupied by five SOAF pilots and an RAF cook. Taff, Red Vine and Russ Peart, all those with whom I had been talking the night before, were there and we tried to piece together exactly what had happened. It appeared the radar had been right and that the adoo had crept down to the plain under cover of night, fired three 75mm shells into the camp and then retreated back to the safety of the foothills. The first two shells had done little damage, one landing in an empty car park, the other putting some holes into a row of unoccupied sleeping quarters. The third had come through the trees outside the officers' mess and had landed on a corner of the patio, exploding just behind a sofa. Most of the blast and debris had continued in the same direction, away from the assembled company. It was incredible that no one had been killed, but we had taken eight casualties, six pilots, an RAF Air Traffic Controller and the cook.

Peter Hulme and Bill Cooper, the Air Traffic Controller, had been sitting at either end of the sofa with their feet on the ground. Both had their legs severely damaged. Peter Williams, an ex-Royal Navy fighter pilot who had only recently returned to active duty after damaging his back ejecting from a Strikemaster, was sitting between them but with his feet on a low table; he escaped unhurt.

Peter and Bill had been patched up by the FST but, because of the severity of their injuries, they had been evacuated immediately to the RAF hospital at Akrotiri, in Cyprus. Peter was to spend many months in hospital before he recovered. Bill, despite the excellent treatment he received from the FST, later had to have his foot amputated in Cyprus. I was told he was playing squash again within a year. A piece of hot metal had passed through my right calf, fortunately without hitting either bone or tendon, and had ended up in Russ Peart's knee, still with a bit of my trousers attached, and there was a strange, unexplained hole in my left shoe. Taff and Red both had leg injuries. Red also had a small fragment of shrapnel lodged in his earlobe. The RAF cook had been injured in both legs.

There had been many heroes that night, but none more so than Geordie, the mess barman. He had admitted to us in the past that he had been sent to Salalah by the RAF as a form of punishment, but on this night he more than made up for any past indiscretions. Within seconds of the explosion he was tearing up clean bar towels to use as bandages and tourniquets; the surgeons later said he had most probably saved the leg of one pilot by tying it to a table, preventing further damage as he thrashed around in pain. Geordie was awarded a Queens Commendation for his efforts and never was one more richly deserved. He did acknowledge that he received almost as much satisfaction from being allowed to assist in an operation, extracting the shrapnel from Red's ear!

No praise could be too high for the FST. Two surgeons, one anaesthetist and a small team of orderlies had started work that afternoon on the casualties from Mainbrace. Twenty-four hours later they had completed more than twenty operations, all carried out in the small, tin-roofed hut set up as an operating theatre, and using a tent as an X-ray room. It was fortuitous that their professional services had been required before the party had started; otherwise they, too, might have featured on the injury list. Even more fortunate had been Gerry Honey's decision to make the party in-house; if he had not, some of the civilians from Salalah, perhaps including their wives, might have become casualties!

Of all the staff at Salalah we were probably in the safest place on camp—in the hospital. For days after the attack all the able bodied personnel were to be seen walking around the airbase armed to the teeth, jumping at the slightest sound and scuttling to the shelters whenever the siren blared. On one occasion as we lay, legs swathed in bandages, we heard an explosion from within the perimeter. Five of us rolled on to the floor and under our beds, leaving the cook, who had both legs immobilised, cursing us for not helping him. "Tiny," the six-foot six-inch wardmaid, came in to reassure us: the explosion had been from one of our own mortar bombs! We were told that a newly joined member of the RAF Regiment had been ordered to lay down some harassing fire on the jebel edge, and had forgotten to check which way the mortar tube was pointing. We were told he was returning to the UK for retraining. Tiny was in sole charge of the ward and helped us through that first week. He ruled our lives, although his sense of humour was, to say the least, macabre and not always appreciated. It was he who administered the four-times-daily injection of antibiotics and once entered the ward, blunting the hypodermic needle with a large file while asking who was first for the jab!

After a week we were flown out in a Hercules C130 of RAF Transport Command, initially to Masirah, then for a grinding ten-hour flight to Akrotiri. The lack of military overflying rights across Syria forced us to route via Iran and Turkey, before turning south to Cyprus, and by the time we landed we were all very pleased to be taken to a ward and a comfortable bed. Our reception at the hospital was mixed, and we were given the impression by some people that we were something of an embarrassment. The young ward maid who came to take our particulars for their records was a little confused to find I was a Flight Lieutenant without an official number; my explanation that I had been in the Fleet Air Arm but was actually a civilian served only to confuse her further. We must have been the worst patients there. Our stock with the senior sister on the ward reached an all-time low when some of Taff's friends, in Cyprus with their Lightning squadron, discovered he was in the hospital and came visiting with several crates of beer. We compromised and kept the crates under Peter Hulme's bed, since he,

being a Squadron Leader, had his own room. When Red Vine comman-
deered a wheelchair so that we could all visit the nightlife in Limassol
the writing was on the wall. As soon as our stitches were removed we
were put on the first VC10 heading for the UK!

Jane met me at Brize Norton and drove me home to Plymouth.
When the stitches had been removed from my calf the wound had
opened up, leaving a hole about the size of a penny in the muscle. I had
been assured it would heal in time and was told to see my local GP in
Plymouth for further treatment. He took one look at it, said that he had
no experience in treating such injuries and recommended I should go
to the Royal Naval Hospital at Stonehouse. There, the naval surgeon
told me he would have to insert wire stitches for the wound to have any
chance of healing, and for this I would have to go back to the operating
table. He also agreed to x-ray my left foot which was hurting every time
I put any weight on it. The photograph revealed two small pieces of
shrapnel embedded in the sole of my foot, possibly explaining the hole
in my left boot, although he could find no sign of an entry wound.

I spent the next few weeks convalescing at home, watching the
Olympics on television. Then, since I could walk unaided, I declared
myself fit to travel back to Oman and, once more avoiding a night stop
in Muscat, I arrived at Salalah just as the monsoon lifted. I had missed
very little flying, the monsoon having effectively grounded the airforce
that year. The adoo had, however, received a savage mauling at Marbat.

The Battle of Marbat has rightly entered the annals of the SAS as an
example of their courage and endurance under fire, and has been fully
described in several records of their exploits. Suffice it to say here that
the adoo had gathered together a force reported to be in excess of two
hundred and fifty men and, under cover of the monsoon cloud, had put
in a dawn attack on the little fishing village of Marbat. The defenders,
some askars and a few of the SAS, beat off many attacks, but were near
the end of their tether. The cloud lifted marginally, sufficient for the
strike squadron to launch some aircraft from Salalah to assist the

defenders, and the helicopters to airlift in some reinforcements. Our troops did not escape unscathed. Several of the askars were killed or wounded, and the SAS lost two killed and two wounded. The adoo had suffered more. At least thirty bodies were found at the scene, several of which were paraded in Salalah town for the benefit of the local population, and it was reported that many more had died of their wounds. It was almost the last time the adoo attempted such an attack and in many ways it was the major turning point in the war, although hostilities were to continue until 1976.

Chapter Eleven

We began to return our troops to the jebel. There was still much cloud around and I was amazed to find their tops were tinged a delicate shade of green. As I let down to the surface I discovered that the ground had been transformed. Gone was the brown, wispy grass, the leafless thorn trees covered in reddish brown dust and the stony landscape. Instead, I was confronted with rolling hills covered in lush, green grass. I could have been flying over Salisbury plain in late spring! The route to our positions near the Wadi Darbat took us close to the Darbat Falls. After the monsoon the streams from the springs in the surrounding area flowed together, forming a river that cascaded over the cliff in a waterfall, and the wadi floor was covered with huge pools of fresh water that would supply the inhabitants of the villages for the rest of the year.

We established a new position on the jebel edge, to the west of the Darbat and overlooking the other adoo stronghold in the Wadi Arzat. Because we could approach it from over the plain we decided we could dispense with top cover and a second pilot, but were proved wrong. I was making a run into Sycamore, as the new position was called, when I became aware that someone on the ground had taken exception to my presence. I could hear the crack of the bullets as they passed the helicopter, and then felt the shock as they began to hit the tail cone. Pulling up sharply, I took refuge in some friendly cloud and then returned to Taqa to await developments. The firefight died down and soon I was able to return to complete the resupply.

A few days later I met the British army officer who had been in charge of the troops at Sycamore, and his description of the incident did little to boost my confidence. After the action, one of his Baluch sergeants had come to him. and said. "Sahib," he said, "When the helicopter was approaching, I could see the adoo shooting at it!"

"If you could see them, why didn't you shoot at them?" asked the officer, gripping him warmly by the throat.

"Oh no Sahib," he replied. "If I had shot at them, they would have stopped shooting at the helicopter, and shot at me!"

Pure logic, I suppose, but it hardly commended itself to us!

By now we had persuaded the staff we should carry out the resupply missions using the nylon cargo nets and strops that had been lying unused in the hangar for several months. Using the belly hook on the aircraft we could both pick up and release a netted load from the hover, thus saving time at both ends since the cargo no longer had to be loaded and unloaded from the main cabin by hand. After some tentative test flying we also discovered we could still employ the Salalah Spiral, although we never dared to calculate the added weight on the aircraft hooks caused by the "G" force we pulled during the manoeuvre.

We also succeeded in obtaining some armour plating for the pilot's seat. This was not the fully armoured seat used by the Americans in Vietnam, but consisted of three carbon fibre plates, one on the lower half of the pilot's door, the other two placed under and at the back of the pilot's seat. It was better than nothing, but still left the co-pilot totally unprotected. To remedy this, we were issued with flak jackets, two curved sheets of carbon fibre that fitted like a carapace around our upper body. Theoretically the flak jacket was able to stop a .762 bullet, but we preferred to retain the psychological protection it provided and never put the theory to the test. I wore it religiously whenever I flew up to the hills, although it was uncomfortable and hot to wear and added an extra fifteen pounds to the load I already carried strapped to my body.

We were required to carry small arms with us at all times, not only when we went flying, but also whenever we left the camp to visit Salalah town or the beaches. There were many adoo sympathisers on the plain, and no way of differentiating between a friendly or an unfriendly Dhofari. All the males carried arms. They would have considered themselves improperly dressed without a gun of some form. However, it might be considered ironic that we went to the beach armed to the teeth, and there met up with the unarmed and mostly unguarded wives and young children of the European families from Salalah! The Taylor-Woodrow camp, with maybe fifteen or twenty families, was guarded by an aged askar with an obsolete rifle. He sat at the camp gate with twenty or thirty yards of barbed wire on either side of the entrance, a charming old man who was at his happiest teaching the Taylor-Woodrow children to count in Arabic, and whose son, Said al Shanfari, was later to become the Omani Oil Minister. The rest of the camp was open to the world, especially the fifty and more miles of golden beach between Taka and Rizut.

The staff at the British Bank of the Middle East in the town must have been unique. The tellers would not turn a hair when a customer leant his rifle against the counter while he signed a cheque, and the manager, "Gordon-the-Bank" (I never knew his surname), would invite us into his office, guns and all, and discuss an overdraft over a gin and tonic. In fact, the ease with which we could obtain an overdraft from him was really quite reassuring, if a little surprising, considering our occupation. It was pleasant to find at least one person who seemed to have confidence in our ability to survive.

Our weapons were varied and depended primarily on personal choice, the .762 FLN or the Armalite being the most popular. I had acquired a Czechoslovakian copy of the AK47, captured from the adoo by the Battmen, and this, with a .38 automatic, seldom left my side. There was no shortage of ammunition and we all became quite proficient with our guns, although my training in the use of firearms had ceased at the Naval Gunnery School at Portsmouth nearly twenty years before. The only instructions I had ever been given in the use of a handgun had been from a Petty Officer Gunnery Instructor at the Naval Gunnery School at Portsmouth, who had told me that, if I ever got close enough to use it, the best thing to do was to throw it! Apart from those who had army or Royal Marine training there were few of us with much experience, yet there were only occasional incidents. Among them was the pilot who shot himself in the knee when cleaning his automatic, having forgotten to clear the round in the breech.

Whenever I went flying I went out to my aircraft staggering under the weight of the flak jacket, AK47, .38 automatic, and pouches filled with spare ammunition, including two full magazines for the handgun. If we were unfortunate enough to be shot down it was hoped we would be able to defend ourselves until a rescue helicopter appeared. I hoped I had rationalised the situation and had no intention of being captured alive, but have no idea why I carried all those rounds for the .38, except perhaps that I was a lousy shot.

The adoo had become braver. They seemed to have realised that the strike pilots could not see much detail on the ground when they were in an attacking dive, and no longer kept their heads down. They had also taken to remaining closer to our positions after a firefight, as I discovered when making an approach into an LZ. I was surprised to see the Battman who was marshalling me in, suddenly throw himself flat on the ground; then I saw the telltale spurts of dust stitching across the ground towards me. Turning away sharply, I went and hid behind a tree, the only cover I could find. It was a very little tree but, like the flak jacket, provided a formidable psychological shield. Shortly after returning to Salalah I was approached by an aggrieved engineer who complained he was going to have to change a rotor blade on my aircraft. I pointed out to him that he could hardly blame me for bullet holes. He took me across to the aircraft and pointed to the blade tip. There was no doubt as to what had caused the damage: the end was severely mangled and bore the unmistakable signs of contact with a tree. I had not even felt a rise in the vibration level on my journey home!

A few days later I was carrying out a Hawkeye and began to feel that the adoo had it in for me personally. Orbiting above the jebel at the usual five thousand feet, I watched as the jets roared down in their attacking dives. I could see the little balls of green tracer lazily curling up towards the fighters, and from the height the bullets were reaching it was obvious the adoo were using a .50 calibre machine-gun. My sense of detachment evaporated as I realised these fluffy balls were now heading in my direction and I moved, hurriedly, to a safer position. If a Spargen bullet had hit my little 206, they could have carried home the remains in my flak jacket.

This feeling of personal involvement was strengthened when I returned to the camp from another foray to the beach and dropped in to the operations room. Glancing out of the window, I was surprised to see everyone throwing themselves flat on the ground. Simultaneously, the adoo landed two 75mm shells on the hardstanding about thirty yards from me. They bracketed several aircraft, including a couple of Strikemasters that were fuelled and armed, ready for a mission. The aircraft received little more than minor shrapnel damage and were soon made serviceable again; but orders were now received to disperse the aircraft around the airfield in revetments. It seemed to be a case of shutting the stable door after the horse had bolted and as far as I know the adoo never attacked the field again.

As an ex-navy pilot it was assumed I knew how to winch people up and down from ships at sea. HQ Dhofar conceived the idea of sending one of our naval vessels, a bum armed with two .50 machine-guns, to bombard the adoo positions in the western sector. I was told to take an army liaison officer, Peter Gordon-Smith, and lower him to the boat when it was out of sight of land. It had been some time since I had done anything like this, and even longer since I had flown a single-engined helicopter over the sea without flotation gear. If we had any problems it was going to mean a long swim home. Stan Stanford came with us as winchman. We found the bum, but it took many violent hand signals before we could persuade the Captain, Gordon Gillies, to turn his vessel into wind and swell. We came to a hover over the quarterdeck, the single mast swaying perilously close to us as Stan lowered Peter on the winch. It was a tight fit, and he was in danger of being disemboweled by the machine-guns every time the ship rolled. We managed to deposit him in one piece and they steamed off into the dusk to carry out their mission. Whether it had any lasting effect on adoo morale I never knew, but Peter enjoyed the change of scenery and Gordon, who had once been the skipper of a Hebridean ferry, entered into the spirit of his new role with great gusto.

In October 1972 we received reinforcements. The Sultan had visited the Shah of Iran and negotiated the loan of eight hundred troops and a squadron of 205 helicopters. It was very much in the Shah's interest to help Oman achieve a victory in Dhofar. Defeat could have placed an unfriendly, communist government right on Iran's doorstep in a position to threaten the Straits of Hormuz, the seventeen-mile wide entrance to the Arabian Gulf through which passed most of Iran's oil, and more than thirty percent of the western world's oil supplies. The Shah's response to the request was swift and emphatic, and within three days the first of the Iranian C130 transport aircraft was touching down at Salalah. Three days later the eight hundred troops were in Dhofar and the helicopters, also transported in the C130s, had been reassembled and made serviceable. The troops deployed to a position at the western end of the plain but there the momentum ran out. We were told the deep-freezers had been mislaid and the troops were unwilling to move any further without them.

The helicopter pilots of SOAF were none too impressed with our counterparts from Iran. With the exception of the squadron commanding officer and his deputy, the remainder were very inexperienced, some were nothing short of dangerous. Worse still, they were not allowed to show any form of initiative; if it was not written in their instruction manual they were not allowed to do it. This could prove dangerous if we became too closely involved with them in the field.

During their first few days in Dhofar we flew with the Iranians as co-pilots in our aircraft to show them the area of operations, then they joined in with their own aircraft. It was on one of these joint operations that we discovered just how hidebound by the rulebook they were. We were withdrawing some troops from a forward location, and had been briefed that the adoo were believed to have a machine-gun post about a kilometre due north of the LZ. Dave Duncan, who was orbiting in the area in a 206 and co-ordinating the operation, was somewhat surprised to see an Iranian 205 flying low and slow in a northerly direction away from our troops. He called them on the radio, suggesting they might be in some danger, and received the response: "Our main cabin door has dropped to the ground. We are looking for it."

Obviously not fully appreciating the true significance of this, Dave repeated his warning, telling them to turn and get out of the area.

"Very well," came the reply. "You come down and look for our door!"

Dave's reply was unprintable. The adoo must have been just as bewildered, for they never opened fire.

There were some other people in Oman who appeared to be equally hung-up on the rulebook. The situation at Mainbrace had become tense; the adoo had closed in on the position and were mortaring the airstrip every time one of the fixed wings landed. When they damaged one of the Caribou it was decided it was too risky for the fixed wing, and that the helicopters should shuttle in all the supplies for the location from Manston, a dirt strip about forty miles from Mainbrace and in safe country for the fixed wing delivery flights. Four 205s were moved to Manston, the crews living in tents, myself among them. At least we did not have to use the strip at Mainbrace and could vary our point of touchdown in dead ground at will, but the descent was hairy and we came under fire from the adoo on many occasions. As a result we used to hold the aircraft in the Salalah Spiral to the last possible second.

Dave Duncan and Steve Watson, in a 205, came under fire during a descent, left their pullout a fraction too late and struck the ground, moving sideways at about forty knots. The aircraft rolled several times before coming to a stop, a total wreck. All three crew members climbed out unhurt, although the Omani crewman said he had nearly been crushed by the five forty gallon water barrels they were carrying in the main cabin; these were never lashed down in order to speed up the supply missions. The army commander at Mainbrace was rather terse about the affair, saying the wreck was attracting adoo fire and had to be removed. For the rest of the helicopter pilots it was a case of "There, but for the grace of God, go I."—and there the matter should have rested.

It was not to be. A signal was received from Muscat, informing us there was to be an Official Board of Enquiry. The President of the Board was to be Jim Cobb, a retired RAF Wing Commander serving with SOAF (Tac), the rest of the Board being Nick Holbrook and myself as the helicopter experts and Bob Ponter, an ex-Fleet Air Arm fighter pilot. We were none too pleased when it was rumoured that, if the Board found the two pilots to be at fault, they were to be severely disciplined. Everyone at Salalah knew it was their "fault"—if that was an adequate description of a misjudgement in airmanship while coming under fire from a Spargen machine-gun! The margin between a successful conclusion to a Salalah Spiral and splattering the aircraft on the ground was small enough at the best of times; when coming under fire at the same time the margin was minimal.

The decision of the Board came as little surprise to anyone at Salalah. Bob and I were unashamedly biased, being used to the Fleet Air Arm system. For years the navy had accepted that "Pilot error" was not necessarily "Pilot negligence"—possibly because of the frequency with which pilots had impaled themselves in the barrier on a flight deck and written off their aircraft. We were all agreed that any concept of blame attached to Steve and Dave would have the inevitable effect of inhibiting the helicopter pilots from carrying out what was already a difficult and dangerous task. The official verdict was reached quickly and unanimously. The accident had happened as a direct consequence of the aircraft coming under enemy fire, and no blame was to be attached to the pilots. Privately, it was considered by many that there were some people in Muscat who were out of touch with reality.

November rolled into December. From the information we received from the ever-increasing stream of SEPs, it seemed as though we were beginning to wear down the enemy; but the war was nowhere near over, especially for me. I should have known better, but on the 17th December I stopped off at the operations room on my way back from the beach; as I did so, a call came in from the jebel for a casevac. Nick Holbrook, the duty pilot, asked me if I would go with him. By the time I had gone to my room, put on my flying overalls and grabbed my weapons, Nick had the aircraft started and ready for takeoff. I climbed into the left-hand seat and we took off. For the first time for many months I flew without wearing a flak jacket.

On the way up to the hills Nick briefed me on the situation. Acting on information received, the army had laid a company-sized ambush for the adoo but had, themselves, been ambushed and pinned down near the Midway road. They had taken casualties and one, a Baluch, had been hit in the head. If he was not brought down to the FST it was considered he would probably die. Our troops had reported that the original firefight had died down, and that the adoo were believed to have retired.

We located their position and spiralled down towards the LZ, but came under fire immediately, taking some bullet strikes—obviously the adoo had not pulled back all that far. We retired from the scene to an SAS location, inspected the aircraft for damage and found there were one or two bullet holes in the tail boom, but that nothing vital had been touched. During our first approach we had noticed a shallow wadi leading towards the LZ. It would provide us with a dead ground approach for most of the way, the final run in being no more than a few hundred yards up a slope from the south before we would be over the LZ and once more in dead ground. The adoo were believed to have retired to the north, so we decided to give it a try.

We spiralled down to ground level without prompting any interference from the enemy, and began a high-speed run along the wadi. As we began the final turn up the slope, I glanced left out of my cabin window and was surprised to see about a dozen men walking up the hill in line abreast. The nearest were no more than fifty yards from us and there was no mistaking their identity. Dressed in blue Chinese fatigue uniforms, sweat stained and ragged at the edges, they were carrying AK 47's. They were adoo!

I screamed at Nick to weave the aircraft but it was too late. The first burst of enemy fire shattered the bubble window beneath my feet. I looked down to discover the big toe of my left foot was sticking up through my boot. It was not actually hurting, but I knew that it should not be like that and leant forward to rearrange it. The movement probably saved my life as the next burst of fire came through my cabin door, one of the bullets passing where my head had been a moment before, and burying itself in the electrical panel in the cabin roof.

At first I was able to regard our position quite dispassionately. We were low, but still flying towards the LZ. As we slid over the top of the hill and into dead ground, Nick called for me to come onto the controls with him. The cyclic appeared to be jammed and together we wrestled it free (it was subsequently discovered to had been jammed by a stray bullet). By that time it was too late to land. We passed over a cliff and immediately received another burst of fire from directly beneath us. The engine was groaning like a creature in pain. There was a strong smell of aviation fuel. Red lights were flashing on the instrument panel and needles gyrated alarmingly. At this point I lost interest as my foot started to hurt and claimed all my attention. Nick managed to nurse the helicopter to the SAS location we had left only minutes before and landed. He was unhurt, as was Salim, our Omani crewman, although how this had occurred was nothing short of a miracle. An inspection of the aircraft later revealed that more than twenty bullets had entered the cabin area.

As we touched down, Salim leapt from the cabin, opened my door and I fell out into the arms of the SAS. They carried me to a sangar, gave me a shot of morphine and bandaged the foot, boot and all. Nick came over and reassured me that Charlie Parsons was already in the area in a 205, and was on his way to airlift me back to Salalah. I heard the familiar sound of the helicopter approaching, and then the equally familiar sound of mortars exploding nearby: the SAS position was now under attack! It was at this point I realised my sangar was built of mortar bomb boxes, and from the regular traffic to and from my shelter, and the sound of outgoing mortars, the boxes probably contained live ammunition.

The firefight was short lived. Soon I was being bundled into a 205 and Charlie was flying me to the welcoming arms of the FST, only forty-five minutes elapsing between my being hit and finding myself once again on the operating table. I lay there counting down from one hundred as the anaesthetic took effect, and can remember silently bewailing the fact that I would have to go to Akrotiri again.

The damage to my foot was not severe. The bullet had tracked up through the sole of my boot, neatly taking out the middle joint of my left big toe. When I regained consciousness after the operation, Martin Melsom, the RAMC surgeon, told me there had been enough tissue left to sew the top joint back on to the foot, and he was confident it would heal. He did warn me, however, that I might have difficulty balancing on my left foot. This didn't worry me unduly for countless aircrew medical inspections had proved I had been plagued with this affliction for years. Martin's prognosis would have been one hundred percent correct if he had added that I would have a permanently ingrowing toenail—a very small price to pay.

I did not have to go to Akrotiri. Friends from the Taylor Woodrow camp knew of my aversion to the place, and one of them, Doug Stevenson, suggested to Martin that I could convalesce in their bungalow at Salalah. A week later I was taken in an ambulance to the Taylor-Woodrow camp and, my foot swathed in bandages, I entered the Stevenson's house hobbling on a pair of crutches, feeling very sorry for myself.

Ann, Doug's wife, was cleaning the carpet with an upright carpet sweeper. She greeted me, took away one of my crutches and replaced it with the sweeper. "Now you're here," she said, "you might as well make yourself useful!" As she told me later: "You were feeling quite sorry enough for yourself. You needed no help from me!"

I had not been entirely happy with the move. Ann and Doug had two sons, Peter aged seven and Michael aged nine months. My toe had to be dressed twice daily and I was concerned that the sight might not be pleasant for Peter. When Sister Kay, the resident Taylor-Woodrow nurse arrived with the inevitable cigarette dangling from her lips, Peter insisted on being present throughout, asking endless questions about the toe. He was totally unimpressed with my reaction to the ice-cold antibiotic spray he was allowed to apply, and his interest reached its peak when Dave Duncan visited me, bearing my boot with pieces of toe still attached!

I was declared fit to travel early in January 1972 and flew to Europe for convalescent leave, returning to Salalah in early February. Several of my friends suggested I should leave SOAF, since it appeared that I was fated to attract adoo attention. The anaesthetist from the FST put it even more strongly, pointing out that I might not be so lucky the third time and that my salary was not so good that I needed to take the chance of finding out! I was determined to prove, if only to myself, that I could come to terms with the risks and recommenced flying. I found I was able to put the past in its right place and was not conscious of any inclination to hang back. Having done so, I decided it was probably the right time to leave. I was nearly forty years old, and the longer I stayed in the military flying environment the more difficult would be the transition to civilian aviation. I had no intention of remaining a military contract pilot for the rest of my life.

Neville Baker and the new commander of SOAF, a seconded RAF Group Captain, were very helpful, and it was agreed I could terminate my contract without penalty. I left Oman at the end of March, unfortunately before the actual presentation of the Sultan's Bravery Medal for which Nick, Salim and I had been gazetted.

*   *   *

In many ways I was sorry to leave. Despite everything that had happened I had enjoyed Oman, especially meeting the Omanis themselves. They were a people who had lived for so long in the fifteenth century and yet, when they arrived suddenly in the twentieth, proud and very conscious of their heritage, there was little trace of the arrogance that is apparent in some of the oil-rich Arab countries.

I departed a far more competent pilot than I had been when I arrived. We had been flying the helicopters closer to the limits than ever before, and had been pushed into discovering our own personal limitations, a discovery that I intended to put to good use in the future.

I also left without wearing either dinner jacket. The black one remained mouldering in my suitcase. The white one was worn once, by Gerry Honey when he dined with the Sultan in the palace at Salalah!

Chapter Twelve

Our marriage, which over the previous few years had been less successful than either of us would have wished, seemed to be coming to an end and, when I returned from Oman, Jane and I agreed to a separation. I was faced with the self-inflicted prospect of no home, no job and the overriding necessity of finding a way to earn a living. My time in Oman had enabled me to save a little money and, once the laundrette and boat had been sold, I was left with enough to live on for a few months, and to go back to school.

There were no alternatives. I had to obtain a civilian pilot's licence in the shortest time possible. The best way to achieve this was to go on a crammer course at a college of aviation. I chose CSE at Kidlington, near Oxford, which ran an eight week course tailored for ex-service pilots, and which included the Civil Aviation Authority exams. Packing my worldly goods into a caravan, I hitched it to the back of the car and drove to Oxford. There were fifteen on the course, all but two being fixed wing pilots working for their Commercial Pilots Licence (Aeroplanes). As ex-military helicopter pilots, the two of us had sufficient qualifications and flying hours to go for the Airline Transport Pilot's Licence (Helicopters), (ATPL(H)). In 1973, the CAA had yet to devise licence exams specifically for helicopters and we all were going to sit the fixed wing CPL exam, with a few additions to take into account the different technical problems.

It was back to school with a vengeance as I wrestled with the basic theory that I had not touched for fifteen years. Some of the detail we were having to study seemed to bear little relation to the problems we would face once we were flying again, especially with regard to navigation and flight planning. This was directed towards jet airliners flying at heights and speeds far in excess of anything a helicopter could achieve, and using more fuel to taxi out to the takeoff point than most helicopters could carry. I managed to pass all the exams but one at the first attempt, the one I had to retake being the technical exam on the Bell Jet Ranger. This was required so that my new Professional Licence could be endorsed with a specific type and, since I had been flying the Bell for nearly three years I had neglected to revise the subject!

I had no fixed ideas about what I was going to do. Most ex-military helicopter pilots seemed to gravitate towards oil related flying, but I wasn't sure this was what I wanted. Then, through a friend, I heard of a job working for a wealthy, retired businessman. I knew little about it, apart from the information that the previous incumbent had left after five years. I gathered that his reasons for seeking alternative employment were many and varied, but were mainly the feeling that the experience he was gaining was limited, and that the demands made on him were reaching the point where his family life was suffering too much. It was highly paid by the then current helicopter standards, but involved much time away from home at very short notice. The work was split between the Republic of Ireland, the UK and Europe, but seldom was any long period spent in one place.

I went for an interview and was offered the job. It was very tempting. There were three helicopters to be flown, a Bell 206 and two Hughes 500's, rent-free, furnished accommodation in Ireland, an allowance paid during our travels if no free housing was available and the salary just as expected. I decided to accept.

Once all the arrangement had been made I flew out to Biarritz. The Boss, as he was known by everybody, with his wife and younger son, met me and led me across the hard standing to a gleaming Bell 206 in the private aircraft park. On the way there I received a lesson, the first of many, on working for him. I had arrived with a small suitcase and a shoulder bag, the minimum I reckoned I could survive with for three weeks in an hotel in France. He informed me that if I needed to travel with "all that luggage" I should start to look for alternative employment!

He climbed into the Captain's seat and indicated that I should sit in the co-pilot's. Handing me a map of the area he pointed out our destination and told me to navigate. I had been told the Boss held a helicopter licence and I wondered how good a pilot he was. The aircraft was magnificently equipped with the Sperry Stars artificial horizon and compass, Decca Danac roller map navigation system, VOR and ADF, and yet, among all this high priced gear, fixed on the centre console was what could only be described as a plastic bowled, rotating grid yacht compass. I soon discovered the answers to my unspoken questions.

The Boss was blind in one eye, and the sight in the other was less than perfect. I later discovered that he had difficulty in seeing the numbers on the main compass, but as long as I set the grid to the right heading on "his" compass he could maintain a course. When I was surer of myself I asked him how, with the lack of depth perception, he was able to judge his height for landing. He replied, "By comparing the aircraft height from the ground with the height of the grass." I had, by then, also learnt to curb my tongue a little and forbore to ask him what happened if he were landing on concrete! In fact his basic handling was competent, and I was able to concentrate on the navigation for the twenty-five minute trip to our destination.

"Home" in France was a chateau near Beylongue, a small village deep in the pine forests of the Landes and about twenty miles from Mont-de-Marsan. Our route lay over country that was not easy to tie in with the map. It was flat, heavily forested, and the few roads or rail lines we crossed were all at oblique angles to our track, making pinpoint navigation difficult. The map on the Decca roller was for the northwest of England and therefore of little use. There were no suitable beacons ahead of us, and I was left trying to read the map and use a back bearing on the beacon at Biarritz. I had visions of getting lost on my first trip with my new employer, and it was to my considerable relief when he pointed out a small hill in the distance and said the house was just north of that. He handed over control to me for the landing on a concrete pad at the back of a barn; he and the other passengers disembarked and I was left to put the aircraft to bed.

I was joined by Jimmy, the Boss' chauffeur, who helped me push the aircraft into the barn that served as a hangar, and then drove me to the motel where we were to live for the next three weeks. Jimmy was a Scot, an ex-professional footballer who had given up the game because of injury. He had been married to a French girl from the Mont-de-Marsan area, and had been living and working there when our employer offered him the job of chauffeur. He became my mentor. Without him I doubt if I would have lasted past the first week. The owners of the motel spoke no English, few if any of the locals did, and it was a case of speak French or starve! My grasp of the language was of the schoolboy variety when I arrived, but with the help of Jimmy, who spoke fluent French and was conversant with the local patois, my grasp improved rapidly.

He filled in many of the gaps left by my interview. The "circus," as he referred to our employment, moved at the whim of the Boss, seldom with any warning, but based around a pattern: France in the summer, Scotland in the autumn and Ireland in the winter. In spring we had a rest when the Boss went on holiday for a couple of months. There was no guarantee that we would stay in any one place for long: he tended to get itchy feet after a couple of weeks and had the money to indulge his whims. There was a Hawker Siddeley HS125 business jet for his long journeys, and he used the helicopters as other people would use a car.

It was not that he had no wheeled transport. His collection of vintage and veteran cars was quite magnificent. They were spread between various places, some in France, others in Wales and Ireland. They were all immaculate and roadworthy, and included an 1898 Mors Dogcart, a host of Rolls Royce cars, Bugattis, Mercedes and one of almost every Ferrari ever built. There were modern runabouts of every shape and size; a couple of Rolls, several Mercedes and a Renault. There were also two British Leyland Mini Estates, although these were far from standard, being fitted with Cooper engines and capable of speeds well in excess of one hundred miles per hour. The Boss had told me he would provide me with a car in France, and I had visions of driving at least one of the Mercedes. Jimmy laughed when I told him this and pointed out of the hotel window.

"You see that old Simca?" he said, indicating a battered wreck in the car park. "That is yours. The Boss has very fixed ideas about pilots and cars. None of you know how to drive, and any car you have, you ruin!"

It appeared that one of the previous pilots had suffered a series of accidents and had been banned from driving any of the fleet. The Simca showed obvious signs of its history. It was held together by large patches of rust and, as I discovered when we finally got it started, had an asthmatic engine that belched oily black smoke from every pore. As an added attraction it had loose steering and non-existent brakes.

The next day, in fear and trembling, I drove it to Mont-de-Marsan to get it registered and insured. By the time I got back to Beylongue I had decided to buy my own car, but the beast had a mind of its own and within a couple of days both clutch and engine had given up the ghost. I managed to persuade the Boss it could not have been my fault and he agreed to put it into a roadworthy condition. Nevertheless, he left me with the distinct impression that I had reinforced his opinion about pilots and cars.

One of my duties was to keep the helicopters spotless, inside and out. This passion for cleanliness was reinforced within a few days when he came into the barn to inspect the helicopter. He prowled around it for several minutes then, returning to the tail of the machine, looked closely at one of the tail rotor blades and exclaimed triumphantly: "There's dirt on this blade!"

I joined him and looked at the blade. Sure enough there were the remains of a fly that I had failed to remove. His interest in the helicopter seemed to subside and, remembering a piece of advice I once received when in the Navy, from then on I always left an obvious patch of grime, which he inevitably found; but once found his interest waned and I could happily clean the rest of the aircraft to my own satisfaction!

Flying in France wasn't particularly exacting, but landing was. Helicopter landings made anywhere other than an officially registered heliport had to receive prior clearance from the police. The Jetranger was used for almost all journeys over a distance of ten miles, and the landing sites could range from restaurant car parks to deserted sand dunes near the Atlantic coastline. I could be given as little as twenty-four hours notice of a new destination and would have to leap into the car, reconnoitre the site and then negotiate with the local police for landing clearance. The universal language of aviation is English, but this was a fact not fully appreciated by the Landes police. They usually met my efforts to convey my needs in English with typical Gallic shrugs, while those who showed any signs of understanding what I was trying to say were obviously followers of Charles de Gaulle, since they studiously ignored my requests. I soon discovered that if I tried to speak their language they became incredibly helpful, and my knowledge of technical French improved by leaps and bounds. Although their replies were often spoken far too fast for me to understand, I assume the requisite permission was granted since I was never arrested.

The three weeks passed and my employer departed in the HS125. I was left to return to England on my own, leaving the Jetranger in the hangar at Beylongue. My instructions were given in the simplest terms. They were to get myself checked out on the Hughes 500, and then go to Anglesey. Malcolm Ebbutt, his engineer, would arrange all the details and meet me at RAF Valley to give me further information about my movements.

The Hughes 500 is a pilot's aircraft. Originally designed for gunnery spotting and communications for the American army in Vietnam, it is compact, handles beautifully and also has a startling performance. The engine is the Allison C18 or C20, the same as the engine in the Bell 206, but because the Hughes is several hundred pounds lighter than the Bell it has a rate of climb that exceeds that of most comparable helicopters, even when carrying a full load. If it has drawbacks as a civilian aircraft, they are that the cabin is cramped for the passengers, there is little baggage space and the aircraft is incredibly noisy.

My conversion completed I met Malcolm at Valley. The newer of the Boss' two Hughes was there, and I was to deadhead (reposition on my own) to Kidlington and await his arrival and further orders. The weather was loud and clear for my first solo that gave me plenty of opportunity to consolidate my scanty experience in the aircraft. By the time I reached Kidlington I felt I would not disgrace myself in public.

That evening I learned we were to fly to London the next day, landing at Battersea Heliport. Flying in the London area is rigidly controlled, and helicopters, especially single-engined ones, are restricted to specific, narrow lanes. This is not only to avoid conflict with airliners flying in and out of Heathrow, but also to ensure that a helicopter has somewhere safe to land in the event of an engine failure. Most of these routes lie over main roads or railway lines; mine was via the M4 past Heathrow and Kew, then along the Thames to the Westland Heliport at Battersea. Never having flown into London in a helicopter, I had visions of bringing the traffic at London Airport to a shuddering halt as I flew in front of a landing jumbo jet. Fortunately the weather remained clear, I entered the London Control Zone near Maidenhead and could see the M4 stretching out ahead of me. Heathrow was passed without problems and the turning point over Kew was obvious. I followed the river until Battersea power station was abeam, and there was the heliport beneath me.

The Boss left, and his wife, who wanted to go to East Grinstead to stay the night with relations, joined me. The journey should have been comparatively easy. All I had to do was follow a railway line south from near Battersea, via Clapham Junction, continue over the railway until I cleared the Control Zone and then turn left. Full of confidence following my successful arrival, I set off, but the weather was now rather hazy.

I managed to follow the wrong line out of Clapham and became temporarily unaware of my position. It was too late to retrace my steps so, continuing as best I could, I picked up the navigation beacons at Gatwick and was able to establish my position before I strayed into their Zone.

My passenger had been to East Grinstead by air, but we had to orbit the town a couple of times before she was able to identify our landing spot in a paddock behind the house. Next morning it was back to Battersea, where she left me and the Boss took over again. Our first destination was Baston, in Lincolnshire, where he wanted to view one of his veteran cars that was being refurbished. The weather was glorious as we flew eastwards down the Thames, but was forecast to become less attractive. We turned north over Essex. Soon the cloud from the approaching front began to build and lower and the visibility decreased dramatically. I felt it might be prudent to land but the Boss insisted we continue, so continue we did. I had no idea where we would land at Baston, but he said there would be no problem and on arrival pointed to the village green where, he said, he had landed before. No one seemed to mind, there was no influx of irate police and, after about an hour, the Boss returned and we took off again, this time for Kidlington.

We were now heading in to the teeth of the weather, and before long the cloud base was such that we could only just maintain the legal minimum height of five hundred feet above the surface. The Hughes, as with all of the Boss' aircraft, was well equipped and included both VOR and DME (Distance Measuring Equipment) which between them should have been able to give us an exact bearing and distance from our destination. However, these high priced navigation aids require the aircraft to be flown at such a height that the radio signals for them, which are line-of-sight, can be received. At the height at which we were being forced to fly, both VOR and DME were just so much pieces of electronic junk, and I had to rely on the far less accurate ADF, and map reading.

Narrowly avoiding an American airbase with its all-weather fighters and twenty-four hours a day operations, we crept into Kidlington.

The Boss gave me my instructions for the following day and left for his hotel. Having put the aircraft to bed, I spent the rest of the evening at my bed and breakfast lodgings arranging the details for the next day's delights. First of all he wanted to have lunch at an hotel near Shrewsbury, then continue to Oulton Park to watch some car racing. The Clerk of the Course at Oulton Park was very helpful and gave me exact instructions as to the latest time of arrival, and where to park. Arranging lunch was less easy. To start with, the Boss was not entirely sure of the name of the hotel at which he wished to lunch; all he could remember was that it was on a bend of a river southeast of Shrewsbury! It turned out to be The Swan but, once I had confirmed the lunch reservation, I was rather on my own. The hotel owner was as helpful as he could be, but freely confessed he was not a helicopter pilot and had no idea whether I could land anywhere near the hotel. He mentioned a path on the other side of the river and it sounded as though it might be possible to land there; so I asked him to inform the police of our arrival time, and prayed before I went to bed!

On arrival at the Swan the next day from the air the path looked very narrow, but there was nowhere else, the Boss was getting hungry and had already pointed out that any delay would make us unacceptably late at Oulton Park. We squeezed in, and he and his guest left me to go to the hotel. I was eating the sandwiches he had sent out for me when the police arrived. They were very relaxed about our appearance and stayed chatting with me for nearly half an hour. I got the impression that the helicopter's arrival had made a welcome break in their routine.

Once again in the air, the Boss informed me that the crowds at Oulton Park would be most ill-disciplined, and that I should remain with the aircraft at all times to prevent vandalism. I saw none of the racing, spending my time prowling round the aircraft trying to explain to children of all ages why they could not sit in the aircraft and play with the controls. I failed miserably. As I restrained one group, a small boy rushed up to the helicopter on the other side, leaned against the bubble window in the co-pilot's door, and the perspex cracked from top to bottom. I had visions of being fired on the spot but, apart from inferring that I was an incompetent idiot and that the cost of repair would be deducted from my salary, a threat he never actually followed up, the Boss said little as we continued on our way, this time to the Trearddhur Bay Hotel in Anglesey. I parked on the lawn in front of the hotel for the night, and next morning, deadheaded to Manchester to pick up the Boss' wife and take her to Aberdeen, lunching at Carlisle Airport on the way.

The Boss, who had materialised there in the HS125, met us at Aberdeen. It was August 11th, and he was to visit the Kildrummy Hotel for the opening shots of the grouse season. He did not enjoy flying too high, and anything much above the legal minimum height of five hundred feet was too high. This does not make map reading any easier, but he insisted he knew the way to the hotel and began to give me directions. Before long it dawned on me that at least one of us was lost and that we had probably turned up the wrong glen.. He would not let me climb any higher to get a better view, so I took the next best course and landed in a field near a crossroads. Leaving him at the controls, I walked over and had a look at the signpost. As I did so, a farmer approached, and very courteously pointed me in the right direction.

The Kildrummy Hotel lies in a spectacular setting on the side of a hill overlooking the ruins of Kildrummy Castle, the ancient seat of the Mar family, but as a heliport it left much to be desired. The Boss's intended landing spot was a small lawn, bounded on three sides by low, stone walls with the hotel itself forming the fourth side. The area was surrounded by tall trees that made it necessary to approach on a very steep glide path, and to make a towering ascent when leaving. The Boss told me it was where he always landed so, with a silent prayer that the engine would keep turning, I went in.

Contrary to some expectations, the helicopter was not used to transport my employer to the grouse moors, but I was not left idle. Over the period of five days, I flew his wife twice to Aberdeen for shopping, and the Boss once to Aberlour for a day's salmon fishing on the River Spey. Finally, the grouse shooting over, I flew them both to Aberdeen from where they were picked up by the HS125.

I now had just one VIP with me, Boko, the Boss' black Labrador gun dog. Jimmy had warned me that Boko was of uncertain temperament and had once tried to remove the seat of his trousers. Nevertheless, Boko behaved beautifully on the flight, lying quietly in the rear cabin. My destination was Castlebar, on the west coast of the Republic of Ireland in County Mayo, but after a stop at Mallaig, on the west coast of Scotland, I would also be refuelling at Glasgow and meeting Ann. On her return from Salalah her marriage had gone much the same way as mine, and we had been seeing as much of each other as the job allowed. She was coming with me to Ireland to look at the house that went with the job, and hopefully would be joining me at the end of the year.

My arrival at Abbottsinch, Glasgow's international airport, coincided with that of the first of a series of frontal depressions sweeping in from the Atlantic, and I managed to scrape in under the lowering clouds and landed in the private aircraft park. Ann met me and I asked her to take the dog for a walk on the nearby grassy area, while I visited the Met. Office to obtain the forecast for our onward route. On my return, I found her deep in conversation with a security guard. He had approached her and told her, quite correctly, that dogs were not allowed inside the airfield perimeter, and asked her how she had managed to get Boko into the aircraft park in the first place.

"The dog is a passenger," said Ann, and the guard seemed to relax a little.

"Does he mind travelling in a cage in the hold?" he asked.

"Cage! What cage?" said Ann. "You see that little white helicopter over there? Well, that belongs to the dog!"

Somewhat bemused, the guard stayed with her until I returned. The news was that the weather was foul over the whole of our route to the Republic, but was forecast to clear the next morning.

As predicted, the weather cleared and we took off for Aldergrove, the international airport for Northern Ireland a few miles outside Belfast. Our route took us down the coast of Scotland to Stranraer, from where we struck out across the Irish Sea. Over the next three years I was to cross that sea all too often. It was not so bad in the Bell, which had flotation gear and would probably have stayed on the surface in the event of a ditching. The Hughes had no such equipment and would have sunk like a stone.

At Aldergrove I went to clear customs and check the weather for the last leg of our journey, again leaving Ann to walk the dog. I presented the aircraft documents to the duty customs officer who, after a cursory glance at them, informed me the aircraft was impounded pending a decision on how much duty I should pay. He went on to tell me the aircraft had been originally taken into the UK on a temporary import licence, which had long since expired. I enquired how much the duty might amount to and was told it could be as much as fifty thousand pounds. Clearly I wasn't going to be able to pay *that* out of petty cash! It took me ten minutes of fast talking, pleading everything from ignorance to insanity, before they agreed to let me have the aircraft back. I also had to promise to persuade the Boss to write to them—once I discovered where he was!

I returned to the aircraft to find Ann in conversation again, this time with a soldier dressed in full combat gear with flak jacket, and carrying a gun. We had forgotten there was a state of emergency in Northern Ireland. She had been walking the dog not far from the aircraft when she heard the click of a gun being cocked, had turned and found a very nervous young soldier, obviously uncertain of his next move. He had accepted her explanation for her presence, but had waited until I came back. We thanked him, climbed into the aircraft, and took off.

There was a belt of thick haze blanketing the whole route, reducing visibility to about two miles and making navigation difficult. Another complication was that all the aviation charts for the area were in the hangar at our destination! Ann, who at this time hated flying and would have preferred to have been under the influence of Librium, navigated for me using our only source of information—an Automobile Association book of road maps! She proved a natural and brought us unerringly to Castlebar Airport, where we were to clear customs. Actually, the nearest customs post to Castlebar was at Westport, several miles away on the shores of Clew Bay, but Malcolm had arranged for the Customs officer to meet me at Castlebar. The delay at Aldergrove had meant a late arrival at our destination; the officer had become bored with waiting for us and had returned to his office. Jim Ryan, the airport manager, met us with instructions that we should continue to the "Big House" where Malcolm Ebbutt would meet us and complete the necessary formalities. This was our introduction to the delightfully relaxed atmosphere that was to be a feature of much of our time in Ireland.

Jim bought us a cup of coffee while he told us how to get to the Big House, eleven miles from the airport. It lay in a wooded area on the west bank of Lough Conn, the twin hangars just to the north of the house. As we drew closer, I could see the approaches to the landing site were well up to standard: both were across wind, one over tall trees, the other down a steep hill and over a massive privet hedge just a few yards from the hangars. The touchdown points were small wooden platforms set into concrete troughs in front of each hangar door. Malcolm was waiting for us and marshalled me onto one of the platforms. As soon as the rotors had stopped and were tied down he opened the roller door to the hangar, pressed a button and the whole platform was winched under cover.

Time was short. We were due to take the other Hughes back to Scotland the next day and we still had to see the furnished accommodation I had been promised. Malcolm drove us a couple of miles down the lakeside to Carrickbarrett Lodge. Ann and I fell in love with it on first sight. It was set on a little knoll no more than two hundred yards from a secluded beach, and totally surrounded by an oak forest. On one side was Mephin, one of the highest hills in Ireland; on the other side was the lake, reputed to contain some of the finest salmon in the country. The house furnishings consisted of a few carpets, a couple of night store heaters and some lampshades, but this did not spoil it for us.

The next day, leaving Boko behind, we flew the other, older, Hughes to Inverness. The journey was uneventful, apart from the dire warning from the customs officer at Aldergrove about what would happen if *this* helicopter overstayed its temporary import licence!

Chapter Thirteen

Leaving the Hughes at Inverness and Ann in the Borders of Scotland, I continued south to Beylongue by public transport. The Boss's wife had returned to France for a few weeks and wanted me there to fly her and her guests around the local area. Within a week the plan had changed. The Bell was once again tucked away in the barn, and I was on my way back to Inverness to await the Boss. It was the middle of September and time for the stag shooting. He arrived in the 125 and we were soon on our way down the north side of Loch Ness in the Hughes. It was a bright clear autumn day, the Highlands showing at their best as we switchbacked our way maintaining five hundred feet above the surface. Turning right up Loch Arkaig, we passed through the narrow confines of Glen Pean to Loch Morar. There, a few miles along the south shore, we came to a wide glen with a river flowing through it and into the loch. This was the River Meoble from which the estate took its name.

The Boss directed me up the glen to an open-fronted, corrugated iron hay barn, in front of which was a very basic concrete landing pad. We were met by Neil MacDonald, the ghillie, in a battered Landrover. When he had taken the Boss up to the Big House, a large, single-storey lodge part-hidden in a fir plantation, he returned to help me refuel the helicopter from the barrels stored in the hangar, using a small electric pump. When we finished we wheeled the machine into the barn for the night.

Work for the day completed, he drove me down the rough, rutted track, past the main house, to where I was to live for the next seven or eight weeks. From the outside my accommodation looked exactly what it was—a corrugated iron shack—but the exterior belied the truth. Inside were three bedrooms, a sitting room, kitchen and bathroom, the whole interior lined with wood panelling. Marie, Neil's wife, had already lit a fire in the old-style, black-leaded range and the place was warm and cosy. The MacDonalds had also provided a small stock of food and other necessities. This was to tide me over until I could arrange for my own "messages" to be collected by Sween MacDonald (no relation to Neil), who was the estate boatman and made regular shopping trips into Mallaig, our nearest shopping centre.

I discovered a bottle of whisky among the "necessities" and with the help of several drams Neil and Marie regaled me with details of life at Meoble. There were only four inhabited houses in the valley. The "Big House," Neil's (where he lived with Marie and Sandy, his younger son), and mine were all within half a mile of each other. Sween and his wife, Morag, lived in a cottage at the mouth of the river about one and a half miles from us. There were no roads either in or out of the valley and the Boss had, for years, travelled to the estate in a flying boat, landing on Loch Morar. Now the only access to the outside world was by helicopter, by boat or on foot. The nearest road was at Lochailort, seven miles to the south, and to reach it entailed a walk over country that appeared to me to be all uphill. Neil assured me it was no more than a wee stroll and that it was not unusual for them to be first footed on Old Year's Night by friends and relations from Fort William!

The estate stretched for nearly fifteen miles in an east-west direction, from halfway along the south shore of Loch Morar to Glen Pean. From north to south it was six or seven miles from Loch Morar to a fence on the ridge above Lochailort. Isolated it may have been, but over the next three years Ann and I were to spend some of the happiest months of our lives at Meoble.

This time she was able to join me for only three weeks. Once she had returned Peter to prep school at Melrose, she and Michael were going to drive to Bracora, on the northwest corner of the loch, leave the car with the local priest and take the boat to Meoble. The plan fell to bits when, only a few miles along the way from Hawick, the car broke down. Leaving it at a garage to be repaired, Ann continued in a hire car, but there was no way she could arrive before eleven that night. She telephoned to let me know what had happened. A few hours later, hearing of our predicament, the Boss told me to take the helicopter and meet Ann at Glenfinnan, cutting several hours off her journey. It was a generous gesture and much appreciated by us both. Calculating that she should arrive about eight, just as it was beginning to get dark, I flew the five minutes across the ridge and landed opposite the Glenfinnan Hotel, close by the monument commemorating the landing of Bonnie Prince Charlie at the start of the 1745 rebellion. I spoke to the hotel manager to let him know what was happening. He suggested I should park the helicopter in the hotel car park, pointing out that helicopters in car parks are a comparatively rare sight, and that Ann could hardly fail to see it, even if she was not expecting it. It was dark by the time she arrived, but it was a clear, frosty, moonlit night and presented no problem for the flight back to the valley. We then settled in to a delightfully relaxed routine revolving around the hunting of the stags.

Stag shooting in the Highlands is a necessity as well as a sport. The damage deer can do to agriculture is unacceptable, and I was told Government marksmen cull herds left unculled by the owners of estates. In either case a specific number of stags and hinds must be shot each year. At Meoble, the stalking was conducted in a less than traditional manner. Not for us the early morning start, saddling the ponies and trekking out in the dark. Our day began at eight when Neil and the Boss would decide which part of the estate they would stalk. This depended on the weather, especially the direction of the wind, and could be influenced by the meteorological report I obtained each morning. The Boss required me to get the official weather forecast, and on at least one occasion I had to walk through the pouring rain to the Big House to use the only phone on the estate—to enquire from the Met. Office at Glasgow Airport, a hundred miles away, what the weather was like at Meoble! The Boss would sight in his rifle on the range and, while he went back to prepare himself and his guests, I would fly Neil and Sandy up the hill to the selected landing site.

The flying was about as close as I could hope to get to the freedom I had in Oman. In some ways it was better since I was unlikely to be used as a target by guerrillas, although the calibre of the Boss's gun, coupled with his poor eyesight, sometimes gave me cause to wonder. The Hughes was ideal for the Highlands, small, incredibly manoeuvrable, and quite powerful enough to cope with the turbulent winds that curled over the mountaintops and eddied through the narrow glens. I seldom climbed more than two hundred feet above the ground, accepting there were few places where I could land in the event of an engine failure.

Most of the landing sites were well known to Neil. He would direct me to what appeared to be a totally inaccessible shelf on the side of a precipice, but which always turned out to be quite acceptable; as I got used to the area I began to find my own. Using a helicopter, while perhaps frowned upon by the purist, was a tremendous advantage. Not only could the decision as to where the stalk would commence be left to the last minute, but it was also possible to start in the furthest corner of the estate, something which would have been impossible with more traditional forms of transport. Nowhere on the estate was more than twenty minutes by helicopter.

Leaving Neil and Sandy at the landing site, I would return to the valley, pick up the Boss and his party and take them to the start point. Once back at the hangar, all I had to do was refuel and the next few hours were my own while I waited for the afternoon pickup. Ann and I, with Michael in tow, spent much of our time walking the hills that towered immediately above the house, and I found, somewhat to my surprise, that I enjoyed it.

At about half past two in the afternoon I would get airborne again. The pickup was always a chancy business. I would have a fair idea of which direction the stalking party had moved, normally upwind; but even so this left a huge area to search. Neil always tried to ensure they were in open ground, but the clothes they wore, chosen to blend so well with the background to avoid being seen by the stags, made spotting them from the air very difficult. If I had not seen them within twenty minutes I would land and shut down. Hearing this, Neil would fire a couple of shots that echoed around the hills but at least gave me some idea of where they were. I suggested they should carry some distress flares that gave out a thick, red smoke, and this made sighting much easier. Eventually Neil and I both carried hand-held radios; this allowed him to direct me to a landing with total accuracy.

Once I had taken the Boss back to the valley, I would return to where I had left Neil and Sandy and commence the pickup of the stags. There were never less than two, sometimes three, making at least two trips necessary. Sandy would go back to the hangar first, to position the tractor and trailer near the hangar while I returned to the hills. Neil would attach the carcasses onto a nylon strop attached to the hook beneath the aircraft, and I took them back and lowered them directly onto a trailer which Neil would tow to the stag larder. Finally, once I had recovered Neil and refuelled the helicopter, my day was ended and I was free until the next morning.

Ann left to drive back to Hawick. Two weeks later, and rather earlier than expected, the Boss decided to pack in the stalking. He wanted to go to Baston again and I was to take him to Glenfinnan from where he would drive south. I was to meet him later that day at the RAF station at West Wittering and take him on to Baston. I reached Blackpool but there my journey came to a grinding halt. As I was refuelling I noticed a trickle of oil coming from the bottom of the engine casing. When I opened up the clamshell doors the cause was obvious—one of the main oil supply pipes to the engine had fractured. A helicopter engineer from a firm at the airport confirmed it would be several days before the aircraft would fly again. I managed to contact the Boss and told him the news. He was none too pleased, and after making one or two suggestions with which I was unable to comply he told me to go to Ireland, pick up the other Hughes and come to West Wittering to take him on to Baston.

It was gone midday, and even if I could have got an aircraft direct from Blackpool to Castlebar, I still could not have made Baston before nightfall. This was met firstly by stony silence; then, reluctantly, he told me to leave the aircraft where it was, go to Mayo and meet him at Shannon the next day with the other Hughes. I managed to find a flight to Dublin and caught the last train from there to Castlebar. Next day I arrived at Shannon just before the HS125. The aircraft taxied in, the ladder was lowered and the Boss appeared. Half way down the ladder he stopped, turned, and climbed back into the aircraft. It was raining, really no more than a light Irish mist, but this was sufficient reason for him to decide not to remain in Ireland and extend his journey to Biarritz. I was to stay at Shannon until the next morning, then return the Hughes to Castlebar and get myself to France as soon as possible! I was also to telephone the chateau in France and inform the staff of his imminent arrival. Talking face-to-face to Jose, the Boss's Portuguese butler, was never easy, his command of the English language being only marginally better than my non-existent knowledge of Portuguese. This, combined with the vagaries of both Irish and French telephone services, made the task monumental, and I could not be certain that the message had been successfully delivered. What I could be certain of was that if the plan fell apart I would be so informed in no uncertain terms on my arrival at Beylongue!

After a quick dash to Castlebar, and a rather more leisurely journey by train across to Dublin, I arrived in time to catch a flight to Biarritz. I stayed in France for one week, flying the Bell on three occasions: twice to Mimizan, a grass airfield near Beylongue, to give the Boss's wife some help with her helicopter flying, the third time to take them both to Biarritz to catch the 125 back to Britain. I was left to fly the Bell back to Wales with Tom Whitney, a young Irish aircraft engineer who had recently joined the circus. It was an unhurried trip in perfect weather, refuelling at Tours and Dieppe, clearing customs at Le Touquet and Lympne, and night stopping at Kidlington. Next day, after breakfast, we continued to Llanfairfechan where the Bell was to be left for some necessary maintenance.

I returned to Ireland. There was to be no flying for at least a fortnight, my first break since joining the Boss. Ann arrived at Carrickbarrett Lodge and we began buying furniture and making the lodge into a home. Given a level of patience and an understanding of the Irish way of life we could obtain almost anything we wanted, most especially meat which was some of the best I've ever tasted. We decided to buy in bulk and bought a fifteen cubic foot deep freeze in Castlebar. Unfortunately this proved to be unserviceable the moment we plugged it in, and we were forced to delay our order of meat. The electrical shop in Castlebar passed us on to the agents in Dublin who promised to send us a replacement by train. This would arrive at Ballina, fifteen miles from Carrickbarrett, from where it would be delivered by lorry to our door.

A month later a phone call from Ballina informed us our new deep freeze would be brought to the house that afternoon and we reordered a hindquarter of beef, some pork and some lamb.

The freezer arrived, but in a large pantechnicon that was too big to get up our hundred-yard long drive. The lorry driver helped us to wheel it up the hill in a wheelbarrow but, denying all knowledge of the arrangement to take the unserviceable one away, returned to Ballina. Ann and I removed the first freezer to a shed, positioned the new one in the larder and switched it on. It failed to work. The compressor was broken!

Once more delaying the delivery of the meat, we contacted the agents again, who promised faithfully that their engineer would deliver a serviceable machine within days. He did so, some thirty days later, with the new freezer in a pig trailer behind his car. We carried the old machine out, the new machine in and plugged it in. Great joy, it worked! The engineer prepared to leave, at which point Ann asked him what he was going to do with the two defunct deep freezers. With loads of Irish charm he told us we would have to check with the agents in Dublin. The idea of spending another month cluttered up with two unserviceable freezers was too much for Ann. She walked over to the back door, locked it, and informed the engineer he would be staying with us until the freezers were removed. Fortunately we could all see the funny side of it and, after contacting Dublin, it was agreed that he would take both away that afternoon, one in the pig trailer, the other in the back of the estate car he was driving.

When the Boss finally returned I was kept very busy flying around Ireland, a totally different experience to the rigorously controlled airspace of either Britain or France. Apart from the three main airports of Dublin, Cork and Shannon, and the fifteen-mile radius control zones around them, we could fly whenever and wherever we wished without let or hindrance. No one seemed to worry when I parked the helicopter on the quays in Galway Town, and left the aircraft to go and buy some fish at McDonoughs, the finest fish shop on the west coast. I landed by the harbour at Killala to pick up fresh crab and lobster from the local fishermen. Other landing sites included deserted coves and many of the offshore islands, hotels and pub car parks. All were used with the minimum of fuss.

Castlebar, with its small airport and two thousand foot bitumen runway, was our main shopping centre. It was a town of about six thousand inhabitants, two main streets and a pork and bacon factory producing the finest pork sausages I've ever eaten. It also had more pubs to the acre than anywhere I've visited. Given time, we could obtain anything we wanted, but soon discovered that the Irish equivalent to the word *Manana* had not quite the same sense of urgency.

Our telephone at the Lodge had been modernised. This meant that instead of cranking a handle to rouse the exchange at Foxford, a small village a few miles away, we pushed a button that rang a bell. Once the exchange answered we would be given all the local gossip before finally being connected to the required number. I had to obtain all the weather reports from either Dublin or Shannon, and this could take forever as I was handed on from manual exchange to manual exchange. One evening, at about a quarter past six, I failed to get through, even to Foxford. I sat by the phone, ringing the bell at one-minute intervals, until at six forty-five the girl in the exchange answered me as though there had never been any problem. Next morning I discovered the reason for the delay. The Bay City Rollers were appearing on television, and the exchange had been left unattended during the performance!

In early January I flew to Meoble for the hind shooting. It was bitterly cold, and heavy snow made stalking difficult. We stayed for four days. The Boss went shooting just once, seemingly a small return for the two-way journey for the helicopter from Ireland, done solo, since my employer travelled by other means.

In the spring the Boss went away and we went on holiday. When we returned to Ireland it was to find the flying freedom I had previously known had become a thing of the past. The Provisional IRA had changed the situation by hijacking a civilian helicopter, and using it to spring a member of their organisation from Mountjoy Prison in Dublin. They had followed this up with another hijack but, I was told, had failed in their attempt to bomb Strabane Police Station with milk churns filled with explosives. These two exploits had caused the authorities to tighten up on the use of helicopters within the Republic.

Now, before I could get airborne, I had to inform the local CID at Ballina of my time of takeoff, my destination and my time of arrival. The Guarda would provide me with an armed escort if I were going to remain on the ground near any inhabited area. It was a system that intrigued me. Most of the time I did not know where I was going until shortly before takeoff (and not always then!), and it seemed to me that the IRA would find it easier to hijack the helicopter direct from the hangar rather than wait until they discovered my destination. Our local policeman would have had great difficulty in coming to our assistance.

He lived in Lahardane, a tiny village about eight miles from the hangar, and patrolled an area of over four hundred square miles of some of the roughest country in Ireland on a bicycle, since he had neither driving licence nor car.

On his return from Sri Lanka, the Boss had agreed to give me more warning of any long trips he wanted to make. This system broke down within days when he gave me less than twenty-four hours notice for a flight to Gigha, an island off the west coast of the Mull of Kintyre. This was further complicated by the information, passed shortly after lift-off from Aldergrove, that he wanted to go on to Meoble after Gigha. Fortunately I had refuelled at Aldergrove and had enough fuel to reach the estate where we kept a supply of fuel. Wrong again! I was informed that we were not actually going to the estate. I was to drop him by the road just outside Mallaig and continue to Inverness with his wife, who was with us at the time. I made Inverness with the proverbial teacup of fuel remaining. We stayed in that area for a few days, visiting various large houses and ruined castles, before I went back to the west coast to pick up the Boss from Mallaig and fly him to Skye. He had recently bought a new fixed wing aircraft, a Mitsubishi MU2J, to replace the HS125. The MU2 was a high wing, turboprop aircraft with a very good short field performance, unlike the 125 which needed a long, fully metalled runway. The MU2 could get in and out of many of the small fields near the houses we visited in Europe, such as Skye and Castlebar, and the dirt strip at Rion-des-Landes which was convenient for the chateau at Beylongue.

The new aircraft complicated my life. It seemed to me I was now expected to be able to airlift the Boss from his house to Castlebar airport, and then rush on ahead to meet him at his proposed fixed wing destination. I managed to convince him that my inability to do this was due solely to the low speed of a helicopter and not a lack of interest on my part.

Chapter Fourteen

I had now been with the Boss for a year and it was time for the annual pilgrimage to France. He was going to fly to the strip at Rion-des-Landes in the MU2, but his wife had decided she'd come with me in the Bell. Ann, with Michael, was going to drive across Ireland to Rosslare, take the ferry to Fishguard, drive to Southampton and then take the ferry to Bilbao. From there it was only a short journey across the border to Biarritz and Beylongue. By the time I finished working for the Boss, Ann and Michael were to experience almost every ferry system between Ireland, Britain and France!

I collected my passenger from Battersea and flew to Le Touquet to clear customs and night stop. The weather forecast next morning was for clear skies, good visibility and light winds along the whole route, and I was looking forward to an untroubled trip to the chateau. We were halfway to our refuelling stop at Tours when both the sun and the gods ceased to shine on us. Storm clouds began to build and before long we ran into light rain, quickly followed by a series of heavy squalls. The rain came down like stair rods and visibility was reduced to a few hundred yards. The situation was worsened by the fact that the Bell was not fitted with windscreen wipers; the shape of the windscreen was supposed to shed the rain with no loss of forward vision, but this did not always happen. There was no point in trying to reverse course to get out of the storm; we would then both have been travelling in the same direction, so when a small village appeared out of the murk I landed in a nearby field and shut down.

I needed to find a telephone so I could inform the police of our unscheduled landing, preferably before they came to arrest me, and also to call the chateau and let the Boss know we would be late. I trudged through the rain and wet grass to the village, which was called Beauche, and by the time I found a cafe with a telephone, I was soaked to the skin. The cafe owner was a true Samaritan. He pointed me in the direction of a hot bath, sent a taxi to collect my passenger, and even rang the police and the chateau for me. The weather cleared after about an hour and we were able to continue the journey to Beylongue without further distractions.

Two days later Ann and Michael arrived. The following day, the first time the Boss wanted to go flying, the Bell went unserviceable. It was a rare occurrence, but we had to wait for Malcolm to arrive from Wales to repair it. The Boss decided I should not waste my time but should go and scout for landing sites and obtain police landing permission at some of the places he wanted to visit. Ann, Michael and I spent a pleasant week driving around the southwest of France, from Bordeaux to the Pyrenees. The sites included a magnificent restaurant at St-Etienne de Bagorre, high up in the mountains, and several secluded bathing beaches on the Atlantic coastline.

Malcolm repaired the helicopter and my holiday was over. I was kept very busy flying around the Landes, but apart from one of the beaches, our landing places always seemed to be at local airports. When I went to the beach I would park the helicopter on the dunes and wait there until the Boss and his wife returned. Sometimes Ann and Michael would join me. On one occasion Ann arrived before me and, selecting a spot below where she thought I would be landing, she lay down to sunbathe. She was startled by a very Germanic voice saying, "Have you seen my son?"

She discovered she had encroached onto the section of beach reserved for nude bathing. As she said later, "When I opened my eyes it wasn't so much that I didn't know *where* to look; there was nowhere *else* I could look. He was standing right over me!"

At the end of the month the circus folded tents and left. The Bell was remaining in France and I was able to go back to the UK by car, sharing the driving with Ann. It was almost the only occasion I managed to do this. On the majority of trips she had to trail me on her own.

We had a few days at Carrickbarrett before the next upheaval, once again for the grouse and stag in Scotland. This time Ann was bringing all four of the boys with her to spend a few days at Meoble before the three older ones returned to school. The routine in the valley was no different: flights to the hills for the stalking, picnics on deserted islands off the mainland, or at the shepherd's hut at the far end of Loch Beohrid. If anyone had told me I would be content living in an isolated valley, a small wood-lined shack for my home, and cut off from the rest of the world by a forty-five minute boat ride, I probably would have laughed in their face. This was our situation at Meoble, and I loved it! The flying was great fun and we went where we wanted with no air traffic control to worry about. The RAF aircraft that used the valley as part of their low flying route, and frequently passed beneath me as I airlifted the stags down the hill to the larder, were just something to keep me on my toes.

Ann and I had thirty thousand acres of beautiful Highland to roam, as long as we kept clear of the Big House. Almost our only problem was food; it always seemed to be a feast or a famine. We had no refrigerator, just a wire-mesh meat larder in the garden. Sometimes a stag or a lamb would be butchered, sometimes both, and everyone in the valley would get a piece. When Ann was left with some lamb, a haunch of venison and half a salmon in the larder, we ended up making fishcakes with fresh salmon to stop it being wasted.

There were the occasional traumas. I came back from the hill one morning to find the boys inside the house on a glorious autumn morning and Ann, rather white-faced, waiting for me at the door. She told me the boys had come in earlier and Peter had asked, "Mum, what's gelatin?"

"Stuff for making jellies," replied Ann.

"Does it come in candles?" Peter had continued.

Ann pointed me towards the coal shed at the bottom of the garden. "Have a look in the shed. I think it is dynamite."

She was quite right. It was dynamite, seven or eight sticks, all weeping copiously and in a very unstable state; with it were detonators, wires and batteries, all the makings of a horrendous explosion! I carried it, very cautiously indeed, to where Neil was working in the stag larder, and asked him what it was doing in our coal shed. He explained that some men had been blasting at the dam on Loch Beohrid which supplied the water for the hydro-electric generator that served the estate. The explosives expert had damaged his back, and the party had left the valley quite suddenly, obviously forgetting about the explosives. Life was seldom dull with the Boss!

The surrounding hills made television reception almost impossible, but several years before I joined him, the Boss had bought a lattice mast to carry an aerial. He had decided it was time to erect it, and I volunteered to airlift all the equipment to the chosen site, half way up one of the hills above the house. There were two mast sections and a small wooden hut, which would house the electronic boosters, to be airlifted to the mast site, and several reels of coaxial cable to be distributed along the route. The mast sections were no problem. "Bunny" Warren, who had recently replaced Sween as the boatman, attached them to the hook and they "flew" without any oscillation. The reels of cable were also very stable, although when I released one on a small ledge on the side of the hill it rolled the whole way down to the river, fortunately without damaging anything. The lift of the wooden shed was a totally different matter. As I started to move away, it began to twirl on the end of the sling, and then sway dangerously from side to side. I tried slowing down, but with no effect. The oscillation got worse, and eventually, at about one hundred feet above the ground, I was forced to jettison the load. I feared it would be a total loss, but we found it, upright in a peat bog, and almost undamaged.

There were days when the weather took a hand and made flying more exacting. I had taken Neil up the hill one morning and had arranged to meet him at the same place late in the afternoon. It was a day of scudding cloud and intermittent rain, but the clouds had remained clear of the hills. When I went to collect him he was nowhere to be seen, so I shut down to wait. The clouds began to descend and I became concerned they would soon envelop our route. It became a race between Neil and the clouds, the clouds winning by a distance. By the time he arrived the helicopter was enveloped in thick, clinging mist, and it seemed we were going to spend a damp, uncomfortable night on the hills. Then I remembered that the little stream gurgling past the helicopter ran down to the main valley. We took my cabin door off so I could see, and I hover-taxied the aircraft sideways and downstream, seldom more than five feet from the ground except when we had to leap over a tree. We arrived beneath the clouds and were able to get home before nightfall.

Ann and I returned to Ireland in late October, to be faced with the problem of obtaining some coal for the winter. Our order of thirty hundredweight was accepted by the supplier in Ballina but several days later, when it failed to arrive, I telephoned to find out what had happened.

"Our delivery lorry has broken down," I was told. "But we're going to borrow a horse box, and it should arrive tomorrow." Two days passed and still no coal arrived, so I phoned again. "You see, it's like this," came the reply. "It's the high winds. It was too dangerous to drive the horse box; but if you stay in tomorrow we'll deliver it, never fear."

I returned from work the next evening to find Ann, who had postponed a visit to friends, on the telephone.

"What about our coal then!" she said.

"I have our driver right her," came the reply. "He says he didn't know where you lived, but was told it was up a tarmac drive off the Castlebar road. He says he couldn't get the coal into your shed because it was full of coal, so he left the bags against the door."

The penny dropped. Our neighbour, about half a mile away, had a similar driveway to ours.

"We'll call you back in a few minutes," Ann said.

Our neighbour thought that Christmas had arrived early, for our thirty bags were indeed piled against his coal shed door! We returned to Carrickbarrett and phoned the coal man.

"So, you'll have your coal now?" he said.

"No," countered Ann. "YOUR coal is outside our neighbour's coal shed. When you put it into our shed, *then* it becomes OUR coal."

"It's nearly ten miles from Ballina, and only half a mile from you," protested the coal merchant. "Couldn't you collect it in your car?"

Irish logic battled with Scottish determination, and lost. He delivered the coal the next day and seemed to think the whole affair had been a normal, everyday occurrence.

We spent the rest of the winter in Ireland, apart from the usual visit to Meoble for the hind shooting. Although I always enjoyed the flying at the estate, the journeys to and from Scotland in the winter were less to my liking. The gales that swept in from the Atlantic, funnelling in between the islands and curling up the glens, tossed my small helicopter about like a leaf. Try as I might, I could never find a route that was not affected.

When the Boss returned from Sri Lanka in April he told me to go to Wales, pick up the Bell and bring it back to Ireland. Tom Whitney and I took the overnight ferry from Dublin to Holyhead, but when we arrived at Llanfairfechan Malcolm told me there had been a slight change to the plan. I was now to fly up to Prestwick and bring the Boss back to Wales. I had not been expecting more than twenty-four hours away from home and was ill prepared for an extended trip, having but one set of clean clothes with me. Malcolm couldn't tell me how long the stay in Wales would be, but reckoned it might be two or three days

On our return to Wales, the Boss informed me that I would be staying there until he was ready to move. I pointed out I was a bit short of clean clothing, and received a lecture on the virtues of being prepared for all eventualities. I felt this was a bit unfair, and reminded him of his first lecture on the virtue of travelling light! My suggestion that I should return to Ireland to re-equip fell on deaf ears. He said he might want me to fly again. He came up with the counter proposal that Ann should drive across to Wales with the necessary clothes; he would pay for the petrol and ferry tickets both ways and he also asked if Ann could pick up some papers and a suitcase from his house.

By now Ann was well used to such changes in plans and took the news in her stride. Packing my bag and Michael into the car, she went up to the Boss's house, to find that there was not only some papers and a suitcase, but also a typewriter and a secretary. She drew the line at a photocopier even though it was already packed for travel! We had three days together in Wales before the Boss made his move and told me we were heading south the next day. I pressed him to be more specific and he admitted that south meant Hurn Airport just outside Bournemouth. We left Wales and arrived at Hurn that night, having stopped for lunch at Staverton, near Gloucester. That evening, when I telephoned him to let him know where I was staying, he informed me we would be going to France in the morning! We crossed the Channel to Jersey to clear customs outbound and then flew to Deauville for inward customs and to refuel. At Deauville he informed me we would be night stopping in Paris.

Our destination was Issy-les-Moulineaux, the Parisian equivalent of Battersea Heliport. Issy is also on the banks of a river, the Seine, and even though I'd never been there before, navigation should have presented no difficulty. All we had to do was fly up the river and the heliport would be on our right-hand side. The Boss had been there before, so when our arrival on the outskirts of Paris coincided with a thunderstorm, I left him to watch out for the heliport while I concentrated on flying through the rain. We narrowly avoided a low-flying Lear Jet that appeared to be trying to get into Orly under the cloud, and plugged on through the murk until the unmistakable outline of Notre Dame Cathedral appeared in front of us. We had overshot our destination. To add to my confusion a helicopter appeared alongside us with the word *Police* emblazoned all over it, and they led me, ignominiously, to the heliport. The Boss left in a prearranged hire car, leaving me with instructions to get the helicopter ready for an early morning takeoff the next day, find myself a hotel and then phone him for details of the next day's journey. It was still raining hard and by the time I had finished putting the helicopter to bed I was soaked to the skin.

It was time to find myself lodgings for the night. I discovered that Paris has the same law of diminishing returns as London—the more you need a taxi, the less likely you are to see one. I decided I couldn't get any more saturated and began to walk. By the time I'd found a small hotel I was in no mood to be critical of my surroundings, paid the amount asked, and phoned the Boss. He told me we'd be staying in Paris for at least twenty-four hours and that he would let me know our further itinerary when he was ready.

I retired to bed and within seconds was asleep—but not for long. The walls that separated my room from the adjacent ones were made of thin plasterboard and anything but soundproof. My rest was shattered on frequent occasions, the traffic in and out of both adjacent rooms seeming almost continuous, and with no-one stopping for much more than half and hour. Ann found my story hard to believe, but if it was not a brothel my hotel must have been very close to it. Next morning I moved to more salubrious quarters, but I'm not too sure whether Ann believed that part of my tale either!

Next day the Boss informed me he wanted to leave, that our final destination was to be Nice and that he wanted to be there in time for the Monaco Grand Prix. Unfortunately the bad weather persisted for three more days, resulting in frequent and irate phone-calls from the Boss. At one point I went to his hotel to inform him I had had enough and was quitting! His reaction was to tell me I was trying to engineer a pay rise which, if the truth be known, I had not even thought about, and to offer me an increase I couldn't refuse.

When the weather finally cleared we staged down through France, night stopping at Dijon and then continuing to Nice, with a slight detour to Grenoble for lunch and a refuelling stop at Marignane. The last leg, from Marignane to Nice should have been easy; all I had to do was follow the autoroute. Once again the weathermen led me astray. Despite their forecast of fine weather the thunderclouds were soon rolling down off the hills and it began to rain. I was forced to reduce speed and height until I found myself flying at eye level alongside some high-tension power cables. Navigation was impossible, the lightning cutting out any hope of picking up the navigation beacon at Nice; all I could do was follow the road and the power cables. When I began to have difficulty in seeing them, and fearing I might meet some wires that crossed the road, I decided to land. As I began to reduce speed even further, the rain ceased like magic, the sun came out and we were able to continue our journey.

I didn't get to see the Grand Prix. Helicopters were allowed to land by the harbour in Monaco, but not to remain there during the race and I had to return to Nice and wait in my hotel for a call from the Boss to come and pick him up. This came *two* days later! We flew on from Monaco and I ended up at Beylongue, twenty-one days after leaving Ireland for a one-day trip. The Bell was remaining at Beylongue, and I returned to Ireland by Air France.

The constant moving was beginning to outweigh even the high salary, and it was difficult to maintain any sort of family life without spending on travel expenses anything we might otherwise have saved. I began to search the back pages of *Flight* magazine for another job, preferably one that would give me a chance to break into the commercial market and, hopefully, to fly twin-engined helicopters.

Meanwhile the annual visit to France ended and we returned to Ireland to prepare for the grouse and stag season. Compared to the rush and bustle of the previous few months, our stay at Meoble was idyllic. The weather was superb for most of the time, the Boss enjoyed the stalking, and even allowed Anthony to join him for a day on the hill. Not even a major unserviceability on the Hughes, when the same oil pipe started to leak, broke the spell. Malcolm was immediately available, arriving within hours, and together we removed the engine under cover of the barn, split the compressor to replace the pipe, and had the aircraft serviceable again within twenty-four hours.

The problem did, I think, persuade the Boss it was time to get rid of the aircraft. When the time came to return to Ireland, I was instructed to take it to Blackpool to demonstrate it to a potential buyer, a garage owner from Lancashire. A price was agreed and I took the aircraft on to Wales so that Malcolm could carry out a few modifications for the new owner. The actual sale was complicated. In the civil version of the Hughes, the Captain sits in the left-hand seat, almost the only helicopter with this configuration. Because of his eyesight, the Boss had bought the military version direct from the United States, and these were configured for the Captain in the right-hand seat. There were no other differences, but this was enough for the Civil Aviation Authority to insist it was a new type, and that they would have to check it out before they would accept it on to the British register. I ended up demonstrating the aircraft to the CAA check pilot, but how the new owner managed to get type rated I never knew.

In November the Boss decided to go to Meoble again. He flew in the MU2 to Connel, a disused strip near Oban, from where I ferried him to Meoble in the Bell, and back again four days later. The rest of my journey back to Castlebar was fraught with difficulties. There was a full Atlantic gale blowing, and although the skies were clear my forward speed was reduced to the point where I became concerned I might not have enough fuel to reach Aldergrove. Departing for the short hop across the sea from the Mull of Kintyre to Ireland, I decided I might get some respite from the wind by carrying on down the east coast of Northern Ireland and up Belfast Loch. I could not have been more wrong. The wind, funnelled down the valleys, increased both in strength and turbulence until it reached the stage where, on occasions, the Bell was almost laid on its side. I could not continue and landed on a beach, just above the high water mark, at Cushendall.

Having shut down I managed to find a telephone and inform the police of my predicament, and within a few minutes an armoured Landrover driven by the RUC arrived. The sergeant in charge told me there was no way I could leave the helicopter where it was, and someone suggested that if I could fly it a few hundred yards to the school playground it might be safer behind the chain link fence that surrounded it.

Leaving the Bell in the playground guarded by the RUC, the sergeant drove me in his own car to a nearby hotel where I had a meal. He told me much about the problems he faced as a Catholic member of a predominantly Protestant force, based in a mainly Catholic area. He was a very gentle soul, having no anger over his strange situation but a deep concern to try to heal the breaches in his community. He appeared very conscious of his responsibilities to all sections of the population, and it was distressing to hear of his death in a Provisional IRA ambush a few months later. It was a tragic waste of a life dedicated to trying to bring some peace to that sad, war-torn country.

Later that evening I bedded down on the back seat of the helicopter. I hadn't been there long when there was a tap on the window. It was one of the RAF Police who had replaced the RUC on guard.

"Are you comfortable in there?" he asked.

"I've slept in worse places!" I replied.

"You're sleeping on top of the fuel tank, aren't you?" He clearly knew the Bell layout. "I wouldn't stay there if I was you. The boys around here have some home-made rockets. There's no way the fence will stop those!"

At that moment I heard a sound I hadn't heard since leaving Oman—the unmistakable crackle of automatic rifle fire.

"Is that your lot?" I enquired.

"Definitely not. We can't afford to waste ammunition like that!"

I made it to the Landrover before he did, and spent a sleepless night listening to the horror stories of military life in Northern Ireland. I was thankful I'd never been posted to the Province during the real "troubles." The RAF policemen were very cheerful, considering they were on a hiding to nothing, targets for both sets of extremists. As the sun rose the next morning the wind dropped and I was able to get on my way, via Aldergrove, to the comparative sanity of County Mayo.

I had applied for several jobs, one of them for pilots to fly in the Arabian Gulf in Abu Dhabi, one of the United Arab Emirates. It was unaccompanied, but offered the chance of a conversion to the Bell 212, a twin-engined helicopter in worldwide use. We had recently bought a house in Somerset so that if my job with the Boss had been terminated suddenly, by either side, we would not be homeless. It was not the most convenient time to be separated, but Ann and I decided it held the best opportunity for the future.

From a professional standpoint my time with the Boss had done little for my career. We'd enjoyed much of it, for he lived in, or visited, some beautiful places; but I was finding it difficult to work for him without frequent differences of opinion as to what level of service the high salary actually bought. On top of this Michael had begun to believe his home was a car, and we would soon have to be thinking about his education.

*   *   *

Our time in Ireland had been totally enjoyable. I'd been concerned that, as one of the dreaded English, I might not have been too well received south of the border, but I needn't have worried. Throughout our stay we found nothing but friendship and, if working there was a bit complicated by the Irish ways, for three years it was a very happy home for us. This continued even during the tense atmosphere when one of the Provisional IRA hunger strikers was buried in Ballina. My contact with the CID suggested we should stay out of sight during the passage of the cortege through Foxford, but apart from that we had nothing to worry about.

Even our departure was tinged with "Irish." Having packed all our possessions into a hired van we did a final tour of the house, but all we found was a bottle of potheen. Potheen is an illicitly distilled spirit, having a taste to the uninitiated somewhere between paraffin and diesel oil, with perhaps just a faint bouquet of furniture polish. The only thing guaranteed about the local brew, apart from a very low price, was the hangover. There was no way we were going to carry this bottle across to the UK! The thought of having to unpack the van if it was found by customs was too awful to contemplate; nor could we drink it—not with two hundred miles of driving before us.

Rather than leave it in the house I decided to pour it down the sink and, in doing so, found another good use for potheen. For the first time in three years the kitchen sink ran clear!

Chapter Fifteen

I felt I was better prepared for my new job than on previous occasions. I had seen enough flying to know that there would be no glamour, commercial pilots in modern aircraft rating somewhere between airborne taxi drivers and electronic systems managers. I would be flying the Bell Jetranger for the first few months but at least the future appeared more promising. At my original interview I had been told that the company, a joint venture between World Wide Helicopters and some local Arab interests, was assured of all the oil contracts in the Abu Dhabi offshore oil fields before the end of the year. The first of the Bell 212's, fifteen seat, twin-engined helicopters, would be arriving by the middle of the year and I had been promised an early conversion to the new aircraft. Even so, with all this information to hand, I was still not totally prepared for the reality.

World Wide Helicopters was part of an American owned company registered in the Cayman Isles. They already had a presence in the Middle East; in fact our Jetrangers had been brought down from Sharjah where they had been involved in similar offshore work. In Abu Dhabi they were to service the French owned *Al bu Khoosh* oil field, situated one hundred and ten miles northwest of Abu Dhabi town.

Tom Loosemoore, the only other British pilot with the operation, met me on my arrival and drove me from the airport to the company flat in the centre of town. Until the discovery of oil, Abu Dhabi had been no more than a fishing village perched on a sandbar, surrounded by salt flats. The original sandbar, enlarged by using more sand dredged from the shallow inlets, was now a concrete jungle, grey buildings towering over a square grid system of roads, while the infrastructure struggled to keep up with the feverish pace of new construction.

Our large, four bedroomed flat was subleased from the French oil company. It was on the third floor of a high-rise concrete block, and was served by a lift which, even without the regular power cuts, was of uncertain reliability, and a water supply that caused us equal concern. The flat had to be large since there were five pilots and seven engineers all told living there, the General Manager and the two technical managers having separate accommodation. We worked two on, one off—and at any time there would be eight of us in residence. We used the hot bunk system, mostly in shared rooms; as one person went on leave his bed would be taken by someone returning from leave. I was lucky and fell heir to my own room, if an area curtained off from the dining room, with a mattress on the floor, could be described in that way. I discovered that our Chairman, an American World War Two bomber pilot, had strong views on our work cycle; fifty-six days work to be followed by twenty eight days leave meant just that. Under American aviation rules, to which we worked loosely, there were few limits on flight or duty hours. We flew throughout daylight hours, seven days a week, and maintained a night emergency service.

Almost all countries have their own Department of Civil Aviation, and most are signatories to the treaty drawn up by the International Civil Aviation Organisation (ICAO). The American and British systems, administered by the Federal Aviation Authority (FAA) and the Civil Aviation Authority (CAA) respectively, have the same aim, the safe operation of civil aircraft, although at that time the methods were somewhat different. The FAA used a broader format within which the individual operator had areas for interpretation of the rules; the CAA preferring more tight control, with little latitude given for variation. As the years went by, the FAA, while still being less rigidly legislated, drew closer to the CAA concept. At the time I joined the company the Abu Dhabi Aviation Authority was still in its infancy, and the pilots worked on the strength of their own national licence. I was told that this subject was under discussion and that, until it was resolved, there was no requirement for an Abu Dhabi validation.

Our base at the international airport consisted of two portacabins, and an expanse of concrete hard standing on which all maintenance was carried out. Next door was the main helicopter operator in Abu Dhabi, Bristow Helicopters, with their purpose-built hangar and office complex, upon which we cast envious eyes although we believed it would all be ours before the end of the year.

Our aircraft, both with more than ten thousand hours on the airframe, perched on rubber pontoons to allow them to alight on the water in the event of an engine failure. I had never flown an aircraft with this configuration before; there always seemed to be fresh leaks in the floats for the engineers to patch and I was never totally convinced they would work in an emergency. We were a Visual Flight Rules (VFR) operation, and the aircraft were equipped with very basic flight instruments, the main compass being of the "E2" type, fitted solely for emergency use in all the aircraft I had flown in the past. Because of our limited carrying capacity, and to give the contractor the best payload possible, we flew with one-way fuel and a twenty minute reserve, refuelling on the platform for the return trip. We carried personnel, tools, almost everything the French needed on their production platform. This included food and, since the French did not stint themselves offshore, there was always competition among the pilots as to who would take the flight shutting down on the offshore platform at lunchtime!

The Arabian Gulf is not generally plagued by the foul weather often found in the North Sea. Apart from the rainy season, which may be any time between November and April, there is seldom any cloud, icing does not feature in the forecast and the wind hardly ever gets above forty knots. What it does have is bad visibility. Dust and sand picked up by the prevailing northwesterly wind, the Shemal, from Iran, Kuwait, Saudi Arabia and other desert areas of the Gulf, often reduce the surface visibility to less than five hundred metres. The dust layer can reach as high as six thousand feet and, apart from immediately beneath the helicopter, obscures the surface from almost any altitude. Oily black smoke from the countless flares that mark the oil fields mixes with the dust and becomes trapped beneath the inversion, the temperature at the heights at which we flew frequently being more than five degrees centigrade higher than at the surface.

The combination of these factors results in conditions that can be compared to flying in a fishbowl. There is little or no horizon, the blue sky above and the sea immediately beneath are the sole reference points, and actual visibility can be established only when an oil rig or ship is sighted. In the worst of this weather the pilot must place great reliance on his flight instruments, and navigation is equally dependent on radio aids. Our aircraft were equipped with VOR, which we could tune in to Abu Dhabi airport out to a range of about sixty miles at the heights at which we flew, and an ADF with which we could pick up the Abu Dhabi and platform beacons. Even so, on one occasion in minimal visibility, one of our pilots managed to fly past the platform and ended up on the island of Halul, in Qatari waters, where he was promptly arrested and the aircraft impounded for a while by the army garrison!

The rainy season, if it comes, brings with it gale force winds, heavy rain, low cloud and thunderstorms embedded in the cloud cover. The weather forecasting from the local aviation services tended to concern itself more with airports, and the high level transiting of jet airliners, and less about the lower levels in which we flew. Good sense dictated that we should avoid flying in areas of heavy rain, but the pressure to complete the task was heavy, and good sense and reality occasionally did not coincide. It was possible to fly around an area of rain but, having done so, find a solid barrier of squalls ahead. Then, when courage failed and the decision made to return to base, equally solid belts of rain and line squalls could block off the line of retreat. There were few, if any, qualified meteorological officers on the rigs and platforms, and weather information from our offshore destinations tended to take a very basic form. I have asked a drilling rig for an estimate of the cloud base and a description of the prevailing cloud, to be told only that "We have some black cloud and some white cloud!" and estimates of visibility could vary with the numbers and importance of rig personnel going on leave—all the radio operators knew our minimum visibility limits!

Another feature of flying in the Gulf is the temperature. Helicopter cockpits are designed to give the maximum field of vision to a pilot working his machine in confined spaces, and have vast areas of perspex window. When ambient summer temperatures by day seldom drop below thirty-eight degrees Celsius (one hundred Fahrenheit), the temperature in the cockpit can be forty five degrees Celsius and more, producing a working environment akin to a vibrating sauna bath. The hottest I ever experienced was in later years in Qatar, when the afternoon air temperature at Doha airport once peaked at fifty-two degrees Celsius. I do not know what the temperature was inside the cockpit; I do know that as I climbed into the aircraft the skin on my fingers stuck to the metal!

My first two months in Abu Dhabi passed quickly. Following leave, I returned just as the first of the Bell 212's arrived and was given the conversion to the aircraft. This had been my main reason for joining the company since job opportunities in the wider world of helicopters would be restricted without twin-engine experience. It was being rumoured that the CAA was to make it mandatory for the ALTP(H), and some of the major offshore operators were getting rid of all their single-engined machines. As soon as the conversion was complete I found myself back on the Total contract flying the Jetranger. More 212's arrived and more pilots were hired. Some of them already had experience on the 212, others were given the conversion and put on to the contracts we were acquiring from Bristow Helicopters. I languished on the Jetranger, but took every opportunity to fly in the co-pilot's seat of the 212's. The pilots were more than happy for me to share their load, for they were all flying over one hundred and twenty hours per month!

October came and went, by which time we had taken over all the off-shore contracts from Bristow, but I was still languishing on the Jetranger. Feeling that something was amiss I spoke to Tom Loosemoore, now my contract manager, who told me it was his opinion that I was too useful to the company flying the unpopular Jetranger. I decided to look for alternative employment.

Qatar, another oil-rich state about one hundred and fifty miles west across the Gulf from Abu Dhabi, had its own offshore helicopter operator, Gulf Helicopters. I had tried to join them in 1973, when I left Oman, but lack of a licence had prevented this. In 1976 the Chief Pilot was an old friend of mine, John Hoskins, who I had known at Culdrose when he was on loan from the RAF as a helicopter instructor. Gulf Helicopters had leased four of the Bristow Bell 212's displaced from Abu Dhabi, and also operated two old Bell 205-A1's, the civilian version of the Bell Huey flown by the military in Vietnam. Although my experience on the 212 was limited, I had many hundred hours on the 205 from my time in Oman and this stood me in good stead. In May of 1977 John offered me a contract and I accepted with alacrity. It was accompanied, and Ann and the boys joined me within a matter of weeks.

Qatar is an independent Emirate situated to the south-east of Bahrain, and pushes up about one hundred and twenty miles north into the Arabian Gulf from the mainland border with Saudi Arabia. British influence had extended into Qatar as far back as the time of the East India Company and early in the twentieth century treaties had been signed with all the Gulf States to guard the supply of oil for the Royal Navy, which was in the process of turning over from coal to oil. More treaties were signed at the end of the First World War to safeguard the many small emirates and sheikhdoms from attack and, to a great extent, Britain rather arbitrarily took over arrangements for their defence and foreign policy. Between the wars, and having no oil, Qatar languished as a backwater of the Gulf, subsisting mainly on fishing and the natural pearl industry. The standard of living was further reduced with the advent of the Japanese cultured pearl.

Onshore oil was found on the western coast of Qatar in 1939, but the field was not developed until after the Second World War. This development was by British companies, and they paid a very small royalty to the Emir, the world price of oil at the time being four dollars a barrel. In 1972, His Highness, Sheik Khalifa bin Khalid al Thani became the new Emir after a bloodless coup, and at the same time there was a massive increase in the world price of oil. This produced an equally staggering increase in the revenue paid to Qatar. The development of the country began at a frenetic rate and, by the time I arrived, Qatar was booming. The offshore oil fields, discovered in the early 1960s, were being further developed and work for the helicopter company was on the increase.

Gulf Helicopters operated out of Doha, the capital of Qatar, and the only town of any size in the country. The offshore helicopter support had been supplied in the past by several companies, Bristow and World Wide among them. Gulf Helicopters was formed in 1973 as a partnership between Gulf Air and British Airways. This partnership was later dissolved, and Gulf Helicopters became an autonomous subsidiary of Gulf Air, owned by the States of Qatar, Bahrain, Oman and the United Arab Emirates. They had been operating five, single-engined Sikorsky S62's, boat hulled helicopters inherited from World Wide Helicopters, but in 1976 Shell Oil, who were partners in the offshore production, decided that they wished to go for twin-engine safety, and that the preferred aircraft was the Bell 212.

There were seven pilots, myself included, five of them British, the other two American. The Americans had been hired to fly the 205's on a construction contract for the building of a stadium in Doha for the Arabian Gulf Football Championships, which had since lapsed. Maintenance was carried out by our own, CAA licensed, engineers, and others who had come with the machines from Bristow, and who would stay with us until our own engineers had enough experience on the aircraft. It was expected that this would coincide with the arrival of six new 212's from Bell Helicopters, due early in 1978. The four 212's were employed on the offshore oil contract, with one 205 on fixed floats as a backup. The remaining 205, also on fixed floats, flew for an Italian company, Saipem, who were laying gas pipelines from the offshore fields to the onshore gas terminal at Um Said, thirty miles south of Doha.

We worked essentially to CAA regulations, with some local modifications. Shell Oil limited the pilots to eighty hours flying a month, as opposed to the one hundred allowed by the CAA, a reasonable reduction considering the temperatures in which we worked. Days off were dependent on the number of pilots on site at any time. One of the pilots, Eric Shelmerdine, told me:

> When I joined the company we had four pilots, and I worked three days on and one day off. Now there are seven, and I am working six days on and one day off. I hope we don't get any more pilots!

The rest of the routine was much as in Abu Dhabi. Our aircraft were on call seven days a week, although most of our flying took place between Saturday and Thursday midday, Friday being the Islamic equivalent of Sunday. The daily flying programme started at 0630, was completed by nightfall and consisted of about twelve flights each day to the oil fields, and we also provided night emergency cover. Daylight flying was carried out under VFR rules and single pilot, at night we flew normally with two pilots. In all we had six regular offshore landing sites, the offshore terminal on the island of Halul, three oilfield platforms and two drilling rigs. The furthest of these was no more than forty minutes flight time from Doha. Occasionally a drilling rig would be brought in to continue the exploration of the North Field. This was a sea area about eighty miles north of Doha known to contain massive quantities of natural gas, which has, in more recent years, been developed in to one of the largest gas fields in the world.

Before the end of 1977 John Hoskins left and was replaced from within the company by Richie Richardson, an ex-RAF wartime pilot who had spent much of his time as a "Pathfinder" in Bomber Command. He had run his own airline after the war, based in the Isle of Wight, but had subsequently retrained on helicopters. Over the next few months we began to recruit more pilots and engineers, the industry was still booming and money was available for further development of the offshore fields. Our new helicopters arrived as scheduled and the Bristow aircraft and engineers were returned to their owner. We now had six, brand new, Bell 212's, five on contract to QGPC (Qatar General Petroleum Company) as the oil company came to be called after nationalisation. We leased the sixth aircraft to Mitsubishi Heavy Industries, a Japanese firm who were building new production platforms for the three offshore fields. Natural gas was now a saleable commodity; the wasteful burning (flaring) of the associated gas from oil production was to cease and it would be pumped ashore via the newly built pipelines to the plant at Umm Said. The pilots took it in turn to fly on this contract, relieving some of the monotony of our normal work.

It was a very slick operation. All the structures, three for each field, had been prefabricated in Japan and towed to Qatar on lighters. Mitsubishi had even constructed some ocean going tugs for that purpose. The first part of the construction was the pile driving of the foundations for the platforms, and a Dutch work barge, an old oil tanker with the engines removed and fitted with a crane capable of lifting more than two thousand tons, arrived to carry out this operation. I watched some of the pile driving when I was shut down on the barge helideck, and later on, the installation of the platforms themselves. The lift of the largest section, the two thousand ton compressor platform with its huge turbine engines that would pump the gas to shore was very impressive. The crane driver handled the colossal load with great skill, despite the swell that was running at the time, lowering it on to the legs and holding it there while the welders swarmed all over it.

The two Americans and I, who were licensed to fly the 205's, had a slightly more varied, if unenviable, choice of destinations. Saipem had three barges in the area, laying the liquid and gas pipes from the oil fields. These barges were rectangular and flat-bottomed, held in position by eight anchors and manoeuvred over short distances by varying the length of the anchor cables. The direction of the pipelines ran at right angles to the prevailing wind and swell. In anything other than a flat calm these barges rolled and heaved with a sullen determination that left our Texan pilot, Jim-Bob Pickrell, heaving in sympathy; the other American, Bryan Novak, declared that he was immune to the motion. I occasionally felt sick, but nothing would induce me to go below for lunch, to join thirty or forty Italians wolfing down yards of spaghetti!

The Mitsubishi contract lasted for eighteen months, after which we had to find other work for the helicopter. We picked up a short term, wet lease in Dubai, flying for the local oil company. All went well for a couple of months. Then we heard that the aircraft had suffered engine problems and had ditched while it was deadheading to pick up some passengers from offshore. The pilot was safe; the helicopter had floated but was upside down, having turned turtle when one of the pop-out flotation bags burst as it hit the water. It had been towed into Dubai harbour but was considered a write off. This was the first loss we had suffered with the 212's. We had the occasional engine failure but these had not been catastrophic and the aircraft returned to base safely each time.

It was not so with the 205's. They were two of the oldest civilian operated 205's in the business and were rather past their prime. Keeping them serviceable was an ongoing problem and, despite much tender loving care, over a period of less than a year both aircraft ditched, fortunately with no loss of life. The first one suffered a total engine failure, followed by a copybook autorotation into the sea. The second ditched when the chain drive controlling the pitch of the tail rotor blades broke, and the aircraft spiralled towards the surface under only partial control. The pilot, Henry Domingues, told us he had waited until the aircraft was about fifty feet above the sea, still in a spiral dive, and then pulled in full collective to cushion the impact. The technique worked and the aircraft remained afloat on the pontoons. The level of confidence in these old aircraft, from both pilots and customers, took a tumble and they were relegated to onshore, ad-hoc work and later sold to a Canadian company. The replacement for the ditched 212 went on contract with QGPC.

Flying operations from the oil company heliport were never easy. The operating area was small and hover-taxiing from parking spot to takeoff area when all the aircraft were on the ground was sometimes like trying to thread a needle. The rest of the facilities were old and basic. The whole area lay immediately alongside Doha harbour and we had to take off either over the harbour and approach to land over the oil company workshops and offices, or the other way round, depending on the wind direction. This had not been so much of a difficulty while the company had been operating the single-engined S62's, since in an emergency and under certain wind conditions the aircraft could have alighted on the water. We now had twin-engined machines, and were required to work as far as possible to the CAA Group A parameters. These specified, among other essentials, the need for a takeoff to be rejected to the ground if an engine failed before safe forward flying speed had been achieved. This we could not do, and the Qatari Department of Civil Aviation gave us a waiver so that we could continue operating from the site until we could move to the new heliport at the Doha International airport, which was being constructed at government cost.

This move was made in December 1981, and with it many of our operating problems vanished. There were comfortable, air-conditioned offices and crew rooms, a large hard standing and a hangar that would accommodate our entire fleet. We were able to use the main runway for all takeoffs and landings and, since it was just short of three miles long and at that time, I think, the third longest in the world, we had no difficulty in finding an area for rejected takeoffs! Not long afterwards a glut of oil, and a downturn in the oil market occurred. The number of aircraft on contract to QGPC was reduced to four and we held our breath to see what would happen to our staff. There were few jobs available in the helicopter world, and anyone made redundant would find it very difficult to regain employment. The North Sea, for so long a haven for any CAA licenced pilot, was suffering, and there had been many redundancies from UK helicopter companies. Fortunately natural wastage took care of most of our problems, and those of us who wanted to stay were able to do so.

Chapter Sixteen

Many of our staff were married and had their families with them. Accommodation varied in many respects, with the exception of rent which was high by almost any standard, but was paid by the company. Our three-bedroomed villa was brand new, built of concrete blocks, with a flat roof and a tiny sand garden, although the rusty steel reinforcing bars sticking skyward from the roof gave it a somewhat forlorn and unfinished air. It was fully air-conditioned, a necessity in summer temperatures, although the year on year increase in demand for electricity in Qatar put heavy demands on the generating station, and power cuts were not unknown. In one respect Ann and I were lucky: our supply came from the loop containing the new hospital which ensured that we were normally among the last to be cut off.

Water arrived every other day by tanker and was transferred into a 500-gallon tank in the garden, from where we pumped it to a roof tank. On one occasion I forgot to switch the pump off and the roof tank, somewhat smaller than the one in the garden, overflowed. We were made aware of my error when we heard the sound of a stream flowing down the stairs and through the hallway! On further investigation we discovered that the rainwater drains on the roof were higher than the roof itself and the water had taken the line of least resistance, through a hole in the roof straight into our bedroom, from where it was cascading down the stairs.

Despite the huge amount of oil money that was being poured into building the infrastructure of Qatar, in 1977 there was still some way to go. These were the years known as 'B.C.'—'Before the Centre'— a massive American Style hypermarket that opened almost exactly a year after we arrived. The new sea port had been completed and cargo boats could now unload from alongside jetties, a modern international airport was open, and there was talk of fresh meat being flown in from abroad; but shopping, especially for food, was still a matter of skill and knowledge. Isabel Camp, our Chief Engineer's wife, took Ann in hand. When the papers announced the arrival of a boat containing fresh food, and knowing which shops were most likely to have the goods required, she led Ann around the many small, mainly Indian run, supermarkets and cold stores. These contained everything that was needed for western style life, although people with a passion for hygiene might have been troubled. Ann, however, had shopped in the souk at Salalah and was well used to making sure, for instance, that the rice sacks contained live weevils—if they were dead there was probably something wrong with the rice!

A car in Doha was an essential since there was no public transport. Modern cars of all shapes and sizes, from huge American gas-guzzlers to small Japanese saloons, were immediately available, and at prices which might make a U.K. car dealer wince. In the mid-1980's I was able to buy a brand new, fully air-conditioned Mazda 323 for the equivalent of about £2000, and petrol was so cheap that when the price was doubled overnight, the increase caused little comment and hardly affected the cost of living! A Qatari driving licence was easy enough to obtain as long as you held a current British licence. I went to the Traffic Police office, presented my British licence and received an application form in return. The form was filled in for me, in Arabic, by one of the many typists sitting under their multi-coloured umbrellas outside the police station, and then I returned to the office to identify some road signs from a poster. I found this last part very easy. The policeman pointed to the picture of a sign, I told him what I thought it referred to and he nodded in agreement; whether the answer was correct neither of us could be absolutely certain since the policeman was from the Sudan and spoke little or no English. The licence was issued within a couple of days. The only real difficulty in the system were the visits to the office counter, which was besieged by all the other foreign applicants and seemed to include half of the population of the Indian subcontinent.

For Ann it was easier still. Because she was a woman she was not required to go anywhere near the counter. We were ushered into the senior Sergeant's office and given a glass of heavily sugared tea while the form was filled in. Then the Sergeant, who spoke some English, turned to Ann and said, "Now you must go and look at the road signs, Madam." He hesitated before continuing, "No, *you* stay here and finish your tea; your husband can read the signs for you!"

Having spent nearly a year in our first villa, we were moved to what was regarded by most as the pick of company accommodation. These were about fifteen or twenty years old, built on what might be described as colonial lines, and consisting of three huge bedrooms, kitchen, dining room and sitting room, and a large, mature garden surrounded by an eight-foot high purdah wall. They were fully air-conditioned and very comfortable to live in, but occasionally suffered from a lack of maintenance. John Kirk who, at the time of the incident was our Chief Pilot, had complained that the wiring in his villa needed replacing; fuses blew regularly and the average life of a light bulb was about a week. The agent agreed that repairs would be made and the old fuse box renewed. Some days later the electrical engineer arrived. The delay was because the electrical engineer was also the plumber, and as such he had been repairing the plumbing in our villa. He brought with him a new circuit breaker system to replace the old box, and it took him only a few minutes to disconnect the thirty or so fuses.

It took him nearly a week to identify the wires he had disconnected, and because it was high summer and the temperature well over thirty-eight degrees for most of the time, the lack of air-conditioning in his house did little to improve John's demeanour. Once the wires had been identified, it took the engineer no time at all to connect them and cement the new box into the wall. Unfortunately for all of us, while the cement was still wet the box fell to the ground, tearing all the wires out of the back. It was yet another week before he had re-identified the wires!

There were no licensed hotels or restaurants in Qatar, but non-Muslims above a certain income level could obtain legally a more than adequate supply of alcohol from one of the two liquor syndicates. It was for home consumption only, although it seemed that, within reason, a blind eye would be turned on those of us who took a cold box to the beach, and woe betide anyone who resold this alcohol to those who could not obtain it, especially followers of Islam. In the main we all regarded it as a privilege, and it was well known that almost any abuse would bring immediate and severe action. Within a year of our arrival a major problem occurred, not—I hasten to add—of our making, and the ration was promptly halved.

The legal system in Qatar is that of Shari'ah Law. Shari'a seems to raise hackles with some people in the western world, and there is no doubt that by western standards some of the punishments inflicted may seem harsh. As a matter of interest, I lived and worked in the Middle East for nearly twenty years, although never in Saudi Arabia, and I have only once seen a person who had had their hand amputated as a result of Shari'a, and *he* was living in Scotland! Ann felt safer when out shopping alone in Doha than in some big towns in Britain. As long as you broke no laws, there was no problem; rape did occur, but I never heard of anyone who committed the act twice! I was once the guilty party in a car accident and, apart from the fact that the trial was held in a Shari'ah court and in Arabic, I could easily have been in a court in Britain. I was fined about the same amount for the accident as I would have been in Britain, although it was automatically increased by ten percent, the extra being given to the Palestine Liberation Organisation. A car accident after 6 p.m. resulted in a blood test, and anyone caught driving with even the slightest trace of alcohol in their blood almost always went to jail for thirty days, and was deported on release. As a result, few of us combined driving and alcohol.

The social life in Doha was superb. Most entertaining was done at home and few days went by without either going out to a friend's house for supper, or entertaining in our own villa; barbecues could be arranged months in advance with the knowledge that the weather would be fine. A friend of ours, Richard Blennerhasset, said that he had once started to count the availability of sports and hobbies in Doha, and stopped when he reached one hundred. They ranged from angling, through the alphabet to yachting, and if there is a sport or hobby starting with 'Z' I am sure it could be found in Qatar. There was a golf club, although it was very stony. Players carried a piece of Astroturf on which they were allowed to place the ball before they played their shot from the fairways, while the greens were actually browns and consisted of oiled sand. By the time I left, in 1993, Qatar had a tennis complex running ATP contests, squash courts for international competitions, and was already building the desalinisation plant to provide water for an eighteen hole, championship standard grass golf course.

Michael received his education in Doha from the age of five to seventeen. There was an English speaking primary school working to UK standards, and by the time we left he had completed his education at the Doha College, which took students from many nations to the UK 'A' level standard. The arts were well represented and the Qatari Government granted a piece of land on which the European community were allowed to build a fully equipped theatre and produce western plays, as long as the scripts were first vetted by the boycott office. When we first arrived in Doha there was one, Arabic speaking TV channel which very occasionally showed an English language programme. I confess I became alarmed when I discovered I could almost follow the plot of some of the more exotic Egyptian dramas—but worse still was beginning to enjoy them! Fortunately Qatar TV began to transmit two TV channels, one Arabic speaking, the other one English. If there was a drawback it was the amount of football televised, and during one

Football World Cup competition every match but one was shown, either live or recorded!

The first ten years of my flying in Doha were spent mostly rotating around the local oil fields. Although part of Gulf Air, we had little work outside Qatar. Bahreini oil was from areas very close to the coastline, and needed no helicopter support. The Emirates had their own, indigenous, helicopter companies that guarded jealously against any infiltration from outsiders, as did we. Oman had no offshore oil, and although the nature of the countryside lent itself to helicopter operations, there was a locally owned civil aviation company that held a monopoly on all internal civil flying, and a military helicopter force which, at that time, was allowed to offer its services to civil contractors.

In 1979, however, I had been offered a lifeline by Richie Richardson, who asked me to become the Company Training Captain. I had never thought of becoming an instructor. It is a job that requires immense patience and the ability to be a good passenger, but not necessarily to be a brilliant pilot, no matter how instructors may assess themselves! My job did not involve ab-initio instruction since all our pilots were fully trained on type. The requirements before anyone could join us were that they had to have a minimum of two thousand hours total flight time, fifteen hundred as Captain of a turbine powered helicopter, and at least one hundred hours on the Bell 212. In fact, few of our pilots had less than five thousand hours in total; two of them had more than ten thousand and there was little new that I could teach most of them.

Under the CAA rules our pilots were required to have two check flights within any period of thirteen months. They had to display a high degree of technical knowledge of the aircraft and, during a flight that could last anything from forty minutes to an hour, by day and by night, show that they knew how to cope with any emergency that might occur. For the first few years I was one of only two training captains, and at least once a month would find myself sitting in the left-hand seat of a 212 putting my fellow pilots through their paces.

The flight check simulated as closely as possible the many emergencies that could occur, and allowed the pilot, if necessary, the latitude to remain at the controls to the last possible second before I took control to avoid damage. Some of the emergencies, especially those involving the electrical systems, required only a detailed knowledge of the circuitry and back-up systems, and how to operate the various change-over switches to ensure that all the instruments, lighting, radios etc. required for the particular conditions of flight remained on line.

Most of the flight, therefore, was devoted to allowing the pilot to practice the more far-reaching emergencies. These involved engine malfunctions, ranging from minor problems with the fuel systems, engine fires leading to a deliberate shutdown of one engine in flight, through single-engine failures to the ultimate double-engine failure and autorotation. All pilots are taught how to carry out autorotations during their initial training, and military pilots are given ample chance to practise them during their normal flying career. Within an operation such as ours, as in most civilian companies, practising emergencies when carrying passengers was expressly forbidden. Almost the only time the pilots could rehearse the handling of such major failures was during the six-monthly company base check.

We carried out the simulation of a double-engine failure over the airfield, but did not continue the autorotation to touchdown. Years of experience throughout the helicopter industry has established that more damage can be caused by practising the final ten feet, than results from a real emergency due to lack of practice of the actual touchdown. Although much of our flying was over water, where the selection of touchdown point was of little importance, the ability to recognise a suitable landing area on dry land, and fly the aircraft in autorotation to its limits were still an essential. I could do little about the selection of the target area on the airfield, but I could make it as difficult as possible for the pilot to reach it.

In the mid-1980's we obtained a contract with an oil company in what was then North Yemen, based at Saan'a, the capital of the country. The flying was principally to check the oil pipe from the oil field in the desert, through the mountains passing south of Sana'a, and ending up on the coast of the Red Sea at Hodeida. Part of the route lay over the ancient province of Saba, with it's capital and main oasis of Marib on the edge of the desert east of Saan'a. Saba was at the peak of it's power about the 7th century B.C., but even now there is a large lake, and the ruins of the Marib dam, over five hundred metres long, which collapsed in about the 7th century A.D., all part of the irrigation system that watered nearly four thousand acres of the desert near Marib,

As Training Captain I was needed to go there to give the pilots their six-monthly flight check. On my first visit I arrived at Sana'a International Airport just after three in the morning. Jabril, our Yemeni driver, who spoke immaculate English (having spent some time living in a Brighton boarding house) drove me to the oil company living quarters where our staff were accommodated. It was about a ten-mile drive during which we were stopped at every road junction by members of the Yemeni Armed Forces, mostly eighteen-year-old conscripts armed with an AK 47 and obviously chewing qat. Qat is a leaf containing a mild narcotic which most Yemeni men chew when they are not working, and sometimes when they are, which leaves them with puffed out cheeks and a green slime dribbling down their chin. I was told it is like chewing privet hedge and, although a mild stimulant, dulls any form of sex drive! I never tried it, the almost permanent headache I had from being unused to living at seven thousand feet above sea level being sufficient for me.

Our aircraft were limited to flying immediately over the pipeline, and at all times we had to carry an armed guard. This was, among other things, to ensure that if we had to land in the outback, we would not be abducted and held to ransom by local villagers. Kidnapping of foreigners in the Yemen had been a feature of life for years, and is often done to try to put pressure on the government to get them to spend money in the remote areas of the country. The flying restriction also extended to flying over the airfield, and we had to do the flight check over the pipeline, again with an armed guard in the back of the aircraft.

In 1987 came the start of what became known as the "Tanker War." The land war between Iraq and Iran had been rumbling on for six years, but we would have been little aware of it had it not been for the world press. Local press and television tended to play the news down, and although we occasionally saw Iraqi aircraft on their way down the Gulf, there were no restrictions on our flying. The trigger was the missile attack on the *USS Stark*, and the decision by the Americans to reflag Kuwaiti tankers to protect them from attack by the Iranians.

The Gulf was invaded by the world's press and television. Shortly before all this happened Gulf Helicopters had positioned a Bell 212 in Oman to try to conjure up some onshore work, and I was sent down to Muscat to ferry it to Dubai, where most of the TV companies had set up their headquarters. Within two days we had secured a contract with NBC, the American TV company, and I flew exclusively for them for the next three months.

NBC set up a second office in Doha, taking a suite in the Gulf Hotel, while we stripped the aircraft of all unnecessary weight and fitted even longer range fuel tanks, extending the endurance from two and a quarter to four and a half hours. Using Doha as a base we could cover the Arabian Gulf between the "no-go" area just north-west of Bahrein set up by the Saudi Arabian authorities, almost to the "no-go" area organised by the Omanis around the Straits of Hormuz. Operating out of Dubai we could search the eastern end of the Gulf and cover the Indian Ocean off Fujairah, from where the tanker convoys and their escorts started their run up the Gulf to Kuwait.

It was a free-for-all for the Gulf aviation companies. The major TV networks from both Europe and the United States were desperate for anything that could fly, and helicopters were at a premium. NBC had also chartered a Twin Otter fixed-wing aircraft from a company in Abu Dhabi, and it was fitted with radar to help them find the convoys.

The US navy, as a result of the attack on the *Stark*, had put out a warning. Any unidentified aircraft flying near their ships, especially using any form of weapons radar or failing to answer a radio challenge, would be regarded as hostile and might be fired upon. The aviation distress frequency was allocated for these challenges. The Arabian Gulf is a crossroads for many of the flights between Europe and the Far East, as well as local traffic, and the frequency became heavily overused; an aircraft with a genuine emergency might have found it very difficult to get a word in edgewise!

It became obvious that the military were monitoring all civil aviation traffic. I was outbound from Doha in the NBC aircraft, callsign A7-HAL, heading towards the northern end of Qatar, and at the time no more than ten miles from base, when I heard an American voice on our company frequency using my callsign: "*Hotel Alpha Lima*, are you off to harass our navy?"

It was an American AWACS aircraft, somewhere over Saudi Arabia, keeping a watching brief on our movements!

The US navy established a two-mile exclusion zone around any of their warships, and also tankers in convoy under their escort. This could be extended at a moment's notice to five miles when any Iranian ships or aircraft were discovered nearby. Our cameraman, even though he was using a hi-tech, stabilised zoom lens, was seldom able to get any good shots from outside the two-mile zone; but when there was no immediate danger the Americans would sometimes ignore us as we slid in closer to get a better view. At other times US navy helicopters would indicate their displeasure at our presence and place themselves between us and the ships, sometimes no more than a rotor span away. One even hovered immediately above me, trying to make me pull away. I had some sympathy with them, having suffered from the press while in the Royal Navy, but I was on the other side now and had my own job to do.

Nothing, however, would induce me to go inside the five-mile zone, when the tension that crept on to the airwaves was obvious.

There were some lighter moments. An Iranian frigate shadowing a convoy trained one of its gun turrets past an American destroyer, and a laconic drawl was heard over the radio: "Iranian frigate, you have just pointed a gun at me. Please do not do that again!"

That evening, as she left the area, the Iranian ship radioed to the Americans: "Good night, and safe sailing. We have no plans to attack you tonight!"

The other navies in the Gulf were friendlier. Most of them made no comment if we came in close to obtain our film, many of the crews standing and waving to us. The only exceptions were the Russians who stolidly ignored our presence.

NBC used "Their" helicopter almost every day searching, often unsuccessfully, for the tanker convoys, but apparently even a ten-second clip of film shown on prime time TV in the States was regarded as a triumph—but it had to be a "new" clip; file film was not acceptable. I also spent much time en-route between Doha and Dubai. It was necessary to search the sea area east of Fujairah, but I wondered sometimes whether a more pressing reason was that Doha hotels were dry, while all those in Dubai had thriving bars.

It was on one of our forays east of Fujairah that I ran into trouble. Close inshore there was a major anchorage, not only full of rusting tankers laid up awaiting an upturn in the oil market, but also the assembly point for tanker convoys to Kuwait. This time we had found nothing unusual and prepared to return to Dubai. Climbing to six thousand feet to clear the mountain range between us and our destination, I called Dubai for a weather report. To my dismay they reported a sandstorm, with visibility of less than five hundred metres, which had not featured on the forecast that morning. I called the new international airport at Fujairah, on our side of the mountains and which was functional but not formally opened, for permission to land to await an improvement in the weather at Dubai. I was met with a polite but firm refusal. I told them I was short of fuel but their answer was the same, apart from a suggestion that I should land in the gardens of the Fujairah Hilton. With no obvious alternative I followed their advice, much to the irritation of the hotel gardener who had just swept some leaves into a neat pile. Nobody else seemed to mind, but obviously someone must have taken umbrage since, a few days later, the crew and passengers of another visiting press helicopter were arrested by the local police and their equipment temporarily impounded.

We sat in the hotel for several hours while the visibility at Dubai crept agonisingly slowly up towards our minimum. As soon as it was reported as one thousand metres I decided to leave. We got airborne and flew alongside the road through the Masafi Pass but, when we reached the desert on the other side of the mountains, the visibility was still very bad. I had the choice of continuing to follow the road, which would bring me to Dubai but with very little fuel, or strike out straight across the desert and trust to my navigation. The Dubai radar controller took the decision for me. He told me he held me on radar and, with a warning that I was still responsible for avoiding any man-made obstacles I might meet, led me unerringly at low level to the threshold of the main runway at Dubai.

We were in Doha when the US Navy sank the Iranian ship *Iran Ajr*, which they had caught allegedly laying mines near Bahrein. We got airborne to go and see whether there was anything worth filming. It was a lousy day for flying, the Shemal bringing with it the usual sand and dust and reducing visibility to under two thousand metres. We were thirty miles northeast of Bahrein when we found ourselves flying alongside an Iranian hovercraft, and knowing that the Americans were in the area I called them on the radio.

"American warships, I am flying westwards in company with an Iranian hovercraft. Please inform me when I am approaching your two-mile exclusion zone."

The answer was immediate. "We hold you on radar: you are already inside our five-mile exclusion zone. Vacate the area—we are about to fire a warning shot!"

I hauled the helicopter into a steep left-hand turn, and if our cameraman, who was busy filming the hovercraft through the open cabin door, had not been secured by a harness he would have been catapulted out like a missile. Thirty seconds later we saw the splash of the warning shot as it landed about half a mile from the hovercraft. I discovered later that the incident, including some of the radio conversation, had been broadcast on BBC radio in the UK.

We began to see more evidence of the war on our daily sweeps across the Gulf. The *Al bu Khoosh* oil platform in Abu Dhabi waters, visible on a good day from the Qatari oil fields, was attacked, first by the Iraqis in mistake for the Iranian *Sassan* field a few kilometres away, and later by the Iranians themselves. The Iraqis then remedied their mistake and partially destroyed the *Sassan* platform.

I had a near miss with an Iranian aircraft. I had just lifted from Halul and was climbing through five hundred feet, when one of their C130 Hercules aircraft flew no more than one hundred feet over the top of me. They were probably searching for targets since their fighter aircraft attacked a small tanker at anchor in the roads off Halul a couple of hours later, and left it burning.

It was inevitable that, sooner or later, there would be an accident. The radar picture, normally busy with civil traffic, was further complicated by military aircraft from both Iraq and Iran. I saw Iraqi fighter aircraft beneath me on many occasions as they hugged the waves on their way to attack Iranian shipping and shore installations—and I seldom flew much above five hundred feet! We should all have been aware that a press card did not provide any form of immunity or invulnerability, but there was always pressure to get in closer. One helicopter pilot from another company was hovering alongside a frigate, while he discussed with his camera crew whether it was flying the French or Italian flag. It was neither, as they discovered when the Iranian anti-aircraft gunner fired a warning burst across their nose! Pilots who flew into the exclusion zones when the Americans were defending tankers from attack by Iranian speedboats, or into Iranian harbours to photograph tankers left burning after an attack by Iraqi aircraft, led charmed lives.

It was tragic that the aircraft to be shot down was an unarmed Iranian passenger aircraft. I do not know who was to blame, but believe that the tragedy should be placed in some form of context. The Iranians had publicly warned the US Navy that they were considered legitimate targets, and the damage caused to the *Stark* by an Iraqi missile must have been very fresh in the minds of all American naval commanders. The area in which the Iranian aircraft was flying was a civil airway, but was also across the Straits of Hormuz, a known "hot spot," and there was nothing to stop a military aircraft using the airway. Techniques for the electronic identification of aircraft are excellent, providing it is transmitting a recognisable electronic code; if the radar target is not showing any identification the decision as to whether it is friend or foe can only be subjective, based on experience and the tactical situation. It must also be remembered that an air-to-surface missile can be launched long before the aircraft can be visually identified.

The press interest in the tanker war waned and Gulf Helicopters looked elsewhere for work. Oman with its large areas of desert, and mountains rising to ten thousand feet, is ideal helicopter country and several companies had tried to break in, but with little success. We now managed to get hold of a Jetranger in the country and started to drum up work. Initially this was limited to ad-hoc charters, mainly survey work in the mountains, but it provided us with a presence which we augmented with a spare Bell 212 from Doha. As one of the pilots with experience not only on both types of aircraft, but also in Oman, I was sent down to cover whenever the resident pilot went on leave.

It was fifteen years since I had last seen anything of Oman, other than Seeb International Airport, and the changes were breathtaking.

Mountain ranges that had seemed impenetrable then, now had dual carriageway roads driven through them. Wadis that once had no more than a stony track leading nowhere were covered with roads and buildings. When I drove from Seeb to Muscat town, through the wadi at Bait al Falaj, I became lost. A major township hid the Bait al Falaj hotel, which had been the only civil building of any size when I arrived in Oman in 1971, and shops, offices and hotels now covered what had been the airfield and main runway.

One of my first jobs there was with the 212, bringing down some construction equipment from a couple of hilltops. Many helicopter pilots, especially those with a military background, will have some experience in lifting underslung loads. However, before a new load is carried by a military helicopter, usually a trial will have been carried out to establish just how it should be slung, and how it will fly. As a result of this trial, guidelines are laid down and pilots given a chance to practice.

In the commercial environment the system tends to be a little different. Some loads, especially those related to the oil world, are carried regularly and their weights and flight characteristics will probably be well known. In many other circumstances the accurate weight of the load will be unknown, and the shape and size may lead it to become unstable at some point of flight. A trial to check on the characteristics of the load would be time consuming and expensive, and contractors usually want the job done as quickly and cheaply as possible. It is not that there is a black art in sling work; much of it can, and should be done on the ground even before the aircraft engines are started. The maximum possible load weight can be calculated, using graphs in the flight manual showing the aircraft capacity for any given height and temperature. Whenever possible, loading and unloading sites are inspected, and routes planned in and out of the area, especially with regard to what may lie beneath the flight path.

No two loads will "fly" alike, but the shape, size and weight of the cargo will give the pilot an idea of what to expect; dense loads normally remain stable, light or irregularly shaped ones tend to swing and rotate in the airstream. Once the load has been lifted clear of the ground it is up to the pilot to assess the situation. As the aircraft moves into forward flight, speed must be adjusted to suit the load. If it begins to oscillate too much, speed must be reduced; if it remains stable, speed can be further increased. Some loads can only be carried at a walking pace; others may be stable enough at the maximum speed allowed for the aircraft, in the case of the Bell 212 this being eighty knots. If a load does go out of control, and this can happen very quickly and almost without warning, the aircraft may be affected so badly that the pilot has no option other than to use the emergency release and drop the load—hence the requirement to plan safe routes. I was once asked to plan the lift of an air-conditioning unit to the top of the Royal Palace in Muscat using our Jetranger. Apart from the fact that the weight was only just within the capacity of the aircraft, no matter which way I looked at it, all I could envisage was the awesome consequences of having to jettison the load over the palace roof, and I was very glad when the contract did not materialise.

Another requirement is that the pilot should be in practice. I had done as much underslung load work as many pilots, and more than quite a few, but this was the first serious work of this kind that I had done since leaving Oman in 1973. The equipment I was to lift was from the top of the Jebel Dawhan, near Buraimi, and at the Sabhan Falls in the Wadi Jizzi, the pass through the mountains between Buraimi and Sohar. Both sites were at three thousand feet, and in each case consisted of some loose gear in nylon nets, and a caravan. I arrived at Jebel Dawhan at first light to take advantage of the lower temperatures. The nets were no problem; they could be attached directly to the aircraft hook and would almost certainly be stable. The caravans, however, were a different matter. The contractor told me they weighed "about three thousand pounds, plus or minus a little." Three thousand pounds was within about two hundred pounds of our maximum lift capacity at that height and temperature, and I needed to be sure that "plus a little" was not "plus a lot." They also told me that the Bell 212 that had lifted the load up the mountain had no trouble with the weight, but this came as no suprise; lifting a load into a site is almost always easier than extracting it.

The start at the Jebel Dawhan was delayed when I discovered that the caravan contained not only some loose gear, but also nearly fifty gallons of water in the kitchen tank, weighing about five hundred pounds. The water had to be drained out and the loose gear put in nets to be lifted down separately before I started the main lift. The caravan was tucked into a little bowl on the mountaintop, surrounded on all sides by rocky outcrops, and I would be hovering over the load without being able to see it while the contractor hooked on the fifty-foot long strop. The load would then have to be lifted vertically some thirty feet before I could move forward and over the cliff edge. I was to be given directions over the radio by one of the contractors standing near the caravan. The calculations concerning the weight proved correct, and I needed more than ninety percent of full power to lift it clear of the ground. I still could not see the load, which had disappeared into a dust cloud as soon as I began to hover above it. The radio remained distressingly quiet, and I was now in a position where I could no longer risk putting the load back on the ground for fear of it toppling over on the uneven surface. Praying that I was clear of the surrounding rocks, I began to ease forward towards the cliff edge until I heard the welcome voice of our engineer on a radio from the valley floor, telling me I was clear of obstructions and could begin the descent. The caravan was remarkably stable, and I completed the journey without mishap. By the time I had descended to the drop point, the increase in available engine power was sufficient to make a hover an easier proposition.

The delays at the Dawhan site meant that our arrival at Sabhan Falls coincided with higher temperatures and a turbulent sea breeze funnelling up the pass. I discovered that in some of the down draughts I needed more than eighty percent of maximum power to prevent the unloaded aircraft from hitting the ground and discretion overtook me. I declined a strongly worded invitation from the contractor to continue and completed the job a few days later.

There was more lifting for me to do the following day, this time in the foothills near Rostaq where a microwave radio repeater aerial was being constructed. The helicopter task was firstly to lift precast concrete blocks, each weighing fifteen hundred pounds and with a five-foot long bolt fixed in the middle, and lower them into holes prepared on the hill-top. Succeeding blocks, each with a two-inch diameter hole in the middle, had to be manoeuvred so that the bolt passed through the hole. The whole construction would provide the base for the actual aerial. I was using a fifty-foot long strop to avoid subjecting the ground party to too much downwash from the rotors and had a crewman with me in the main cabin to give me directions. Due to the long sling, however, the delay between the movement of the helicopter, as I positioned it immediately above the work site, and the corresponding movement of the block, set up a pendulum motion, and the desired accuracy could not be achieved. I returned to the valley, changed to a fifteen-foot long strop and the work continued to schedule.

The final load was the aerial itself. This consisted of a tripod lattice mast and a large, flat plate aerial bolted to the top. This was to be lowered so that the base of the tripod fitted over the bolts in the blocks. The weight was well within the capacity of the helicopter, but I felt that, even with a long strop, the combination of rotor downwash and forward motion would cause this load to rotate and swing quite badly. I offered to try it in two sections, but time was running out—they wanted it in one piece and I had to be back in Muscat before dark.

My fears were realised. By the time I had reached fifty feet above the ground at a slow walking pace, the load was rocking the aircraft fifteen degrees on either side of the vertical; at times, according to my crewman, it appeared to be swinging up almost level with the cabin door! I came back to the hover, the load stabilised and I was able to lower it gently to the only flat piece of ground in the area, which just happened to be immediately beneath me. The tripod stayed upright and I was able to detach it without any damage, either to the tripod or the aircraft.

In mid-1988 Ann returned to Scotland to oversee Michael's further education, and I changed my contract with Gulf Helicopters to bachelor status, two months work followed by one-month leave. Michael intended to go to college in Scotland, and for this a return to the U.K. in good time was essential. For the company, the change in my status was an advantage; I could now work seven days a week, there was no concern about family obligations, and I soon found myself back in Oman flying the Jetranger on a mineral survey contract.

Copper has been produced from the hills near Sohar for more than a thousand years, but now the search for more deposits, and for any other mineral lodes, especially chromite, was a priority. We were based at the mining camp at Magan, just inland from Sohar and close by the main copper mine and refinery at Lasail. Part of the time we spent in the foothills, and while I was shut down I was able to see some of the ancient copper workings, where the signs of the fires used for smelting the ore are still visible. The rest of the time was spent in the mountains.

Flying a Jetranger in the mountains of Oman is not for the faint-hearted. Much of the northern Hajar range lies between four and seven thousand feet, with the highest peak topping ten thousand. Especially in the summer months the temperature, even at seven thousand feet, can be as high as twenty-five degrees Celsius, and produces a considerable degradation of engine power. The winds are frequently strong and are almost always turbulent as they get deflected by the steep cliffs and swirl down the wadis. The aircraft is small enough to be landed on rocky outcrops that are rarely visited other than by mountain goats and these, of course, are the spots that geologists want to look at—there is no point in paying for a helicopter if you can reach the location by a cheaper method.

As with underslung load lifting, many ex-military pilots will have been through a course in mountain flying, but again the techniques they will have learned are less applicable in the commercial world. The ideas of taking time to make low passes over a possible landing site, of avoiding areas of obvious heavy wind turbulence and always approaching in such a way as to leave an escape route have to be modified. When a customer is paying for the use of a helicopter they are unlikely to be interested in surveying potential landing sites; they want to go straight in and commence work at the site of their choice! They will almost certainly want to fill all the passenger seats, carry all their equipment and stay in the field for as long as possible each day, and are not particularly interested in paying for time spent returning to a refuelling base. The pilot will have to maximise the fuel loads, and much of the flying will be done at high weights and high power; this can result in an arrival with little power reserve to cushion an excessive rate of descent, and few places to go in an emergency!

The mountains of Oman are generally of either volcanic origin— jagged rocks and knife edged ridges—or sedimentary layers thrown into tortured shapes by volcanic disturbances, and cut into deep wadis by wind and water erosion. Nothing concentrates the mind quite so keenly as the realisation that, if the engine quits, there are few safe places on which to complete an autorotation. A miscalculated attempt to reach a clear spot on the side of a hill could result in a long roll to the bottom. Most of us decided that if we were unfortunate enough to lose our engine, the best technique would be to head for the bottom of the nearest wadi; it might be rock strewn with nowhere totally clear to land, but at least from there you can roll no further!

The following year the Jetranger was placed on contract with a company making a detailed geological map of the whole of Oman. Much of the map had been completed, but pressure was now on to complete the work to a deadline, and this required the full-time use of helicopters. The expected rate of flying was intense and our resident pilot in Oman could not cover the commitment on his own. The maximum number of hours he could fly in any twenty-eight-day period, limited by regulation to one hundred, would be reached in about three weeks and, as a result, I went down to Oman again to share the flying.

Most of the time the surveyors worked from tented camps, but at Sur on the eastern coast, just northwest of Ras al Hadd, they had rented a small villa. It was close to the local dirt airstrip used by military and civil aircraft, and we parked the helicopter inside the airfield perimeter fence each night for security. The villa was a typical low cost, mass produced concrete building consisting of three small bedrooms, a large living room, kitchen and bathroom. Outside was a small garden surrounded by the inevitable purdah wall and growing little but weeds, gravel, and the tents in which the geologists slept.

We lifted off each morning at 0730, remaining in the field until late afternoon but meeting up with our engineer at a prearranged point in the operating area for lunch, and to refuel the aircraft. The mountains of the Eastern Hajar in which we were flying were mainly sedimentary rock, between three and five thousand feet high but pushed up to over seven thousand feet in places. Despite the inhospitable terrain there were villages in almost all the major wadis, the houses perched precariously on small outcrops of rock. Anywhere water was found, and there was plenty, the hillsides and wadi beds had been cultivated and date palms and alfalfa planted. When we landed and shut down, even in the most desolate spots, the hill people would visit us. They were incredibly friendly, lack of a common language seemed no barrier and custom demanded that they offer the visitors refreshment. Time was to them of little consequence; to us it was money and, with a mixture of our few words of Arabic and sign language, we had to decline their offers.

Sometimes, when I was shut down miles from anywhere and the geologists were on walkabout, I became aware of movement among the bushes and scrub thorn trees that clung to the hillsides. As long as I did not make my interest too evident, curiosity would overcome their shyness and, very cautiously, the "goat girls" would come closer. These were females of all ages sent into the hills to watch over the herds of goats. The older ladies would be fully covered by the abbaya, their faces concealed by a bourka, a heavy leather face mask or "beak." The younger ones were often unveiled, and strikingly attractive. They spent their days, and sometimes nights, roaming the mountain slopes, mostly barefoot, and some of them, seemingly barely into their teens, carried their babies. I would have loved to have been able to photograph them but this was impossible; to have done so without the permission of their menfolk would have been an unpardonable offence, and that permission seemed unlikely to be granted. Although many of the men would pose happily for a photograph when on their own, and did not seem to mind their women being unveiled in our presence, the production of a camera when the women were in view resulted in scowls from the men, and the disappearance of the women.

I had been at Sur for only two days when flying was interrupted. I woke at about three that morning. I knew it was raining, partly because I could hear the rattle of the drops on a tin-roofed shack just outside my bedroom window, but mainly because it was coming through the ceiling and dripping in my face. By the time dawn broke, scudding cloud obscured even the lower slopes of the mountains. The dirt track outside our villa was a raging torrent and the main wadi from the jebel to the sea at Sur, normally a dry gravel bed some three hundred yards wide, had become a fast flowing river more than fifteen feet deep in places. By early afternoon an area of nearly fifty square miles around Sur had been flooded, and the foundations of one of the bridges carrying the main road from Sur to Muscat had been washed away. Twenty-four hours later we were back to sunshine again, but the rain had also washed out all the dirt roads in the district and Reg Bagwell, our engineer, could no longer meet us with the fuel truck. Until the roads were regraded we had to return to the airfield every time we needed to refuel.

The flying was challenging. The sedimentary strata that provided the geologists with information dating back millions of years always seemed to be in the most inaccessible places. I became quite used to hovering a few yards away from three thousand foot high cliff faces, or landing and shutting down on a small rock saddle, with a deep, dark wadi immediately beneath my feet. Landings in the bottom of wadis became commonplace, although restricted space and wildly varying wind directions resulted all too often in rather untidy arrivals. On one occasion, with no alternative to a downwind takeoff and with only just enough power for a very slow climb, I ended up flying for a couple of miles in a narrow wadi, following each twist and turn, as the rocky floor seemed to rise as fast as my helicopter could climb.

On this contract, mountain flying alternated with periods spent in the desert between the southern edge of the Hajar mountains, and the northern slopes of the Jebel Qarra above Salalah. I discovered that since I had last flown in the area, the term "Empty Quarter" had become a misnomer. The increased amount of exploration and new discoveries of oil had resulted in both bitumen and graded roads being driven everywhere. Oil camps, gas flares and well heads littered the desert. Even the nomadic tribes, who still traversed the area with their herds of camels and goats in an unending search for grazing, now did so in Toyota trucks—the skeletons of which can be found in the most unlikely places.

Apart from navigation, mainly map reading from charts with few details and over desert with few landmarks, the flying was less arduous than in the mountains. There was no lack of flat areas on which to land, but the dust and sand raised at every takeoff and landing caused considerable erosion of the engine compressor, resulting in power losses, and wear and tear on all the exposed moving parts, especially the leading edges of the rotor blades.

Fortunately, after several years experience, our contractor had refined their desert living conditions to an art form, and their tented camps were remarkably comfortable. There was always a generator powering lights, a refrigerator for the beer, a clothes washing machine and fresh water shower. The food was excellent. On the down side the campers might have to cope with the occasional sand viper in their tent, camel spiders with a body the size of a tea plate, not to mention the odd scorpion in a shoe when you got up in the morning. It was also just a little disconcerting, when I first enquired for the whereabouts of the toilets among all this comparative luxury, to be offered a toilet roll, a shovel and the keys to a Toyota Landcruiser!

Chapter Seventeen

The Sultan of Oman had been cautious about allowing unlimited tourism, and in the early days it was not made easy for those just seeking sun and sand. However, while I was working in the country I was required to have a Resident's Permit and, with that in hand, could obtain a visitor's visa for Ann. On one of my leave periods she joined me and we spent three weeks in Oman, staying with Dave and Isabel Camp, Dave then being the Chief Engineer of the Royal Helicopter Flight.

We hired a four-wheel drive vehicle and were able to tour over much of North Oman, visiting many of the small towns and villages that I had only seen from the air. For anyone interested in Arabia and it's history, Oman is a treasure trove. The people are friendly, especially towards those who respect the customs of the country, and many of them, even in the interior, speak very good English. The scenery is impressive, including both mountains and desert, thousand year old castles in superb condition and looked after by a well funded government department, and villages in the interior which still bear the marks of how the people lived many hundreds of years ago. The hotels, while expensive, are modern and comfortable and the Omani government has a very enlightened attitude towards western style living.

The highlight of our holiday was a visit to Salalah. We took two days over the journey down, spending a night in one of the motels that are found about one hundred and fifty miles apart in the desert stretch. The actual journey is a total of over eight hundred miles, through the Wadi Sumail, across nearly five hundred miles of desert and then over the Qarra mountains in Dhofar to Salalah. The province had been transformed. A modern airport replaced the old dirt strip I had known. The sandy beach area occupied by the Taylor-Woodrow camp in 1972 was now covered by immaculate villas and gardens, and modern shopping malls lay alongside the old souk. Metalled roads covered the plain from Marbat to Mugshayl, and even in the area west of Mugshayl a road had been driven through the mountains to the border with the Yemen. On the jebel above Salalah we were able to drive, again on metalled roads, across areas which had been no-go country for me in 1972; there was even a guest house on the jebel edge above the Wadi Arzat from where, during the run in to LZ Sycamore, I had been shot at by the adoo. Three weeks went by all too soon and with regret we returned, Ann to Scotland, myself to Doha.

The invasion of Kuwait by Iraq in August 1990 took most of us by surprise. The debilitating war between Iraq and Iran only recently had ended in stalemate, with both sides apparently exhausted. Even so, it seemed that there was little to stop Iraq from a military conquest of all the oil-rich countries on the south side of the Gulf, if that was the intention. Refugees from Kuwait arrived in great numbers, especially in Bahrain and Muscat, and before long all the local hotels and any empty villas were filled. The build-up of coalition forces ensured that Saddam Hussein was prevented from moving further south, and our operations in Doha assumed a semblance of normality again. As with the tanker war, it was the world media that made us most aware that there was heightened tension in the area; although we were, very occasionally, challenged by the war vessels that continued to cruise the Gulf.

The arrival of several squadrons of American fighter aircraft, soon to be followed by the French and Canadian airforces, changed our lives. The local air traffic control became heavily loaded, and offshore we no longer had priority in what had been, up until then, our own little piece of sky. More Allied forces arrived in the Gulf, and naval task groups, mostly American, became our constant companions on the routes to the oil fields.

In October 1990 I was sent down once again to Muscat to continue with the geological survey. We had bought a second Jetranger for the contract; the rate of flying was to be increased to one hundred and twenty hours per month on each aircraft, and we now needed three pilots permanently in Oman. My first three weeks were spent in the middle of the desert at Haima, the administrative centre for the Bedu tribes. The village was on the main road between Muscat and Salalah and consisted of little more than a police post, a petrol filling station, a motel and twenty or thirty bungalows. There was also a dirt airstrip that could be used by small aircraft and helicopters. Haima was the centre for the government-sponsored plan for the protection of the Arabian oryx which, by 1960, due to almost unrestricted hunting had resulted in its virtual extinction. Sultan Qaboos took a personal interest in the plan for breeding the oryx in captivity, and had authorised the local Harasis tribe in the Haima area to be the guardians of the three herds as they were released back to the wild. When flying in the area we could see the results of the programme, the herds ranging far and wide in their search for food.

Although we had maps of the area, they were of little use. The geologists needed pinpoint accuracy since they had to identify individual, and often small, rock formations protruding maybe no more than twenty feet from the surface. They were working from satellite photographs which, while giving startling detail, were very difficult to use for navigation without first receiving a course in photo-reconnaissance. To assist the pilots we had fitted both aircraft with LORAN, a radio-navigation system that, when used within the optimum operating range of the transmitters, can give a position to within one hundred metres. It was unfortunate for us that the nearest LORAN chain was based in Saudi Arabia, and we were anything between six and eight hundred miles from the transmitters. At that range, hopefully and on a good day, we could obtain a position within two or three miles, but all too often the LORAN would become sullen and neurotic, insisting on more than one occasion that I was flying several hundred miles away from my actual position.

There was still a requirement to maximise fuel loads since the geologists were under pressure to complete the survey, and wanted to spend all day in the field. We could be required to fly anywhere within two hundred miles of the base at Haima and our engineer was responsible for meeting us with a truck load of fuel at some point during the day. We had also placed a few barrels of fuel at strategic points in the desert as an emergency reserve. Our lives revolved around fuel calculations, and it was seldom we arrived back in camp with more than ten minutes' worth left in the tank.

Usually we were away from base from seven in the morning to five in the afternoon, airborne for anything up to seven hours a day depending on whether the geologists were carrying out accurate mapping of a specific formation, in which case we could be shut down for several hours, or merely sampling a larger area. In the latter case we could be at the controls, rotors running, for three or four hours at a time, the geologists getting in and out of the aircraft at intervals to check the rocks.

The flying was great fun although at low level we had little or no radio contact with anyone, and if there was an emergency it would be some time before our plight was recognised. We asked our customers to let us know before we got airborne in the morning the rough area in which we would be flying, so that our base engineer would have some idea of where to start the search. The nature of their requirement meant that pinning the geologists down to even a grid square, an area of one hundred square miles, was like trying to pick up mercury with your fingers. On several occasions, having been told we would be working in one direction from base, within minutes of becoming airborne the plan would be changed and our engineer would see us flying off on a totally different course to that planned!

Following a short break in Muscat I returned to the aircraft flying in the mountains, this time on the southern slopes of the Jebel Akhdar at Ibri. I flew over one hundred and thirty five hours in less than seven weeks, and then returned to Scotland in time for Christmas. The Gulf

War started while I was on leave, and I had to decide whether it was safe to return to Doha. For the first three days the decision was out of my hands, the Saudi Arabian authorities having closed their airspace to all civil flights. In some ways it was a relief when Gulf Air recommenced their service to the Middle East and I decided to return to work. I fondly imagined that I would be spared the continuous TV coverage of the war provided in the UK, with an array of experts purveying analysis (but few facts), but discovered that Qatar TV had turned their one English speaking channel over to almost round-the-clock CNN broadcasts.

Life in Doha had changed. Although situated nearly seventy miles from Dharan, we were still down-track for any stray Scud missiles that Iraq might throw at Saudi Arabia. Gulf Helicopters had obtained some gas masks and protective suits and I believe we were among the only civilians in Qatar to have them. It served to remind those of us who felt relaxed about our chances of being attacked, that there was obviously a doubt in someone's mind. We were being challenged more frequently when flying offshore, again on the aviation distress frequency. The allies had issued warnings that all unidentified aircraft approaching their units would be treated as hostile, and there was always a chance that we could be shot at if we failed to respond to their radio challenge. This was not a happy thought, especially when we discovered that someone was occasionally jamming the frequency.

I was soon off again to Oman. Although the Omanis had stopped all civilian flying when the war started, they soon removed the restriction and the survey had restarted. Both our Jetrangers were there, one in the southern desert working between Haima and Salalah, the other at Adam. After ten days at Haima, I returned to Muscat for a short rest, only to find I was now needed to fly a one day load lifting contract in the hills near Sohar. This meant replacing the aircraft I had brought from Haima with the one from Adam, which had a hook. A small drilling team had finished checking a potential chromite deposit, and the helicopter was to lift them and their equipment from the wadi, just south of the Jizzi, to the nearest accessible dirt track. I then moved to Diba, in the Musendam peninsular, where we were to fly for the geologists for about three weeks.

The Musendam contains some of the more challenging helicopter flying found in Oman. The mountains run down to both coasts, ending frequently in sheer cliff faces dropping a thousand feet into the sea. These are bad enough, but it is also an area where, when the Shemal sweeps across the Gulf, the wind is thrown up by the mountains resulting in severe turbulence. To add to my interest on this visit it was also the rainy season, and if anywhere in Oman is going to get rain it is the Musendam. It rained and the clouds hung low for five days on end, effectively grounding me. The few graded roads were swept away, nearly stranding one of the geologists who had driven up into the mountains in an attempt to continue with his work as best he could without the helicopter. On his return journey that evening he discovered that the track was impassable no more than fifteen kilometres from our base. He was forced to retrace his course and make a one hundred and fifty kilometre detour, via Khasab and Dubai, to get home. I tried to fly whenever the clouds looked like lifting, but all too often the clearances were "sucker traps." I found myself not only having to fly at very low level to remain in contact with the ground, but also make major detours to avoid overflying cloud-filled wadis.

The geologists wanted to check the coastal cliff faces and islands and this required us to take them over water at low level. This could not be done with our Jetranger, which was not equipped with floats, and we had to ferry a float-fitted 212 from Doha to Oman to complete this particular flying task. I flew the Jetranger to Seeb Airport and waited in the company office for the arrival of the replacement aircraft. At about 1400 we received a message from Seeb air-traffic control saying that our 212 would be arriving shortly, refuel, and proceed immediately south into the desert. This was somewhat strange, since the Musendam was northwest of Seeb.

The 212 landed and we went out to greet the pilot, John Beattie, to learn that the Jetranger operating out of Adam had reported having an engine failure in the desert, and we were to go and rescue the crew! We found them two hours later, in a shallow wadi more than eighty miles from the nearest inhabitation. Paul Dobson, a recently joined Australian pilot, had been taking off from a rock outcrop and had climbed no more than ten feet when the engine compressor failed and the engine temperature went off the clock. He managed to land without further damage, either to the passengers or aircraft. He had been too low to raise Seeb Air Traffic Control, or any other land station, by radio but had managed to talk to a civilian airliner that was passing overhead, and they had relayed his distress message to Seeb. We left the broken bird sitting forlornly in the wadi, and took the crew back to Adam to work out some way of retrieving it.

It was not until I got back to Seeb that night that I realised how lucky I had been. If it had not been for the load lifting contract during my week off, I would have been flying the now broken Jetranger in the mountains of the Musendam; an engine failure there could have had awesome consequences!

The Gulf land war had both started and finished by the time I went on leave from Muscat. When I returned to Doha, Gulf Helicopters had taken delivery of two new aircraft, Bell 412's, which had replaced two of the 212's on the QGPC contract. The 412 had been in operation for some years elsewhere in the world, and was a marked improvement. It had upgraded engines, a four-bladed main rotor system and was a delight to fly. Gone was the heavy, two-bladed beat of the traditional Bell helicopter! It was faster than the 212 by some twenty knots and nearly vibration free. The pilots had seats of armchair comfort and there was one more attraction—QGPC had insisted that the new air-craft were to be fitted with air-conditioning. If they had a drawback for me, it was that QGPC had also decided that the passenger seats should face forward. In the 212 the back of a row of seats provided a definite division between pilot and passengers; in the 412 they could now lean forward and peer over the pilot's shoulder!

In 1991 we had picked up a new contract, this time in South Yemen. It was for an oil company working in the mountains about two hundred and fifty miles east of Aden. They had been there for some time, but initially the area had not been considered very promising. A Canadian helicopter company was already on site, with a Bell 212 and two Aerospatiale Lamas, but the discovery of considerable amounts of oil during test drilling had accelerated the need to complete the seismic survey. We sent first one, then a second 212, stripped to the bare essentials to lighten them for under slung work. We were working at heights between two and four thousand feet and slinging loads of up to two thousand five hundred pounds on the end of a one hundred foot long line. I went there in August for a three-week stint. It was high-pressure work because, to get the job done within the time limit, we had to start flying at first light, finish at dusk and fly seven days a week.

We had negotiated a waiver to our operations manual with the Qatari Aviation Authority which allowed us to fly without days off, up to seven hours a day and one hundred and twenty hours a month. The pilots flying for Liftair, the Canadian company, worked to the Canadian Department of Transport rules, and this allowed them to fly an unlimited number of hours each day, with a maximum of one hundred and eighty hours a month. They were not required to have any rest days, as long as they did not exceed four hundred and fifty hours flight-time in a three-month period and were given a minimum of thirteen days off at the end of the three months. We sent a third pilot to the camp, but even so we all flew more than ninety hours in three weeks, and there was a constant stream of pilots travelling between Doha and Yemen.

My three weeks flashed by and after ninety hours flying in eighteen days it was time to return to Doha. Only very senior members of the oil company were flown out of camp; the rest of us had to go by road to Aden—a memorable journey indeed. It started with a four-hour drive over rough tracks in an oil company four-wheel drive Toyota to Mukalla, on the coast about 200 miles east of Aden. This was followed by a ten-hour taxi ride to Aden. It was difficult to decide which part of the taxi journey was worse, the desert or mountain section. Our transport, an old Peugeot six-seater, was decrepit, and in the desert we had to stop every thirty miles to top up the leaky radiator, and then push start the beast since the starter motor was inoperative. In the mountains, on badly metalled roads with a sheer drop of several thousand feet on one side or the other, the driver made up for lost time, especially downhill when it became increasingly obvious that his brakes were defective! It made the flight from Aden to Doha in one of the Russian-built *Ilyushins* of the local airline, Alyemda, a distinct pleasure.

Chapter Eighteen

My stay in Doha was short-lived, and I was once more on my way to Muscat. The Jetrangers, which had been brought to Doha for major maintenance, were required back in Oman to complete the survey contract. I was not to be involved in that work, but was to fly for about a week for a firm surveying sites in the Western Hajar mountains and the Sohar area, for a new TV rebroadcast network. The ferry flight from Doha, overland to Seeb via Abu Dhabi, took just over five hours. As soon as we had completed customs and immigration formalities and refueled, Mel Prince, my engineer for this contract, and I got airborne again and headed back along the coast to Sohar. We landed at the back of the Sohar Motel, which was to be our base for the week, and met up with the four surveyors who would be flying with me.

That evening we planned the operation for the next day. All my passengers had flown in helicopters before, and were confident in what they would be doing. Their combined weight, plus the equipment they needed, did not allow me to carry much fuel and we planned to meet up with a lorry carrying fuel barrels two or three times during the day. They wished to remain for only a few minutes at many of the landing sites; it would be uneconomic and time wasting to shut down, so they were briefed on the safety requirements for exiting and entering the helicopter with rotors running. This was quite normal procedure without which much of the work we did in the mountains would have been impossible. Next morning, as usual, I went through the full safety briefing with my passengers and we headed for the hills. We spent the day there, landing nine or ten times.

We returned to the motel at half past four that afternoon, landing some twenty five yards from, and facing, the rear entrance. The passengers asked if they could disembark while I completed the engine run down. The two on the left hand side of the aircraft got out and stood by the skids, while a third, who had been sitting in the right hand, rear seat climbed out and moved forward around the front of the helicopter to join the first two. I turned to check the fourth passenger, who had been sitting in the middle of the rear cabin, but he was nowhere to be seen. I thought he must have climbed out of the left-hand door and would be standing by the baggage bay, so leaned across the cockpit to check, and as I did so I felt two jolts through the rudder pedals. Mel Prince, who had been walking across to the helicopter from the hotel started to run, and signaled me to cut the engine immediately. I think I knew what had happened but did not want to believe it. As I climbed out of the aircraft and looked towards the tail, I saw the fourth passenger lying underneath the tail boom. He was quite clearly dead.

The police told me later that an onlooker had seen the him step out of the right-hand door and, instead of following the other surveyor around the front, had turned right and walked towards the tail, ducked under the tail boom immediately beneath a "Danger" sign with a large, red arrow pointing towards the tail rotor. Even then, had he turned right towards the front of the helicopter and the motel, he would have been safe, but he turned left into the path of the tail rotor blades

An ambulance and the local police were called and, after statements had been taken from the bystanders, the passengers and I were driven to the Sohar police station. Formal statements were taken from all of us and I was breathalysed to eliminate any suspicion that drink was involved. The passengers were released but I, as the captain of the aircraft, remained under arrest until a bail bond of five thousand Omani riyals, about seven and a half thousand pounds, was posted. It was not until after midnight, and a series of faxes between the police, the company in Doha and our Omani sponsors, that the police accepted a faxed letter from our sponsors agreeing to be responsible for my continued presence in Oman, and allowed me to return to the motel.

The following day a fuller investigation was held including the police, and senior members of the Omani Civil Aviation Department who had driven to Sohar from Muscat that morning. At the end of the meeting I was told that both authorities had decided it had been a tragic accident, and that no blame was attached to anyone involved. The passengers had been fully briefed, with particular reference to the dangers of the tail rotor, and no one could offer a rational explanation for the actions of the dead man. The helicopter, which had been impounded by the police, was released to us and, after Mel had given it a thorough check for any damage, we flew it to Seeb Airport to await further developments and instructions. The police, meanwhile, instructed our sponsor that they should retain my passport to ensure that I did not leave the country. This was no more than I had expected. Someone had died, however accidentally, and a formal investigation was required to establish the cause. I was told that this would take no more than three weeks.

Taking into account all the advice I was given, I sat back in the Gulf Hotel at Qurm. It was not an easy period although, in many ways, I was fortunate. I had lived in the Middle East for twenty years, some of the time in Oman itself, and while finding it difficult to do nothing, knew that the system would have to take its course. I was also lucky that Julie Lawry, our Omani representative, her husband Garry, Pete and Kate Williams and many other friends in Oman made it their job to keep me occupied. When three weeks had passed, and nothing seemed to have happened, I started to devil for myself.

The police asked me for a full copy of the Department of Civil Aviation (DGCA) report. This was not immediately available; in fact, when I asked the DGCA for their report they replied by asking me to obtain more information from my passengers, one of whom was now in a survey camp in the Wahiba Sands! I was asked for extracts from our Operations Manual, translated into Arabic, and a statement from Gulf Helicopters that the extracts did, in fact, have the force of law for the pilots. The police also wanted an explanation as to why we did not carry flight attendants. This is not normally required for an aircraft carrying less than nineteen passengers, and the relaxation was mentioned in Omani Aviation Law. They wanted the originals of all this information—faxed copies would not be acceptable.

The Omani National holiday was fast approaching, which would mean a five-day break with no action possible, and I was anxious to return to Doha. It was now six weeks since the accident and a Sudanese lawyer, Abbas Siddiq, had been appointed to look after the legal requirements. The documents were obtained and Abbas and I drove them the two hundred miles to Sohar, where he hoped to be able to look at the police files. Much to our surprise, and within an hour of arriving at the police station, I found myself in front of a judge in his private chambers. The hearing, quite naturally, was in Arabic, and when it was over I was told that the judge needed to see the DGCA report and a full copy of our Operations Manual before he could close the case. Meanwhile, all sides had agreed I could return to Doha, but would have to return to Sohar for the final hearing.

Once again it was time for leave, and on my return to Doha on New Year's Eve I hoped I would be able to spend a few weeks there, especially as I could expect to be called back to Oman at a moment's notice for the hearing. I had been back less than a week when Dennis Laird, our Chief Pilot, called me into his office and broke the news. Ray Poss, one of our American pilots, had gone to Aden to cover a pilot shortfall on the seismic contract, and on completion had flown a 212 from there to Sana'a. It had been intended that he would fly one of the Saa'na aircraft back to Doha for major maintenance, but fate had taken a hand; the aircraft had gone unserviceable, and rather than leave Ray twiddling his thumbs in Sana'a, he was being recalled. I was to go there as soon as the aircraft was ready, which happened a few days later.

The direct route from Sana'a to Doha is about eight hundred miles but we could not obtain clearance to fly over Saudi Arabia; instead we were to fly by way of Oman. Even with full ferry tanks and six barrels in the main cabin, a total of three thousand, five hundred pounds of fuel, we were limited to five hours flying, about five hundred miles, between refuelling stops. My flight on the first day was to be from Sana'a to Salalah. We would complete the journey to Doha, via Muscat, on the following day. Dave Gigg, one of our radio engineers, accompanied me to transfer the fuel from the barrels to the tanks.

Saan'a to Salalah would involve at least seven hours flying. If the wind were adverse it would push us to the limit of daylight operations so we had planned to start at first light, a plan that was both logical and sensible but did not take into account Yemeni officialdom. First light was at about six thirty and we arrived at Sana'a airport in good time, with Jabril, our Yemeni driver, to help us talk our way through the ranks of those who were not so much determined to stop us, as uncertain of how to cope with the unusual. Most people passing through Yemeni Customs and Immigration at Saan'a airport are passengers on a civil airliner, have a scheduled flight to catch and a ticket to prove it. We were the crew of a helicopter, were not a scheduled flight and did not issue tickets to our passengers, let alone our crews! The situation was further complicated by the fact that it was a couple of hours before the next airliner was due to depart and the immigration officer, who was needed to stamp our passports, was in bed and seemed reluctant to join us.

It took an hour to get through immigration, but I finally made it to the met. office. Our aircraft, a Bell 212, was equipped for no more than basic VFR, and I needed to know that I would not meet any bad weather on my route to Salalah, by way of Riyan, on the south coast of Yemen near Mukalla.. What I got was a three-hour old weather report for Riyan, nothing for the route and nothing for Salalah—apparently aircraft from Sana'a never went there! The weather was fine at Sana'a and had been good at Riyan, so I decided to leave.

Sana'a airfield is at seven thousand feet above sea level and, with an overload of fuel, we just managed to stagger into the air. The mountains on either side of our route climbed to over eleven thousand feet but fortunately we were heading downhill all the way to our first turning point at Byhan, a small town on the edge of the desert. The next eighty miles was over featureless sand and stones, before we climbed over more mountains and finally dropped down to the coast at Riyan. We had been lucky up to the end of the desert leg, the visibility had been good with little or no cloud, and the LORAN had been working remarkably well.

As usual, everything happened at once. We were climbing up towards the mountain tops when we ran into low cloud, some no more than four hundred feet above the ground, and the LORAN, which had been working beautifully up to that point, took the opportunity to become neurotic. I stayed beneath the overcast and was attempting to match up a distant peak with something similar on the map when I noticed a puff of dust on the ground ahead of me. It was a helicopter taking off, miles from anywhere, and it came directly towards me before passing out of sight beneath us. It was probably an aircraft working one of the other oil concessions in the area, but served to remind me that even in this wasteland I should keep a good lookout.

We picked up the beacon at Riyan as we dropped down off the mountains towards the sea. I had been there before, but only in a civil airliner and I had not seen the military side of the field. I discovered that it was littered with ageing MiG fighters, and something that looked remarkably like an old Gloster Meteor. There were nearly twenty aircraft all told, but it seemed obvious from the dust that covered them that they had not been flown for some time.

The authorities at Riyan were as helpful as they were able, but there were a couple of hiccoughs. The airport manager was away and his secretary had no idea of how much he should charge me for landing fees; we finally compromised, and he agreed to send the bill to our office at Sana'a. The main problem was fuel. I had been told before leaving Doha that the only way to obtain fuel at Riyan was to pay cash, and had been given a fistful of dollars for the purpose. At Riyan I was told that someone had paid for fuel with counterfeit dollars, and the refuelling party had been ordered not to accept currency of any form. They wanted me to go to Mukalla to talk with their manager, but this was a half-hour drive in each direction and I could not spare the time, even if I could be sure that it was legal under immigration law for me to leave the airport. After much argument, and not a little table tapping, they agreed to accept my dollars as long as I signed as having given them each individually numbered dollar bill. The rest of the journey to Doha was uneventful, if tedious, as persistent head winds dragged out the flight next day to over ten hours.

In March 1992 I received instructions that I was to return to Oman and go to Sohar for the closing of the accident file. The Sohar Police were still insisting that they considered there was no case to answer, and the report from the DGCA stated that the operator had taken all necessary precautions to ensure the safety of the passengers. It came as some surprise, therefore, when the day before I was due to drive to Sohar with Abbas Siddiq, we discovered I was being charged with "unintentional killing." The trial produced a guilty verdict, I was fined ten Omani riyals, about fifteen pounds sterling, and given a jail sentence, suspended for six months. Outside the courthouse the young Omani prosecutor approached me and explained, in perfect English, that the judge felt he had no aviation precedents to work with, and had decided to try the case as he would a car accident. He pointed out that included in the judgement was leave to appeal, which was, in fact, an automatic right, and finished up by saying, "Of course, you must appeal."

I was torn between conflicting arguments. It had been a harrowing period and I had little desire to reopen old wounds. My manager assured me I would not be expected to fly in Oman for at least six months, and although my love of the country and its people were in no way diminished, this was certainly a relief. Winning an appeal was probably the only way that I could have returned to work there with any real peace of mind. There was also pressure on me to appeal from some of the pilots, both in Doha and Oman, if only to clarify the legitimacy of an Operations Manual. If we followed the rules but could not rely on the protection they should afford, there could always be a problem for anyone involved in an accident. I decided to appeal.

The case came before the Omani Court of Appeal in September 1992, almost eleven months to the day of the accident. The language used was, once again, Arabic, but I gathered that the appeal was being allowed primarily on the basis that the judge, in his written summary of the trial, had stated that he had chosen to ignore both the report from the DGCA, and the decision by the Sohar police that there was no case to answer. After a short discussion between the three appeal judges, the President of the Omani Appeal Court spoke a few words in Arabic. My interpreter turned to me and said, "The President has asked me to tell you that you are totally innocent." My feelings of relief were considerable.

Any form of transport, including aviation, is inherently dangerous; if it were not, the rules and regulations that abound would be unnecessary. For this reason, among others, every National and International Aviation Authority, and any reputable company, create a framework of rules, which are refined and amended in the light of experience. These are for the protection of passengers and anyone contracting to use the aircraft. Woe betide any pilot or engineer who, in the event of an accident, is found to have transgressed; justice is summary and if there is a lack of concrete evidence, all too often the cause may put down to negligence. The Operations Manual is the bible, but as well as the protection it offers the passenger, it must also offer protection to the operator.

My sixtieth birthday, when I would have to retire, was rapidly approaching and I spent my last year in Doha much as I had spent the first ten, rotating around the triangle. I had been flying for thirty-seven years, thirty four of them in helicopters, and would be quite pleased to stop. I was also very happy to have confounded all but one of my instructors from RAF Valley. In 1958 I had been ferrying a Gannet from

Eglinton to Culdrose and had stopped to refuel at Valley, where I had met one of my instructors. He told me that of all the confidential assessments that had been made of me when I completed my training, his was almost the only one that suggested I would last much more than three months in aviation!

Chapter Nineteen

The question I have been asked most often during my flying career is "How safe is a helicopter?" There have always been, even among fixed-wing aviators, those who accept the fixed-wing aircraft as an everyday part of life, yet distrust the helicopter, regarding it as dangerous and noisy. This attitude was probably best summed up by Harry Reasoner, an American news commentator, who said in a broadcast in 1971:

> *The thing is, helicopters are different from aeroplanes. An aeroplane, by it's nature, wants to fly, and if not interfered with too strongly by events, or by a deliberately incompetent pilot, it will fly. A helicopter does not want to fly. It is maintained in the air by a variety of forces and controls all working in opposition to each other, if there is any disturbance in this delicate balance the helicopter stops flying, immediately and disastrously. There is no such thing as a gliding helicopter.*

He went on, "This is why being a helicopter pilot is so different from being an aeroplane pilot and why, in general, aeroplane pilots are open, clear eyed, buoyant extroverts, and helicopter pilots are brooders, introspective anticipators of trouble. They know that if something bad has not happened—it is about to."

The humour is apparent, and if he had said this in 1951 there might have been some truth in his comments, but by 1971 the advances in technology made a nonsense of them.

An accident is defined as something without an apparent cause, something unforeseen. Since it is unforeseen it cannot be guarded against, and a true accident-free record, therefore, must depend more on luck than good management. However, since most people refer to any unintentional act resulting in death or damage as an accident, so shall I.

So how safe is a helicopter, both as a flying machine and in comparison with fixed-wing aircraft? Assuming that the pilot does not become incapacitated, why should some flights end earlier than intended, sometimes tragically? The most obvious reason is that no form of transport can be made totally safe. From the moment anything starts to move risk is involved; mechanical parts fail, human beings are fallible and errors of judgement are made in assessing risk levels.

At this juncture I believe it is necessary to separate some of the accidents occurring to military helicopters from those involving civilian aircraft. They may be caused by the same malfunctions, either mechanical or human, but many of the advances in helicopter technology originate with, and are tested by, the military. If failures occur a remedy will be found, and civilian operators reap the benefit. It is also a fact that, of necessity, the military are allowed to fly their helicopters far closer to the limits than would be acceptable in a civilian environment.

There are three major mechanical breakdowns that can cause an immediate catastrophe, probably beyond the ability of any pilot to control. The first of these is the total failure of a main rotor blade, which is the equivalent of a wing falling off a fixed-wing aircraft, and about as common. Rotor blades are, in fact, incredibly strong. There is a photograph taken during the Vietnam war of a Bell 205 that had sustained battle damage. One of the maintenance personnel is sitting on top of it, with his head and neck poking through a shell hole near the root of a main rotor blade. The helicopter had, in fact, flown many miles back to base with that damage!

The other two are the failure of the rotor gear box if it causes the main blades to cease rotating, of which I know of one instance, and the failure of the controls to the rotor system. A problem with the tail rotor system, while being considered a major emergency, should not result in catastrophe, since there are ways of flying the helicopter which allow the pilot to reach the ground without crashing; an untidy arrival perhaps, but not inevitably fatal.

All moving parts are tested to destruction by the manufacturer before regular use in the industry. Modern materials, detailed inspections and maintenance, and regular replacement of all moving parts long before they reach their Mean Time Between Failures (MTBF), make such failures rare.

Modern aircraft engines, used in both fixed and rotary wing aircraft, have an excellent record for trouble-free operation. As with other moving parts, they are subject to regular maintenance, and replacement at intervals well before their anticipated failure rate. If there is an engine failure it should not be catastrophic, unless it causes major collateral damage, because the regulations require helicopters to be operated in certain ways. In general, a multi-engined helicopter must be flown so that the flight can be continued to a safe landing with only one serviceable engine. A single-engined helicopter must always be in a position to make a safe touchdown by autorotating to the surface.

If, following an emergency, a fixed-wing aircraft has to make an immediate landing, there is a major requirement for this to be completed safely. The aircraft must be moving at, or above it's stalling speed up to the moment of touchdown, and must also have a suitable length of reasonably smooth surface to slow to a stop. Assuming the pilot is trained and in practice, the unique capability of the helicopter to complete the landing vertically with a fully cushioned touchdown and on a piece of generally unprepared ground little bigger than it's own rotor span, in my opinion makes it safer than the fixed-wing aircraft.

I can think of no other technical failures which are any worse for a helicopter than a similar failure in the fixed-wing environment, or that are any more likely to be found in rotary-wing machines.

The other major cause of accidents is the human element. Commercial fixed-wing aircraft, with the possible exception of those involved in crop spraying and display aerobatics, spend as little time as practicable close to the ground. They are usually equipped to fly on instruments and have little or no reason to fly close to the surface in bad weather, except at takeoff and landing. They tend to be employed on reasonably fixed routes and between commercial airports. The pilots are assisted by well-equipped met offices, by air traffic control throughout most of the flight, and modern radio and navigation aids. This in no way detracts from their skill and professionalism, and are shared by the pilots working, for instance, the fixed and regular routes in the North Sea oil fields.

It is not so with many other helicopter pilots. Although they can work from airports, they operate frequently over rough country and out of contact with meteorological offices, air traffic control and ground-based navigational aids. They may be carrying passengers one day, lifting loads of wet cement up a mountain the next, and flying a power line survey on the third, to name but three of the many jobs for which the helicopter is suitable. The aircraft is frequently flown at or near the surface, in close proximity to solid objects, some natural and others man-made, and often flying in bad weather while maintaining visual contact with the ground. The very nature of the machine's capabilities places them in a risk-laden environment.

Accepting all these premises, there may still be no obvious reason why a helicopter should not be safe. If the weather gets too bad the pilot can land almost anywhere. If he is unfortunate enough to be over water at the time, he should be fitted with some form of flotation equipment, giving him and any passengers time to get into a dinghy. His judgement should be such that he does not come into contact with solid objects, nor should he get lost or run out of fuel. Some accidents may be caused by genuine incompetence, but what of the rest.?

The answer, I believe, lies in the training, including continuation training, of the pilots, their experience, and the level of equipment fitted to the helicopter. For the first twenty or thirty years of helicopter operations the largest pool of skilled pilots was in the military, where they received their training in almost all of the specialised flying techniques required for helicopter operations at government expense. In the civil world the high cost of training a pilot to commercial licence standard, and the flying hours required before many companies could consider employing him, produced a "Catch 22" situation for the novice; how was he to obtain the necessary skills?

For those who were unable to find some form of sponsorship the personal cost was high, the prospects of employment low, and for many the only answer was to work on the fringes of the industry. Most survived to become competent pilots; some, mainly I believe from lack of supervision, picked up self taught and dangerous habits.

Dangerous habits are also acquired by some holders of Private Pilot's Licences, who tend to be even less well supervised. As helicopters have become more commonplace, and some models little more expensive to buy and run than many top of the range cars, they have come to be not unusual transport for many rich business, sports and entertainment people. Some are rich enough to employ a professional pilot, others prefer to do the flying themselves. Flying is a tremendous thrill and I would never want to deprive the private pilot of that buzz; however, the number of flight hours required to keep a Private Pilot's Licence current are, I believe, too few. Although the ability to control a helicopter on a trouble-free flight from A to B, like riding a bicycle, is never really lost, unless the skills required to handle emergencies are maintained by regular and reasonably frequent practice, trouble will ensue. If you lose your balance on a bicycle you do not have far to fall; making a mistake, even a small one, while airborne in a helicopter can have disastrous consequences. How many private pilots can put their hand on their heart and say that they have practised emergencies recently? How many know, without prompting or hesitation, the flight and mechanical limitations associated with their machine and, just as significantly, their own limits? As an ex-Training Captain I know there are some professionals who need the occasional nudge in this respect!

A Company Operations Manual is usually written to allow the most experienced pilots to fly to their safe limits. There will be a range of ability among pilots in any company and, since they cannot be supervised at all times, the acceptance of their own limitations is essential for the professional. More than this, because there will always be pressure placed upon them to complete the job, they must be able to recognise that a serious situation is developing before it has gone beyond their ability to control it. They must also have the courage to tell their passenger that the flight should be curtailed, for whatever reason and with whatever results. 'Get-homeitis' is a recognised disease in aviation, and can have fatal results! I have no doubt that most pilots have been faced with such decisions, and that they know a fellow professional who has succumbed to the pressure to make, or continue, a flight, and may have paid a high price for doing so.

There is another, more subtle, stress involved in such situations. It may be irrational, seldom intentional and I know there are those who will deny that it exists. It is called "Peer pressure," and stems from a desire not to look bad in the eyes of your fellow pilots.

Unlike fixed-wing flying, where a large number of pilots learn their trade flying as co-pilots, it is only in comparatively recent years that some civil helicopter companies began to train their own flight deck crews. In the UK these were almost exclusively those companies involved in the North Sea oil business. Once having acquired the licence, they flew mainly as co-pilots until they had acquired sufficient flight hours and experience; even then it was possible that they would not have had the necessary training for the more specialised techniques. There was also a marked, and reasonable reluctance within the company that paid for their training, to release them into the wider world.

This leads to the question as to why the majority of commercial helicopters, like the majority of commercial fixed-wing aircraft, are not flown with two pilots? It should produce increased safety margins and provide valuable experience for new pilots. The answer is that, especially in some operations involving smaller aircraft, restriction on payloads is still a factor, and under some conditions the workload may not justify a second pilot. As helicopters have increased in size and complexity, and especially in the offshore oil world, more legislative authorities, contractors and employers insist that two pilots should be the standard—but some do not. It may have been because helicopter payloads were limited; often it is because of cost. A second pilot needs to be paid, and his weight must be subtracted from the payload.

When the Bell 47 and other helicopters of that era were first used in commercial operations, they were flown almost exclusively by day and under visual flight rules. Payloads were small and there was a reluctance to fit anything but the minimum of instrumentation, plus a map and a pilot with a Mk 1 eyeball. In today's world, autopilots, flight and radio-navigation instruments, satellite navigation, aircraft radar and other technical advances for fixed-wing aircraft are all available and most, if not all of them can be fitted in commercial helicopters. They undoubtedly increase the safety margins; whether or not they are fitted again depends on cost.

Cost also determines the use of multi-engined aircraft. If the load to be lifted, be it passengers or freight, is within the capabilities of a single-engined machine, why pay the extra cost of a twin? The arguments for using a single-engined helicopter are firstly that modern turbine engines are very reliable, and secondly that the aircraft must be flown in a safe manner and to the rules laid down in the Flight and Operations Manual at all times. This is both straightforward and logical, but does not necessarily match reality. For instance, to complete a job the pilot may have to fly the aircraft into a position from where, if the engine fails, he will be unable to make a safe landing. He will have to make the decision either to ignore the limitations and continue, or plead the cause of safety. The latter course will cause aggravation to the contractor, some of whom have been known to take a Nelsonian attitude to such hazards. Most pilots continue with the job and usually return safely, which makes the argument for the use of a twin-engined helicopter difficult to sustain. The truth of the matter is that the twin is safer but more expensive, and that commercial cost has taken priority over safety.

Legislation is a prerequisite for safe aviation, but can also present helicopter companies operating to their own national regulations, and who are often worldwide operators, with disadvantages. The discrepancy between flight hours allowed, for instance, under Canadian and British Law is by no means the only difference in aviation regulations. New Zealand and Australia both require pilots to undergo formal training for under slung load operations, either during their ab-initio instruction or before they are employed on such flying duties, and the training becomes part of their official qualifications. There is no such requirement in many other countries, where the question of who does the job is left up to the individual company. Training, and continuation training for whatever form of flying, is non-revenue, and the bane of life for company accountants.

With the advances in materials and manufacture for both airframe, engines, and the equipment which can be fitted applying to both fixed and rotary wing aircraft, there seems to me to be no reason why there should be a great disparity in their safety record. As long as the helicopter is operated within the prescribed limits, and the pilot is fully trained and in current practice, there seems to be little or no reason for people to distrust the helicopter. I believe the question should not be "How safe is a helicopter?" but "How safe do you want the helicopter to be?" The answer must lie in the hands of those who hold the purse strings.

THE END